REAL ESTATE

QUICK

A MILLIONAIRE'S GUIDE TO INVESTING

& EASY

FULLY ILLUSTRATED

REAL ESTATE QUICK & EASY

CONCEPTS OF REAL ESTATE CLEARLY ILLUSTRATED

Roy T. Maloney
PRESIDENT, PATHFINDER REALTY

DROPZONE
PRESS
P. O. Box 882222
San Francisco
California • 94188

International Standard Book Number: 0-913257-03-6
Copyright © 1990, 1988, 1985, 1984, 1983, 1980, 1975 by Roy T. Maloney

Manufactured in the United States of America
Printed by Delta Lithograph Co, Valencia, CA
Published by Dropzone Press

Distributed by Publishers Group West, 4065 Hollis St., Emeryville, CA 94608
Phone: (415) 658-3453

Library of Congress Cataloging in Publication Data:

Maloney, Roy T.
  REAL ESTATE QUICK & EASY,
  Concepts of Real Estate Clearly Illustrated

  Includes index.

  1. Real estate investment.   2. Real property.
  I. Title.   II. Title: Real estate quick and easy.
  HD1382.5.M26   1983   332.63'24   83-11702
  ISBN 0-913257-03-6   (PBK.)

Illustrations by Yoong Bae - Cover design by Jody Krul-Greco and Spiros Bairaktaris
Computer-Composed by Jo Liana King, Franciscan Systems & Graphics, San Francisco
and BookPrep, 1630 Salem Dr., Gilroy, California

PRINTINGS:

FIRST:	August, 1980	EIGHTH:	January, 1987
SECOND:	October, 1980	NINTH:	November, 1987
THIRD:	August, 1983	TENTH:	October, 1988
FOURTH:	March, 1984	ELEVENTH:	January, 1989
FIFTH:	March, 1985	TWELFTH:	April, 1990
SIXTH:	July, 1985		
SEVENTH:	February, 1986		

12 13 14 15 16 17 18   90 91 92 93 94 95

PURPOSE OF THIS BOOK

The purpose of this book is to alert you to some of the basic concepts of a successful real estate investment in a clearly illustrated and interesting manner. It is far from a complete discussion of the subject, and nothing contained herein should be construed as constituting legal advice.

Examples given to illustrate concepts and systems are considered representative of Federal and State law, but with fifty states each having a different rule book, precise interpretations must come from the reader's own attorney or accountant.

It is hoped that you will find this volume a useful guide in addressing your particular needs.

As the midget standing
on the giant's shoulder
can see farther...
I dedicate this book to
all the giants who have
helped me.

The Author

CONTENTS
(Index page 337)

SIMPLE ARITHMETIC

CREATIVE FINANCING
&
MONEY MATTERS

REAL ESTATE LAW
&
TAXES

ARCHITECTURE
&
APPRAISAL

PREFACE

Success in real estate investing depends on coordinating many diverse disciplines. It requires knowledge of property values, management, legal aspects, taxes, financing, construction, remodeling, government regulations and creative concepts.

No one book, or person, has all of the answers on how to make an investment fortune, but there is a common denominator of knowledge that the author will try to present in the simplest form. As one sage has said, "It takes all of our knowledge to make things simple."

All of the sixty or more real estate millionaires that I have known use one or more of the concepts on the pages that follow. They also have access to a real estate broker, an accountant, an attorney, and on large projects, an architect and a manager to provide the required expertise and support.

This book in itself can not assure your success. Your own personal motivation and practical experience are the missing ingredients. It is believed that no significant money-making real estate idea has been overlooked, and as a minimum this book should help prevent the more obvious blunders.

Buy low, sell high,' (or trade up) and have *cash flow in the interim*. This seems the distillate of how to be an 'instant millionaire,' or if not in an instant, then in a five or ten year period. Real estate is so unique that even if you 'buy low, sell *low'* you can still make money, since an 'equity value' is created with the paydown of the loan. You can also make money by *not* selling. Simply take out the equity value by refinancing, or by taking out an 'equity loan' (a second loan).

In over twenty years of investing in real estate, reviewing over 300 books on the subject, lengthy talks with sophisticated investors and seemingly endless seminars on 'how to get rich quick,' I believe that 'buy low, sell high' is as "Quick & Easy" as investing can be defined. If you already know how to do this you needn't read any further. But be cautioned, there may be a few hitches along the way.

For each problem there is a solution. Leaky faucets, call a plumber; building burns down, you should have adequate insurance; seller dies in escrow, the contract should cover such a contingency. *You can think of problems as solutions looking for the right questions.*

The author wishes to thank the hundreds of people who have been kind enough to contribute their time and thoughts to enhance these pages. Inclusion in this book is based on two criteria: (1) the idea must be of general interest, and (2) have usefulness in the real world. The goal being to create an easy to understand book on real estate concepts.

As real estate investing is an ongoing process, any reader's thoughts or comments, that can improve the state-of-the-art are most welcome.

Good luck in your investing.

Roy T. Maloney

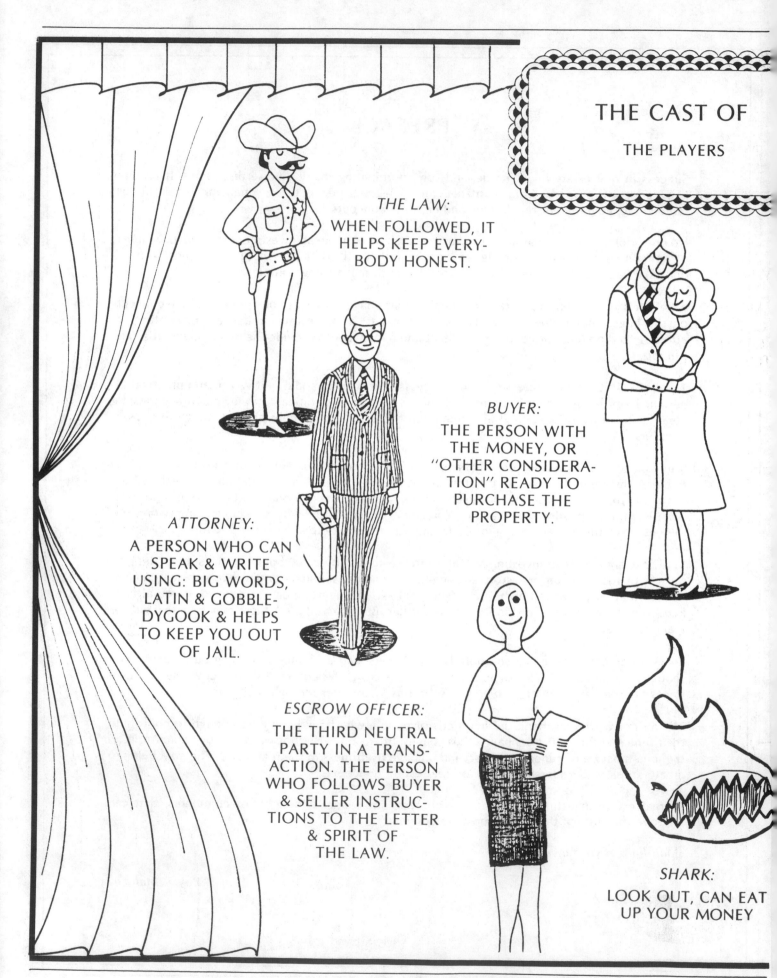

THE CAST OF
THE PLAYERS

THE LAW:
WHEN FOLLOWED, IT HELPS KEEP EVERYBODY HONEST.

BUYER:
THE PERSON WITH THE MONEY, OR "OTHER CONSIDERATION" READY TO PURCHASE THE PROPERTY.

ATTORNEY:
A PERSON WHO CAN SPEAK & WRITE USING: BIG WORDS, LATIN & GOBBLEDYGOOK & HELPS TO KEEP YOU OUT OF JAIL.

ESCROW OFFICER:
THE THIRD NEUTRAL PARTY IN A TRANSACTION. THE PERSON WHO FOLLOWS BUYER & SELLER INSTRUCTIONS TO THE LETTER & SPIRIT OF THE LAW.

SHARK:
LOOK OUT, CAN EAT UP YOUR MONEY

CHARACTERS

MAKE THE MARKET

REAL ESTATE BROKER:
THE PERSON WHO HELPS TO QUICKLY MOVE MONEY FROM ONE PERSON'S HAND TO ANOTHER'S.

ACCOUNTANT:
THE PERSON WHO WORKS WITH ALL OF YOUR NUMBERS & MONIES, & DOUBLE CHECKS TO BE SURE YOU ARE NOT PAYING TOO MUCH IN TAXES.

WISE OLD OWL:
A SMART BIRD ALWAYS READY WITH A PITHY WITTICISM, OR A PROFOUND STATEMENT.

SELLER:
THE PERSON WHO IS WILLING TO ACCEPT MONEY, OR "OTHER CONSIDERATION."

BANKER:
THE PERSON WHO PROVIDES THE DOLLARS TO COMPLETE THE TRANSACTION & WHO MOVES THE MONEY AROUND

CHAPTER
I
INVESTMENT
CONCEPTS

INVESTMENT CONCEPTS OVERVIEW

One man's obscurity is another man's gold mine.

Some of the most basic concepts are considered in this chapter. Of particular importance are the concepts of cash flow, leverage, upgrading and pyramiding. It is important for the reader to link this information to form a continuum of knowledge, and not to minimize thoughts which appear to be unimportant or obscure.

On any one particular investment, bits and pieces of information found in any chapter can and must be tied together in a unified flow of ideas and documentation, in order to consummate the transaction. You might combine ideas such as; equity pyramiding from chapter one, tenancy in common from chapter two, assessed valuation from chapter three, 'wrap-around' loan from chapter four, tax-deferred exchange from chapter five, and a market data appraisal from chapter six. How well you can tie all of these concepts together will, in large measure, determine the success or failure of a particular venture. With experience, the successful investor uses these ideas without consciously thinking about their inter-relationships, and they become rote, similar to driving a car—you don't think of the degree of pressure on the brake and accelerator, you just do it. With enough experience, making money becomes rote.

FLY SPECKS

There are no chapter divisions when you are dealing in real estate. There are no air-tight compartments of thought which are not allowed to intermingle with other thoughts. As we divide and classify in science to aid our understanding of animal, vegetable or mineral, for example, so we can divide real estate information. There is nothing sacred about using six chapters and one appendix, other than seven sections seems like a reasonable compromise and a good number. Knowledge doesn't always divide itself into categories. All the writer does is try to separate the fly specks from the pepper. Great labor pains were taken so that each page would give birth to a relevant thought. It is not necessary to wade through ten or more pages of text to reach the message, the medium of each page is the message, not unlike a slide show with each page being represented as a slide. Just as you would click-click back and forth on a carousel slide projector, you can rapidly turn the pages of this book using a quick review of all pages, or, linger on pages of particular interest.

The author would like to believe that a similarity exists between Dr. Mortimer Adler's Syntopicon, the guide to the *Great Ideas and Great Books*, and this book as a Syntopicon to the great ideas of real estate investing.

ODE TO AN INVESTOR

For everything in real estate
there is a time.
A time to buy
and a time to sell,
a time to option
and a time to lease.
A time to mortgage
and a time to trade;
A time to refinance
and a time to wraparound.
A time to MOF
and a time to be MOFED.
A time when your expenses
are greater than your income,
and it seems that the whole
world is closing in on you.
It is a time to trade down
or sell enough property.
A time to reach a positive
rate of return
on what's left.
In time, the reinvestment
of profit creates wealth.
*Do not eat
the seedcorn.*
It is time to prevent
losing it all.
Reflect on triple net,
and cash on cash edifices.
Enjoy, and delegate authority,
but don't lose control.
In time, the dinosaur lost
to the dogs, which ate his tail.

—*R.T.M.*

PYRAMID OF INVESTMENT

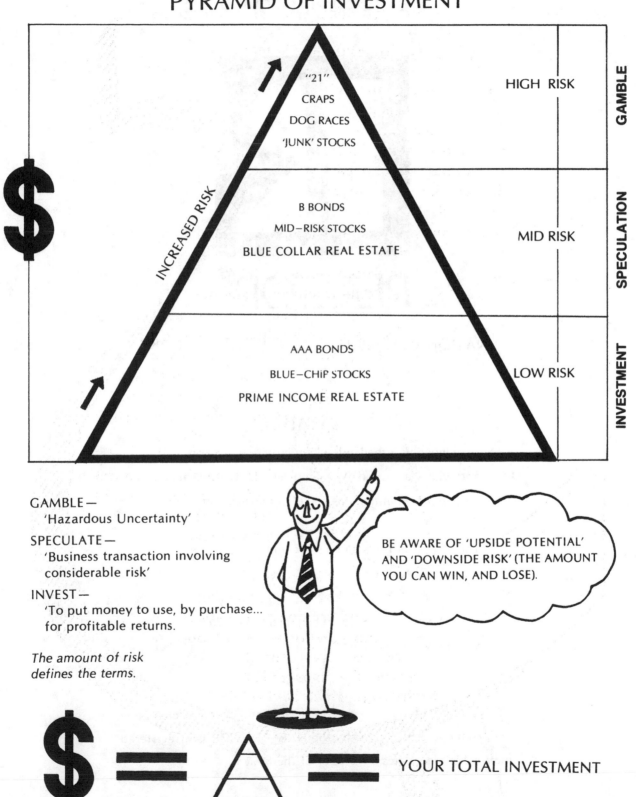

$ INCREASED RISK

"21" CRAPS DOG RACES 'JUNK' STOCKS	HIGH RISK
B BONDS MID–RISK STOCKS BLUE COLLAR REAL ESTATE	MID RISK
AAA BONDS BLUE–CHiP STOCKS PRIME INCOME REAL ESTATE	LOW RISK

GAMBLE

SPECULATION

INVESTMENT

GAMBLE—
'Hazardous Uncertainty'

SPECULATE—
'Business transaction involving considerable risk'

INVEST—
'To put money to use, by purchase... for profitable returns.

The amount of risk defines the terms.

BE AWARE OF 'UPSIDE POTENTIAL' AND 'DOWNSIDE RISK' (THE AMOUNT YOU CAN WIN, AND LOSE).

$ = △ = YOUR TOTAL INVESTMENT

CODE OF ETHICS

REALTOR®

NATIONAL ASSOCIATION OF REALTORS (NAR)*

PREAMBLE

Under all is the land. Upon its wise utilization
and widely allocated ownership depend the survival and
growth of free institutions and of our civilization...

The REALTOR can take no safer guide than...
the GOLDEN RULE:

"Whatsoever ye would that men should do to
you, do ye even to them."

*This page is intended to be educational and does not claim any
endorsement of this book by the NAR. REALTOR is a registered
mark which identifies a member of the NAR.

VALUE & GROWTH

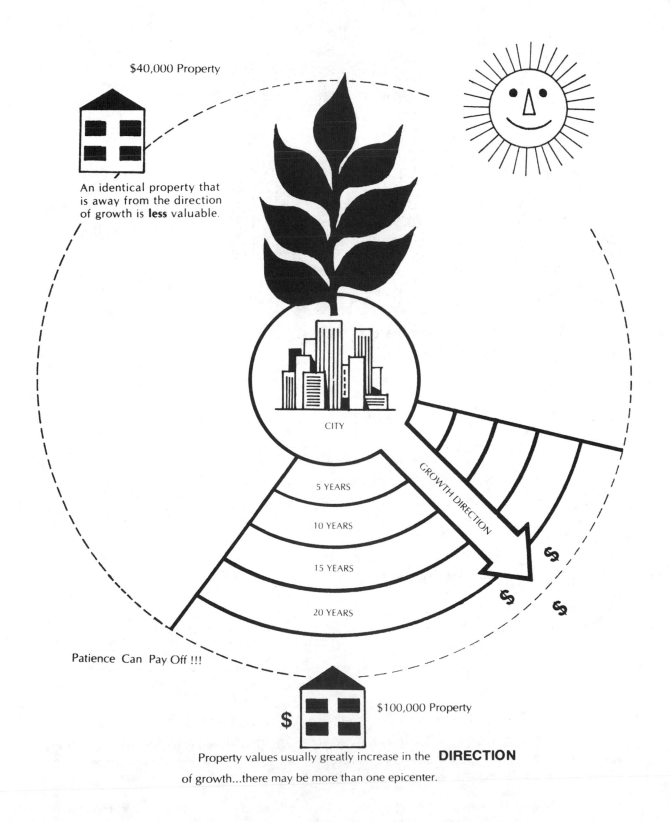

$40,000 Property

An identical property that is away from the direction of growth is **less** valuable.

CITY

5 YEARS

10 YEARS

15 YEARS

20 YEARS

GROWTH DIRECTION

Patience Can Pay Off !!!

$100,000 Property

Property values usually greatly increase in the **DIRECTION** of growth...there may be more than one epicenter.

ZONING

R - 1   = Residential = One-Family Dwelling

R - 2   to   R - 5   =   Multi – Family Dwelling

C   = Commercial (Stores)

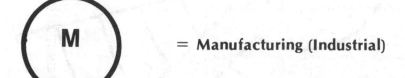

M   = Manufacturing (Industrial)

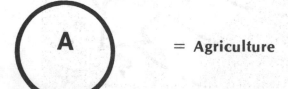

A   = Agriculture

Check with city planning officer to be sure a sewage plant, or the like, can not be built near your income property.

Exact zoning designations can vary widely from city to city. There are even cities without zoning restrictions. The above simply gives a broad brush look at zoning. For details in your area, purchase a copy of the zoning ordinances from city hall.

If you are politically oriented, try changing a few acres of agricultural land to commercially zoned income property. . .that should gross you about a million.

DIVIDING THE PURCHASE PRICE DOLLARS

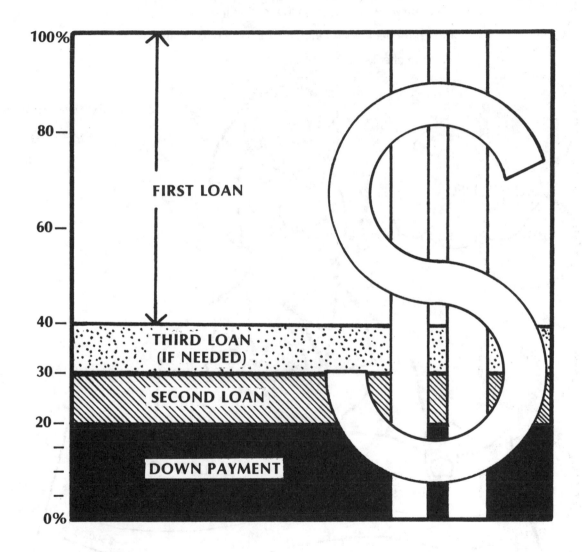

PERCENT OF
TOTAL PRICE

DEPOSIT WITH DEPOSIT RECEIPT

When giving a deposit with your Deposit Receipt
(Uniform Agreement of Sale and Deposit Receipt), which
is a contract, you may wish to write on the Receipt
and your check...particularly in multiple offers with
multiple checks, as follows:

THREE MOST IMPORTANT RULES IN BUYING PROPERTY

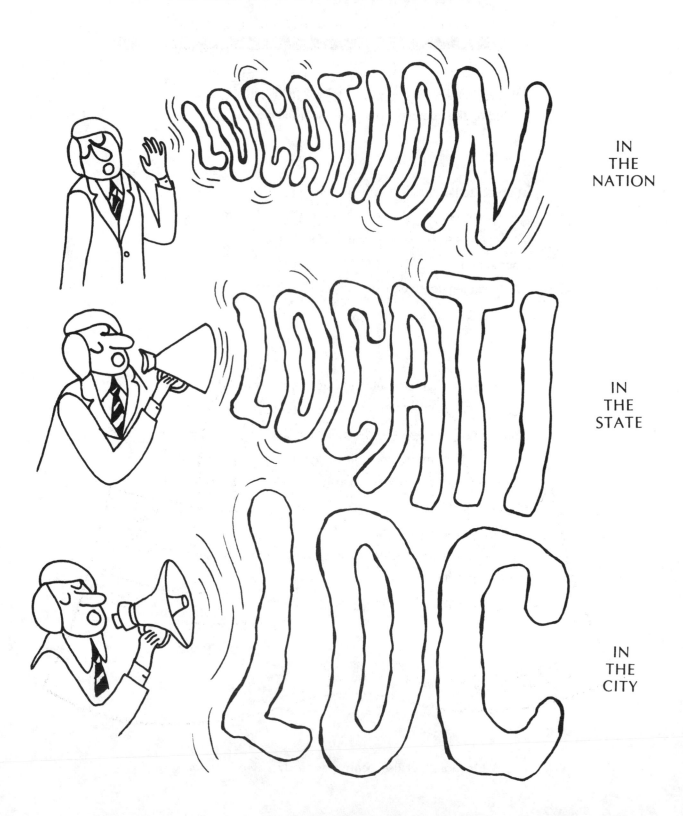

IN
THE
NATION

IN
THE
STATE

IN
THE
CITY

DEPOSIT RECEIPT CLAUSES TO CONSIDER

1.   Purchaser to pay $............CASH down payment,

   including the above deposit, plus the usual closing costs.

2.   Subject to Purchaser obtaining a new FIRST LOAN in the

   amount of $– – – – – – – – – – –payable at approximately

   $– – – – – – – – – – –per month including interest at– – – – – – –%

   per annum.

   A. Loan fee not to exceed– – – – – – –points.

3.   Purchaser to sign and Seller to carry a note secured by a

   SECOND DEED OF TRUST (OR MORTGAGE), in the

   amount of $– – – – – – – – – – –payable at $– – – – – – – – – – –

   per month, or more*, including interest at– – – – – – –% per

   annum, with the entire balance due– – – – – – –years from date

   of note.

   A. Or upon sale or transfer of the property.

   B. Or with right of one transfer upon approval of new

   buyer's credit by– – – – – – – – – – –.   Approval

   not to be unreasonably withheld.

*"Or more" clause permits an early pay-off of loan.

DEPOSIT RECEIPT CLAUSES TO CONSIDER

4.   Seller to deliver to Purchaser copies of all leases and rental agreements within – – – – –days from acceptance of this agreement.

5.   This offer subject to Purchaser's approval in writing of a PEST CONTROL INSPECTION REPORT made by a company of his choice, at his expense, and within – – – – –days from acceptance of this agreement.

6   The sales price includes all furniture and furnishings and any other personal property used in the operation of the building, including– – – – – – – –.*

7.   Possession of the property shall be delivered to the Purchaser upon recordation of the deed.

CLAP =ACRONYM

CASH   LOANS   AGREEMENTS   POSSESSION

*Note: Use "Bill of Sale" if extensive list.

REMARKS: 'Acronym' is a word formed by the initial letters of a name, or by combining initial letters, as 'Radar' is for RAdio Detecting And Ranging.

Please note Litigation Prevention pg. 379.

FAIR MARKET VALUE

FMV of a Property.

Elements:

1. A buyer and seller who are ready, able, willing and
   informed, and under no compulsion.

2. Property exposed on open market (many people) for
   a reasonable length of time; 3 to 6 months.

3. Sale to be for money, or with financing
   typically available in a given area.

EQUITY

Equity is the dollar amount of ownership; the difference between fair market value
of property and existing loans.

Property A:

Fair Market Value: $130,000

All Loans: −100,000

Equity $ 30,000

Property B:

Fair Market Value: $150,000

All Loans: −110,000

Equity $ 40,000

Property B has $10,000 more equity than Property A.

Please note Letter to Author pg. 383.

TWO-WAY EQUITY EXPANSION

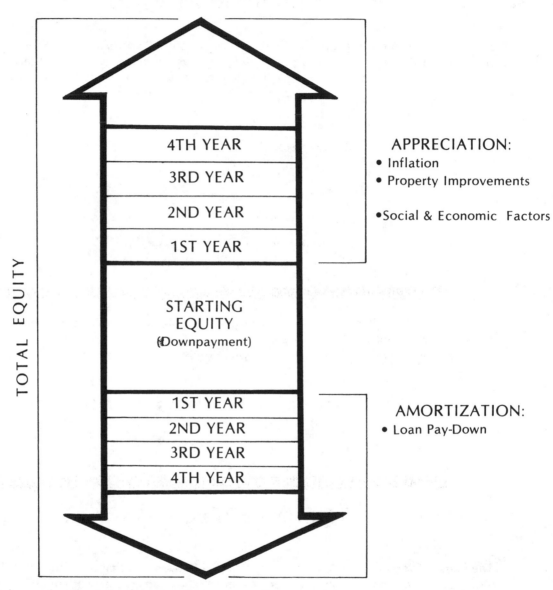

With the purchase of real estate there is a two-way equity expansion.

First, the equity increases with the increased value of the property due to inflation—property inflation usually exceeds the general inflation rate. This appreciated value can be further increased by improving the property, i.e., painting, landscaping, etc., as well as by factors of social and economic importance. For example, your area is selected for a television documentary expounding on the marvelous architecture, way of life and advanced public services; or, a new, efficient transportation system and feather massage health spa are installed within only walking distance from your building. Note that a 10% increase in appreciation, or $10,000 for a $100,000 property, is equal to a 50% increase on a down payment of $20,000: an example of high return on your equity investment.

Secondly, the equity expansion is accomplished by the paying down of the loan using the principal portion of the monthly loan payment.

SELL TO THE SLEEPING POINT

Are you tossing and turning in your bed worrying about your property? Then sell (or trade). Peace of mind and the enjoyment of a productive life is as important as money. Start looking for 'no sweat' properties, that are headache free. Sell to the sleeping point.

WINNERS & LOSERS

A winner knows what he will do if he loses, a loser only knows what he will do if he wins.

If, at some future time, real estate prices (not necessarily *values*) decline, some people will see this as an opportunity to buy. Many of today's great fortunes began in the depression of the 1930's when people of vision saw opportunity, while others only despaired.

THE IMPERFECT MARKET

The market for real estate is an imperfect market in the sense that the items for sale are not alike (compared to cartons of milk in a grocery), and a buyer can not be aware of all property for sale in the area of his interest at any given time. It is the function of the real estate agent to make this inherently inperfect market more perfect, so that both buyer and seller have better information about their available choices.

Real estate can not be sold mechanically like stocks and bonds. One should be aware that any property, real estate or stocks and bonds, can legally and practically be sold to another person without a broker. It is odd that fewer people think of selling stocks without a broker than of selling real estate by themselves. In general, competent professional real estate brokerage is easily worth the cost of the commission.

SWEAT EQUITY

Sweat equity is the equity created in a property by your own hard labor, and usually the ability to obtain a 'home improvement loan.' It is a matter of historical fact that when you take away the incentive for sweat equity (with rent control and the like) you help create 'instant slums.'

Be sure it is worth your time fixing leaky faucets, repairing ceilings, and other repair and remodel jobs . . . as opposed to contracting the work, and spending your hours negotiating for an eight unit complex that can make fifty thousand dollars in profit.

THE MEEK TO INHERIT

The *"meek shall inherit the earth."* Possibly so, but it is recommended from personal experience that the meek have at least ten percent down payment, good credit references, and a complete loan package.

RENT vs PURCHASE

START WITH A $100,000 HOUSE OR CONDO.

RENT		PURCHASE	
		Down Payment $20,000	
$ 500	Per month (Assumes no increase in rent which is unlikely.)	First loan cost per month . . 800 (Principal, interest and taxes) PER YEAR	$9,600
		Taxes per year $1,000	
		Loan interest (Say 10% of $80,000) 8,000	
		TOTAL OF INTEREST & TAXES (deductible) . . . $9,000	
		Say 30% tax bracket. Then 30% of $9,000 is a tax saving . . . . (—)	2,700
$6,000	PER YEAR	EFFECTIVE YEARLY OUTGO . .	$6,900

TEN YEARS LATER (OR SOONER) MONIES SPENT FOR HOUSING

$60,000   **$69,000**

GROSS PROFIT ON SALE
(Or equity build up is equal to appreciation plus loan pay down)

$0   **$170,000**
                                                                (Conservative)

If one sale obtains $170,000, why not try for six sales and one million?

Please note Letter to Author pg. 382.

EQUAL HOUSING OPPORTUNITIES

Federal law prohibits
discrimination based on race,
religion, creed, color, national origin
or ancestry in connection with
the sale or rental of
residential real estate.

EMOTIONAL EQUITY

What is the *present worth* to you of your mother, father or a close friend? What is their *future capital asset value* to you? One hundred thousand dollars, a million? Not really. The questions seem unintelligible, for we place values on people and things that have nothing to do with money. Some are irreplaceable and invaluable.

So it is, with certain property. You place a value on a building, usually your home, that transcends equity defined as fair market value less loans. Investors often say 'don't become emotionally involved with a building,' no doubt, an accurate statement when your goal is to create a large bank account, and not monuments. It is not accurate, however, to say don't become emotionally involved with *living*. To invite friends to your home for good food, good music, and good conversation amidst beautiful surroundings creates an emotional value and 'equity' that is not found on a balance sheet.

THE PROPERTY STATEMENT

Location:	100 Baker Street
Lot Size:	81.6 ft. × 70.3 ft.
Zoning:	R - 3
Assessments:	Land . . . . $ 9,600
	Improvements 30,000
Improvements:	Six, 2 bedroom units with...
Income:	Apt's. 1 to 6 @ $366+ each.
	Monthly gross income: . . 2,200
	ANNUAL GROSS INCOME: $ 26,400

Expenses:*

Taxes	$ 5,000
Insurance	300
Water	120
Gas and Electricity	190
Garbage	90
License	20
Elevator	240
Miscellaneous	40
Annual Expenses:	$ 6,000
Annual Net Income:	$ 20,400

Asking Price:	. . . . $240,000

* With a property manager you would have an additional expense *tax write-off*. If you manage yourself and occupy one unit, then in this example, 1/6 is treated as your home and 5/6 of expenses and depreciation are tax deductible. Property taxes and loan interest are 100% tax deductible.

Remember that even a single-family dwelling, if rented,
is income property.

THE LIVES OF A PROPERTY

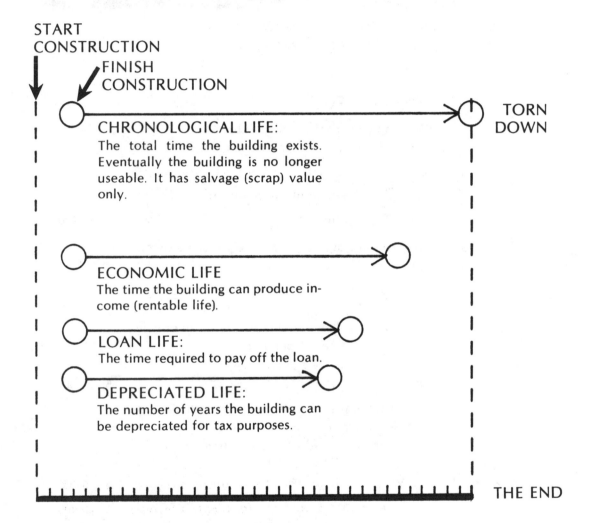

START
CONSTRUCTION
FINISH
CONSTRUCTION

TORN
DOWN

CHRONOLOGICAL LIFE:
The total time the building exists.
Eventually the building is no longer
useable. It has salvage (scrap) value
only.

ECONOMIC LIFE
The time the building can produce income (rentable life).

LOAN LIFE:
The time required to pay off the loan.

DEPRECIATED LIFE:
The number of years the building can
be depreciated for tax purposes.

THE END

TIME IN YEARS

A building has many lives. The actual or chronological life could be fifty, or a hundred years or more. The loan life could be thirty years (to completely pay it off).

Better the building lasts longer than the loan, than the reverse.

CASH FLOW MADE SIMPLE

UNDERSTANDING TERMS:

1. Owner's Asking Price . . . . $ 220,000
   (What an owner asks and what he gets
   can be different.)

2. Purchase Price (Buyer) . . . . $ 200,000

   Selling price (Seller) . . . . $ 200,000
   For buyer and seller, the price is the same on one
   transaction.

3. Down Payment (15%) . . . . $ 30,000
   (Usually in cash, but could be other form of value
   such as gold, auto, second notes, etc.)

4. Annual Gross Income . . . . $ 25,000
   or Scheduled Gross Income (is usually rent
   income), but also includes income from garages,
   washer and dryer, ad sign on building, etc.)

5. Less Vacancy Factor (4%) of Gross Income . . . . $ 1,000
   Can be exact $ amount or % for area.

6. Effective Gross Income . . . . $ 24,000
   Also called Adjusted Gross Income.

7. Less FIXED EXPENSES
    Fixed (T + i = Taxes and Insurance)
    Taxes .... $ 5,000

    Real estate taxes only (not to be confused with income tax).

8. Insurance .... $ 300

    Usually covers: fire, property damage and liability (. . . be sure to analyze if you want to cover earthquake, theft, loss of rentals, etc.).

9. OPERATING EXPENSES:*

    Water .... $ 120
    Gas and Electricity   190
    Scavenger Service   90
    Business License   20
    Elevator   240
    Misc.: janitor, etc............................   40

    Be sure you are aware if tenants are paying for their own utilities and that they are not included in operating expenses.

    Total Annual Expenses .... $ 6,000

* Operating expenses are everything except P.I.P.E. (principal, interest, and personal expenses).

10. Annual Gross Income . . . . $ 25,000

    Less Vacancy Factor 1,000
    Effective Gross Income 24,000
    Less Expenses 6,000
    Annual Net Income (Operating Net Income) . . . . . . $ 18,000

    This 'net income' is more accurately a 'broker's net'
    or 'operating net' as all factors have not been con-
    sidered. It is a handy reference point.

    We must keep going for a more complete property
    analysis . . .

11. Debt Service (Loan Payments):

    1st + 2nd* Loan . . . . $ 170,000
    1st + 2nd Loan Payments ($1,500 month) 18,000
    (P + i = Principal and Interest)
       1st + 2nd Interest Payments (part of loan pay-
    ment)* 13,000
    Principal** . . . . $ 5,000

* 'Purchase money deed of trust, or mortgage' is a loan that the
  seller 'carries' (takes back) to consummate the purchase.

** With an amortized loan, the interest portion decreases, and the
   principal portion increases.

12. Annual Operating Net Income . . . . $ 18,000

13. Annual Debt Service   18,000

14. Annual CASH FLOW   0

    CASH FLOW is income remaining from gross in-
    come after deducting annual operating expenses
    and principal and interest payments. In this exam-
    ple, by increasing the down payment, you would
    decrease the debt service, and increase the cash
    flow.

15. Net Spendable Income   0

    Net spendable is cash flow less income taxes. (In
    this case with zero cash flow there is no income tax
    . . . as the $18,000 net income is 'tax sheltered' by
    $13,000 in interest and $6,000 in depreciation.)

16. Even with zero cash flow, you would have the
    following advantages:

    A. Annual Depreciation (BLDG. $150,000 × 4%) . . $ 6,000
    B. Equity Build-Up (Principal)   5,000
    C. Appreciation (5%) . . . . $ 10,000

A QUICK ANALYSIS OF CASH FLOW
(ACTUAL CASE)

P.P. =Purchase Price = $230,000 = 8.71 x Gross Income

Low Down Payment = 30,000 = 13% Down

1st and 2nd Loans = $200,000 = Balance

Gross Income = $26,400 = Rentals

IN = $2,200 Month

1st Loan = $161,000 = 70% of P.P.

@ 9.5%, 30 years = $1,354 Month

2nd Loan = $39,000 @ 9.5%

INTEREST ONLY, due in 10 years = $ 309 Month

Debt Service = $1,663 Month

Expenses, Month = 517

$2,180 Month

OUT = $2,180 Month

CASH FLOW = $20 Month

If no loans the cash flow would equal $1,683 Month

A PARCEL OF PARADISE
REPRINTED FROM CONDOMINIUM REVIEW

Condominium Review Editor-in-Chief Jack Swig recently sat down with Roy Maloney to discuss Roy's penthouse at the Island Sands on Maui and the reasons for its purchase.

CR: Roy, why did you decide to purchase, rather than rent, for the few weeks a year when it's possible for you to get away for a vacation?

RM: Well, Jack, owning property is important to me. If I may digress for a moment, I'll explain how I view ownership. I think you **can explain whole systems of government and political phenomena as functions of ownership**. I would even go as far as to say that **ownership is the cornerstone of democracy**. It's a pivotal point in any civilization.

CR: Can you expand on that thought with some examples?

RM: War is the transfer of ownership from nation to nation, revolution the transfer of ownership from class to class. Fascism the control of ownership by one man, a dictator. Oligarchy the ownership by a rich few. Socialism is ownership by the state; and Communism, in its pure form, is ownership by all the people. On the other hand, Democracy is ownership by private individuals. I think this is the very essence of democracy. **In my view, the more private individual ownership that exists, the stronger the democracy becomes.**

CR: I see your point, but isn't there a more practical reason behind your decision to buy the unit on Maui?

RM: Yes. The other reason is I wanted to make a buck. I suppose if you wanted to sum it up in one word, I would have to say that I bought it because of the ladies.

CR: Are you telling me that women are the reason you bought? Do you really meet more ladies because you own a condominium on Maui?

RM: No. Let me explain. I use the term "L.A.D.I.E.S." as an acronym, standing for: Leverage, Appreciation, Depreciation, Income, Equity and Shelter. And I'm going for all of them.

CR: Why did you select a condominium instead of a single family home or a beach bungalow?

RM: Well, actually, I would have preferred a single family home. I found a spectacular parcel on Maalaea Bay, on which I wanted to build my own home. But then I discovered that the land alone was priced at $1.1 million. So, I took a more practical point of view and came to the realization that the most affordable location on Maalaea Bay with the best view was the Island Sands Condominium. It met the three most important requirements for real estate — location, location, and location. My requirements were a place on the water with an unobstructed view of 180 degrees, or ideally a 300 degree view. It had to be something affordable, and I preferred fee-simple title, as opposed to a lease arrangement. Within those parameters, the condominium I bought was the only way that I could conceivably fill those needs. I bought a home within a condominium structure to make it economically feasible. It's just that simple. The condominium vehicle offered me the best location at the lowest price. And, of course, the future benefits were quite attractive.

CR: How about the cost picture? Could you outline your monthly costs?

RM: The costs of ownership include day to day maintenance, taxes on the individual unit and the common area, insurance, and, of course, loan payments, if you have a mortgage or deed of trust outstanding. Let me give you some specific figures as examples. Monthly maintenance, which includes common area insurance, is about $170. My taxes are fifty dollars a month. Insurance runs twenty dollars a month. So, each month, I spend about $240. I paid cash, so there is no loan.

CR: Would you say that your monthly costs are less than those on a single family home, in a comparable location?

RM: There's no question that this is true. The obvious reason is that I am sharing the costs with eighty-three other people. We have one acre of land with a swimming pool, a breakwater, security coverage and other amenities. When a group of owners share these costs, the monthly individual cost is very modest. The only conceivable way I know for a person of average means to afford a six million dollar property is to join with others to make it affordable. The condominium allows you ownership. **This ownership can only be possible when it is shared, and the sharing affords this luxury to many people.**

CR: I know you're not a C.P.A. Roy, but could you tell me what tax relief your ownership provides?

RM: That's correct. I'm not qualified to give tax advice. However, because I am the first owner of a newly-constructed condominium, I can take double declining balance depreciation. In this case, it means $16,400.00 a year, not including the $10,000.00 worth of personal property that I put into the unit, that can also be depreciated. This depreciation provides an excellent tax shelter.

CR: The story has been all roses and no thorns, up to this point. How about rentals? You don't live there for much of the year, and you're located a considerable distance away. How difficult is it for you to obtain rentals?

RM: It is extremely easy for me to obtain rentals, because I don't do anything. My involvement in the rental process is zero. I pay the management company 40 percent of the rentals they obtain. It's one of their standard services. Herein lies the ease of renting, and, herein also lies the rub. The first year it was rented less than half the time. Because I am three thousand miles away, I have no control over the rental, it's frustrating. I expect our new management group will be more successful in increasing the rentals. Basically, I suppose, it's lack of control that disturbs me.

CR: Are you satisfied with the percentage of return on your unit?

RM: Hell, no! I'd like to see it rented closer to 90 percent of the time, but I'd settle for 70 percent as a reasonable compromise.

CR: Were there any representations made to you at the time of purchase, as to the percentage of time you'd be able to obtain rental income?

RM: No. They played that point very straight. They said that they didn't know what the rental factor would be, but that they expected an increase in rentals, each year. They did tell me

that there would be a negative cash flow. It was a new construction and it is harder to find rentals while the property is new and unknown.

CR: Does living in a condominium destroy the seclusion you were seeking from a single family home?

RM: In my particular case, I selected an end unit penthouse, with three sides of open air and one thick cement wall. I tested the interior units and found them to be relatively soundproof. Frankly, the people who can afford a place like this are wealthier people buying second homes or retiring, and they make nice neighbors.

CR: How would you assess the quality of ownership on the unit, Roy? Are you disappointed that you didn't buy a single family home, after all?

RM: No. I could not afford, from a cash flow basis, the land I wanted, much less the cost of building a home. I couldn't afford the maintenance, the trees and landscaping, or the security service to look after the place when I wasn't there. In short, without a condominium, I couldn't afford the location.

CR: Now that you've owned the unit for over a year, have you had any second thoughts?

RM: Not at all. The condominium was definitely the right decision, even though it was stated to me that there may be a negative cash flow. I analyze an investment by examining my satsfaction with two major factors. First, for me the location is perfect. The sec-

ond factor is appreciation. There is no question in my mind that the property has appreciated in value. I could not find a unit today that compares with mine, without spending $100,000 more. **The reality is that you make your money when you buy.** I bought right. The old adage, 'Buy land, they ain't making it any more' is particularly true concerning beachfront property on Maui. It is a definite seller's market. I understand a two bedroom penthouse on Kaanapali Beach recently sold for one million dollars.

CR: From what you say about the increase in prices, could I reasonably infer that your appreciation is far outdistancing' your negative annual cash flow?

RM: My opinion of my own unit and location is that the appreciation is on the order of 40 percent a year, that's over three percent per month. So, the answer is yes. Also with no loan payment, I have a positive cash flow.

CR: In a nut shell, Roy, what has owning the condominium meant to you?

RM: Well, economically, it has appreciated in value. And, it's a great place to live . . . in fact, recently I was there standing on my lanai at five in the morning. The surf was crashing below, the sugar cane was whispering in the breeze. In minutes, the moon went down over the mountains of Maui, to the West. And then the sun rose behind the 10,000 foot peak of Haleakala, the world's largest dormant volcano. As I stood there, the world changed from pitch darkness to brilliant sunlight. It's my parcel of paradise, a very warm and sensual place. □

DEPOSIT OF RENTAL CHECKS

In order to facilitate the deposit of checks for your manager, or when you are on vacation ...

You may want to consider a DBA (Doing Business As) name for your property ... it also helps to keep the accounting separate.

You or your manager can then stamp the back of rent checks:

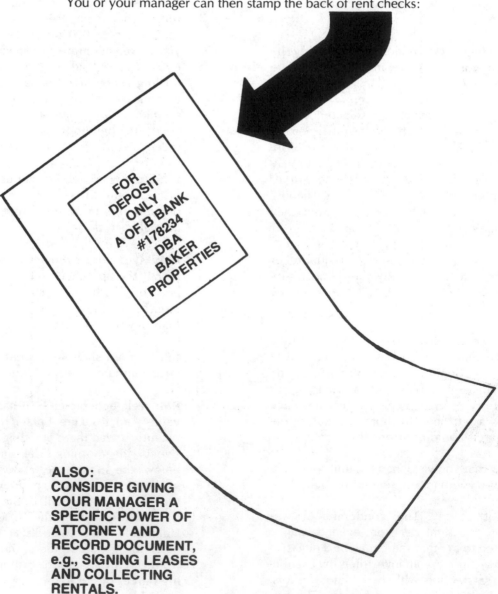

FOR
DEPOSIT
ONLY
A OF B BANK
#178234
DBA
BAKER
PROPERTIES

**ALSO:
CONSIDER GIVING
YOUR MANAGER A
SPECIFIC POWER OF
ATTORNEY AND
RECORD DOCUMENT,
e.g., SIGNING LEASES
AND COLLECTING
RENTALS.**

TENANTS AS AN ASSET

Above property gross income = $ 0

Tenants = Income = Assets

LEVERAGE AND RETURN

	NO FINANCING	FINANCED
Purchase Price:	$100,000	$100,000
Financing:	(−) 0	75,000
Cash Down Payment *Your equity:*	$ 100,000	$ 25,000
Net Income:	10,000	10,000
Loan Interest: *$75,000 x 0.08*	(−) 0	6,000
Net Income LESS Loan Interest *As Yield:*	$ 10,000	$ 4,000
Return on EQUITY: *Return on investment*	10%	16%
Increase in Return Due To Leverage:	0	6%

LEVERAGE

Leverage:

> To use borrowed money to purchase an investment that
> realizes enough income to cover the expense of financing.

PROPERTY "A"

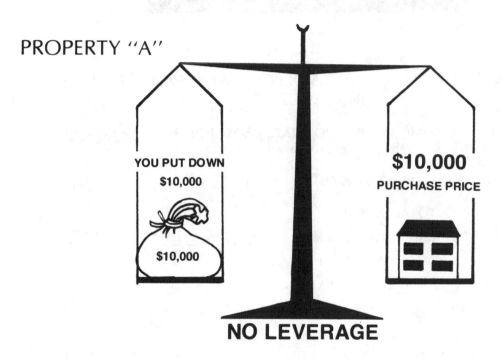

PROPERTY "B"

LEVERAGE & INFLATION

COMPARE $20,000 IN A SAVINGS DEPOSIT WITH $20,000 INVESTED IN REAL ESTATE

ASSUME AN INFLATION RATE OF 8% PER YEAR
(The principle works with any rate.)

BANK SAVINGS DEPOSIT

TOTAL DEPOSIT	= $20,000
BANK INTEREST 8%	= 1,600*
DEPOSIT + INTEREST 1st YEAR	= 21,600
8% RATE OF INFLATION	= −1,600
VALUE OF DEPOSIT AFTER INFLATION	= $20,000
YIELD (AFTER INFLATION)	= 0%

NOTE: For purposes of comparison and
simplicity, the leverage and inflation
are isolated. In the real estate example
(next page), expenses are balanced by
rental income and tax write offs
(depreciation, etc.)

* You are even . . . almost. You must pay
taxes on interest earned.

LEVERAGE & INFLATION

SAME $20,000 INVESTED IN REAL ESTATE

WITH 20% DOWN & 80% LOAN (LEVERAGED).

PURCHASE PRICE @ FMV		$100,000
INVESTED IN DOWN PAYMENT	$20,000	
INCREASE IN VALUE OF PROPERTY AT RATE OF INFLATION (8%)	8,000	
VALUE OF PROPERTY AT END OF ONE YEAR.		108,000
COST OF $80,000 LOAN @ 10% INTEREST.	(−) 8,000	
TAX WRITE OFF (SAY 37.5% BRACKET)	(+) 3,000	
ACTUAL COST OF INTEREST PAID ON $80,000 LOAN AFTER DEDUCTING FOR TAX SAVINGS.	(−) 5,000	
VALUE OF PROPERTY INCLUDING INFLATION & LESS COST OF LOAN		$103,000
AMOUNT AHEAD OF INFLATION (EQUITY)	$3,000	
$3,000 INCREASE ON $20,000 INVESTMENT		15% YR
		RETURN ON INVESTMENT

LEVERAGE ALTERNATIVES

FIXED CONDITIONS:

1. Purchase Price = $500,000

2. Net Income = 11%
   Net Income = $55,000

3. Interest on Any Loans
   (Payable Interest only) per Annum = 10%
   (Tax Write-Off)

VARIABLE CONDITIONS:

1. The $ Amount of Loans
   (Amount of leverage)

2. Down Payment
   (Cash invested)

	Try:	OR A	OR B	OR C	OR D
Purchase Price	$	500,000	500,000	500,000	500,000
Down Payment	$	500,000	450,000	100,000	10,000
Loans	$	0	50,000	400,000	490,000
Net Income (11%)	$	55,000	55,000	55,000	55,000
Less: Interest Cost on 10% Loan	$	0	5,000	40,000	49,000
Investment Return	$	55,000	50,000	15,000	6,000
Divided By: Cash Invested	$	500,000	450,000	100,000	10,000
Return on Cash Invested		11%	11%	15%	60%

Note that the "Return on Cash Invested" increases with the **increase** in the loan amount borrowed (the amount of leverage). The trick is to be sure the net income is factual, and will hold long enough to obtain the return of your cash invested, plus a profit.

The question is will the net income stay above the cost of the loan? If not, then be as sure as possible that you can profit on the appreciation.

In general, the greater the risk the greater the reward.

LADIES

A good acronymn to remember for income property.

L
A
D
I
E
S

LEVERAGE
Low down, big loan.

APPRECIATION
Increase in value of property.

DEPRECIATION
Tax write off each year.

INCOME
Gross income less expenses is net income.

EQUITY
Paying down the loans and building equity.

SHELTER
Depreciation and expenses can shelter income from taxes.

A COMPARATIVE ANALYSIS OF INVESTMENTS

	FIXED YIELD		SECURITIES	
	Bank Savings Account	**2nd Deeds Of Trust**	**AAA Municipal Bonds**	**Blue-Chip Stocks**
Market Value	$20,000	$20,000	$20,000	$20,000
1 Less Loan	0	0	0	0
2 = Equity	20,000	20,000	20,000	20,000
3 Gross Income	1,000	2,000	960	840
4 - Expenses	0	0	0	0
5 = Net Income	1,000	2,000	960	840
6 Yield on Price	5%	10%	4.8%	4.2%
7 -Loan Payments	0	0	0	0
8 =Cash Flow	1,000	2,000	960	840
9 Yield on Equity	5%	10%	4.8%	4.2%
10 Income Tax $\pm$	-300	-600	0	-252
11 Net Spendable	700	1,400	960	588
12 Yield on Equity	3.5%	7%	4.8%	2.9%
13 + Appreciation	0	0	0	+860
14 Spendable + Apprec.	700	1,400	960	1,448
15 − Inflation 3% (Low)	-600	-600	-600	-600
16 =Net Appreciation	100	800	360	848
17 + Equity Build Up	0	0	0	0
18 Total Return	100	800	360	848
19 Total Yield	0.5%	4%	1.8%	4.2%

REAL ESTATE

	Free and Clear (All Cash)	25% Down 75% Loan
Market Value	**$20,000**	**$80,000**
1 Less Loan	0	-60,000
2 = Equity	20,000	20,000
3 Gross Income	2,800	11,300
4 -Expenses	-1,200	-4,500
5 =Net Income	1,600	6,800
6 Yield on Price	8%	8.5%
7 -Loan Payments	0	-5,320
8 =Cash Flow	1,600	1,480
9 Yield on Equity	8%	7.4%
10 Income Tax +−	-192	+453
11 Net Spendable	1,408	1,933
12 Yield on Equity	7%	9.7%
13 + Appreciation	+1,000	+4,000
14 Spendable + Appreciation	2,408	5,933
15 -Inflation 3% (Low)	-600	-600
16 = Net Appreciation	1,808	5,333
17 + Equity Build Up	0	+850
18 Total Return	1,808	6,183
19 Total Yield	9%	30.9%

RAW LAND VS. INCOME PROPERTY

Manhattan island was purchased by the Dutch from the Indians for $24.
The present valuation is about $12 billion dollars.

William Seward purchased ALASKA for $7,200,000.
A cost of 2 CENTS per acre.

There are still many good buys in raw land.

Be sure you can afford to pay the property taxes, make the loan payments
and be able to wait.

Raw land produces zero income.

LOT SIZE IN ACRES

1 ACRE = 43,560 Square Feet

$$\frac{\text{Your lot in sq. ft.}}{\text{Divided by 43,560}} = \text{Acres you have}$$

Or: 1 sq. ft. $= \dfrac{1}{43,560}$ Acres

1 sq. ft. = 0.000023 Acres

Square Feet you HAVE x 0.000023 = Acres you have

Or:

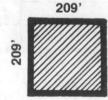

209'

209'

A 209 ft. square is

roughly one acre.

A SECTION

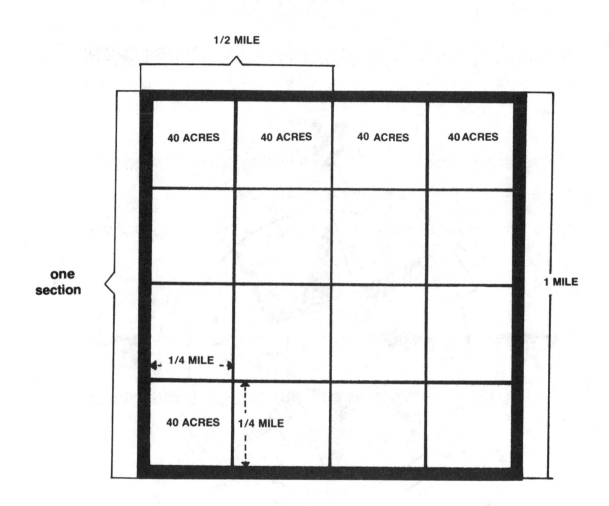

- A ¼ mile square equals 40 acres
- A section is I mile square.
- A section has 16 parcels of 40 acres each.
- A section has 640 acres.

A standard township six miles square contains 36 SECTIONS.

COMPASS ROSE

Directions and descriptions by points of the compass are more specific.

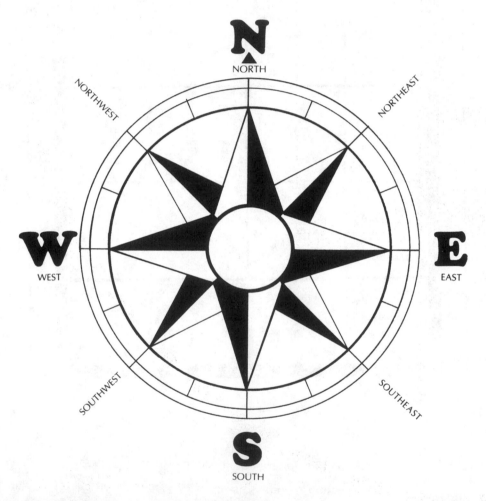

Property can be described in terms of *metes* (measurements and compass directions) and *bounds* (boundary lines), or it can be a *legal description* as follows:

LEGAL DESCRIPTION

BEGINNING at a point on the westerly line of Gough Street, distant thereon 110 feet northerly from the northerly line of Pine Street; running thence northerly and along said line of Gough Street 27 feet and six inches; thence at a right angle westerly 110 feet; thence at a right angle southerly 27 feet and six inches; thence at a right angle easterly 110 feet to the point of beginning.

The best way to read a legal description is to find the first semicolon (;) and *read backwards*.

ACTION OF THE SUN

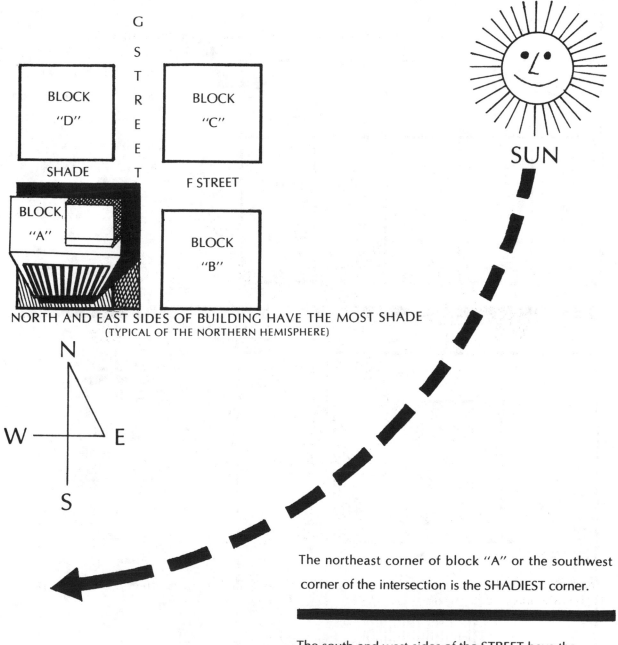

NORTH AND EAST SIDES OF BUILDING HAVE THE MOST SHADE
(TYPICAL OF THE NORTHERN HEMISPHERE)

The northeast corner of block "A" or the southwest corner of the intersection is the SHADIEST corner.

The south and west sides of the STREET have the most shade.

The north and east sides of the STREET have the most sun.

KEY LOT

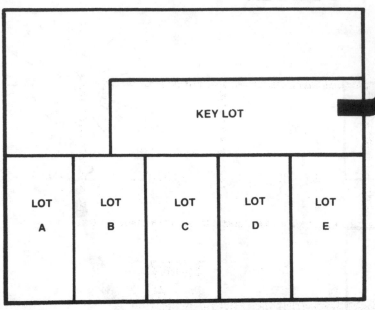

KEY LOT

| LOT A | LOT B | LOT C | LOT D | LOT E |

A lot bounded on **one** side by the backs of other lots which front on another street is usually the *least* desirable lot; too many neighbors —too many barking dogs.

COMMERCIAL ACRE

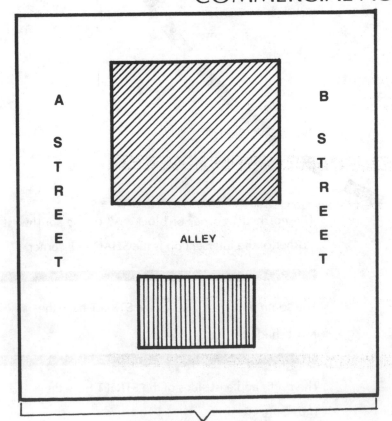

A STREET

B STREET

ALLEY

43,560 SQ. FT. = 1 ACRE

C.A. is the *remaining* portion of full acre after subtracting public streets and alleys.

ASSEMBLAGE & PLOTTAGE

LOT "A" $20,000	LOT "B" $20,000	LOT "C" $20,000

A + B + C = Assemblage

The ACT of combining two or more parcels.

$$\begin{aligned} \$\ 20{,}000 &= A \\ 20{,}000 &= B \\ 20{,}000 &= C \\ \hline V = \$100{,}000 \end{aligned}$$

INCREASE in VALUE

due to assemblage is PLOTTAGE.

W. Zeckendorf, the famous New York Realtor, assembled 17 acres of an odorous old slaughter-house district into the United Nations site...with a resultant skyrocketing plottage.

He also "changed the use"...to "the highest and best use" (*greatest net return*).

ESCROW

An Escrow is a transaction wherein a THIRD NEUTRAL party acts as a stake's holder for buyer and seller and processes all papers and monies to complete the sale.

SELLER

DEPOSIT RECEIPT

BUYER

Escrow Officer acts as agent for buyer and seller.

ESCROW OFFICER

ACCEPTANCE

ALL DOCUMENTS AND MONIES.

ESCROW

CLOSE OF ESCROW...COE

PRELIMINARY TITLE REPORT

As the name implies, a *preliminary title report* is a report issued on a property prior to close of escrow. On any property of interest it can and should be asked for, and then carefully analysed.

The report lists all matters of record relating to a specific property, such as:

1. Assessor's parcel number and usually a street address.

2. Vesting, i.e., how title is presently held. Concerning vesting of title, be sure to get expert advise on the best method of taking title, and be aware of the various Federal and State tax advantages for: joint tenancy, tenants in common, community property, limited partnership, tenancy in the entirety (like community property), etc.

3. A legal description of the property. It is a good idea to trace out the legal description on a plot map, and be certain the property lines form a complete enclosure.

4. Taxes, current and outstanding (if any).

5. Liens, encumbrances, easements, Deeds of Trust, mortgages, conditions (contigencies or qualifications on the property), covenants (unconditional promises), and restrictions (limitations on use) (CC&R's).

6. Judgements or any other matter affecting the vested owner.

7. If in doubt ask for *all* documents specified in the 'prelim.' The documents themselves are just referred to. For example, on reading the actual CC&R document it might be stated (as they have) that "no liquor may be sold, or no animals may be raised." This could be of concern for a potential liquor store or kennel.

ESCROW CHECKLIST

☑

☐ **1.** Prior to escrow be sure there is complete agreement between the buyer and seller on all essential points, and that all contingencies are removed before, or during escrow.

☐ **2.** Be sure all terms and conditions are written specifically, and with definitive times for completion. Remember a court of law, or arbitration committee, may have to interpret the exact meanings if a serious problem arises.

☐ **3.** Prior to escrow, be sure you have analysed the *'Preliminary Title Report'* and are aware of the legal description, and the various matters of record.

☐ **4.** If possible, bring the existing deed.

☐ **5.** Handle building inspection and pest inspection report, as per contract.

☐ **6.** Increase the down payment and notify multiple listing service (if used) of sale.

☐ **7.** Full names of buyer and seller of the property.

☐ **8.** Statement of how buyer wants title to be vested, i.e., joint tenancy, community property, etc.

☐ **9.** Names of all holders of mortgages, or trust deeds including their addresses, phone numbers, loan numbers, and seller's future address and phone number.

☐ **10.** Terms of new and existing encumbrances, and unpaid balance of each.

☐ **11.** Buyer to prepare and deliver a financial statement (necessary for the holder of the loans which are to be obtained or assumed).

☐ **12.** Buyer to obtain insurance for the property, or a 'binder' (temporary coverage), for fire, liability, etc.

☐ **13.** Current tax bills and receipts.

☐ **14.** Appropriate closing costs.

☐ **15.** Copies of all leases, including security deposits.

☐ **16.** Utilities to be in buyer's name at close of escrow.

☐ **17.** Keep escrow number handy for reference.

☐ **18.** Notify tenants of new ownership at close of escrow.

☐ **19.** Keep in touch with your Realtor and escrow officer for other details.

Please note Letter to Author pg. 379.

BUYER'S ESCROW CLOSING COSTS

A QUICK CHECKLIST

(Always contact the escrow officer, or Realtor, for details):

✔	✔
☐ Title insurance	☐ Loan fee
☐ Escrow fee	☐ Credit report
☐ Notary fee	☐ Tax service fee
☐ Recording fee	☐ Appraisal fee
☐ Fire insurance (and liability)	☐ Interest on loan
☐ Pest control inspection fee	☐ Taxes

SELLER'S ESCROW CLOSING COSTS

A QUICK CHECKLIST

✔	✔
☐ Notary fees	☐ Prepayment penalty
☐ Recording fees	☐ Lender's loan fee
☐ Impound funds	☐ Proration of rents
☐ Documentary transfer tax	☐ Security deposits
☐ Real estate sales commission	☐ Repairs to building
☐ Proration of property tax	☐ Proration of interest on loan
☐ Reconveyance fee	☐ Title insurance (if payable by seller)

SIMPLIFIED CLOSING STATEMENT

SELLER   BUYER

DEBIT	CREDIT	DEBIT	CREDIT
	$120,000 Selling Price	$120,000 Purchase Price	
$100,000 1st loan to be assumed			$100,000 Buyer is CREDITED for 1st loan assumed
$20,000 Cash to seller			$20,000 Cash needed to close
$120,000	$120,000	$120,000	$120,000

Note that debits are always to the left and credits to the right.

BANKER'S RULE:

All prorations, *calculations,* based on 360 day year and 30 day month, for determining debits and credits on taxes, insurance, loan payments, rental income, etc.

PEOPLE TO HELP YOU

Names and addresses to obtain and keep handy:

Accountant	Furniture Rental Agent
Appliance Repairman	Gardener
Appraiser	Handy-man
Apt. House Owners Assoc.	Hardware Store Mgr.
Architect	Insurance Agent
Attorney in Real Estate	Interior Decorator
Banker	Manager*
Carpenter	Painter
City Planning Officer	Plumber
City Tax Officer	Realtor*
Contractor	Rental Agency
Electrician	Termite Inspector

The above, if chosen carefully, will help you be successful.

*The two key people are your property manager and your Realtor. If you do not buy, sell, trade and manage properly, all the rest will be to no avail.

AMORTIZED LOAN

A loan in which the principal payments are paid in installments,
AND IS COMPLETELY PAID OFF!

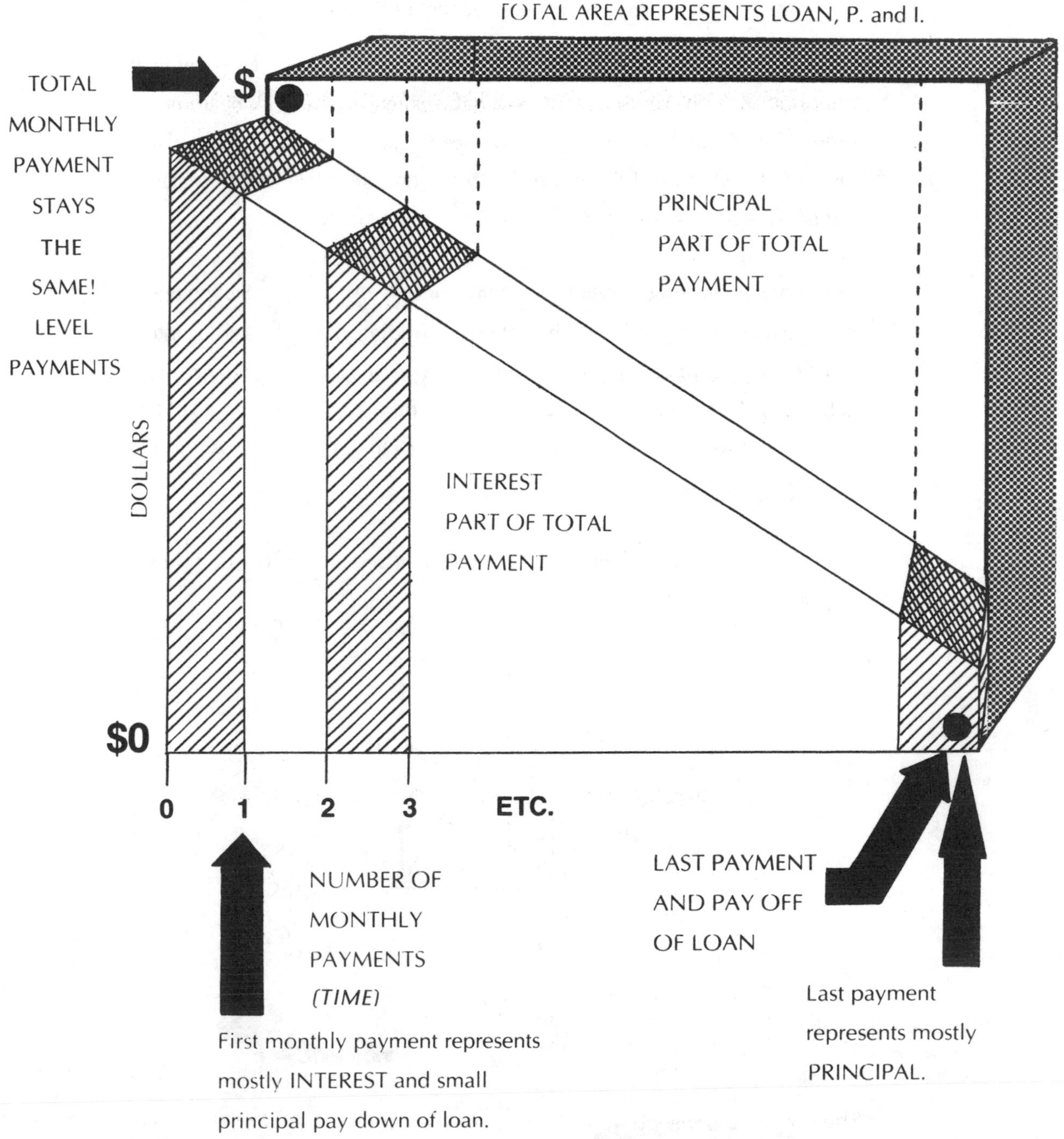

TOTAL AREA REPRESENTS LOAN, P. and I.

TOTAL
MONTHLY
PAYMENT
STAYS
THE
SAME!
LEVEL
PAYMENTS

$

PRINCIPAL
PART OF TOTAL
PAYMENT

DOLLARS

INTEREST
PART OF TOTAL
PAYMENT

$0

0   1   2   3   ETC.

LAST PAYMENT
AND PAY OFF
OF LOAN

NUMBER OF
MONTHLY
PAYMENTS
(TIME)

First monthly payment represents
mostly INTEREST and small
principal pay down of loan.

Last payment
represents mostly
PRINCIPAL.

Please note Letter to Author pg. 374.

TIME IS OF THE ESSENCE

"Time is of the essence" appears to be a trite phrase found on many contracts, especially Deposit Receipts. It is, however, an important requirement that parties involved in a contract must perform punctually or be in default.

In a larger sense Time and Timing are esoteric factors that can be of vital importance in determining your personal wealth. We have all heard many times of the great deal "that could have been" ... if only it was purchased just last year or last week. The question is: Why didn't you? The "good old days" are now.

The other perplexing question is should you sell now or later? Selling now is immediate dollars, but usually higher taxes. Trading up involves going into a more expensive property, but usually defers taxes. A future sale should mean a higher sale price due to appreciation, but you may have missed a golden opportunity to purchase or trade into another building. Also a sale in the future only delays your tax liability.

There is no one easy answer ... good judgement and taking your best shot is the best you can do.

DEGREE OF RISK

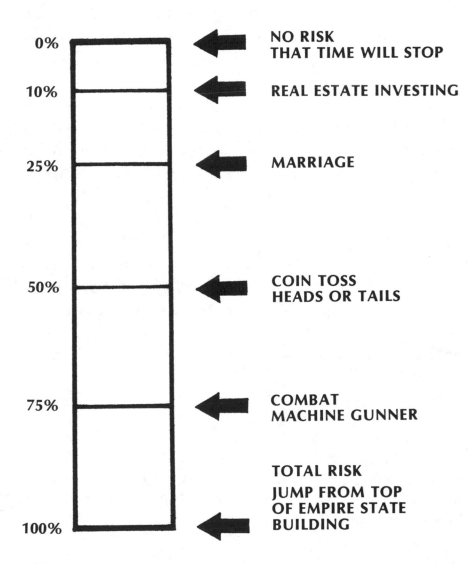

0%	**NO RISK** **THAT TIME WILL STOP**
10%	**REAL ESTATE INVESTING**
25%	**MARRIAGE**
50%	**COIN TOSS** **HEADS OR TAILS**
75%	**COMBAT** **MACHINE GUNNER**
	TOTAL RISK **JUMP FROM TOP** **OF EMPIRE STATE**
100%	**BUILDING**

Life is a gamble. Other than death and taxes, there is little if anything we do that does not contain a degree of risk. We all, at one time or another, "suffer the slings and arrows of outrageous fortune."

Science tells us, with the certainty of its theories and laws, of the comings and goings of our physical universe, yet no scientist has ever been able to predict the exact movements of any one electron. Using the systems outlined in this book, the prediction of disaster by investing in real estate is approaching zero.

But there is an element of success that goes beyond knowledge, goes beyond experience and beyond motivation. The missing link of success, the link that gives an "escape velocity" that can not be stopped, would be called intestinal fortitude. You can always hire brains, but you can't hire guts.

INCOME, PROFIT OR LOSS

BREAK-EVEN POINT

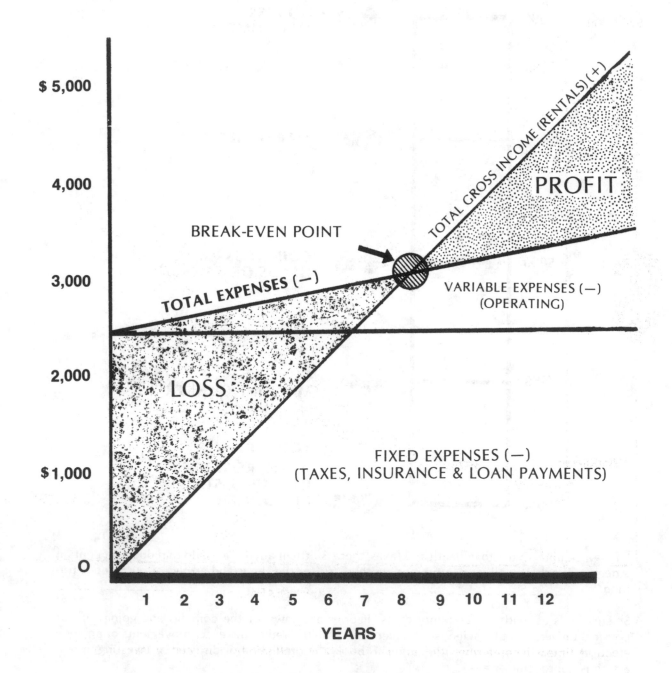

Note that to increase the 'profit area' triangle, the 'total expenses' line must be lowered, or the 'total gross income' line must be raised (rotated to the left). Better still, is to do both.

TIME & DEPRECIATION

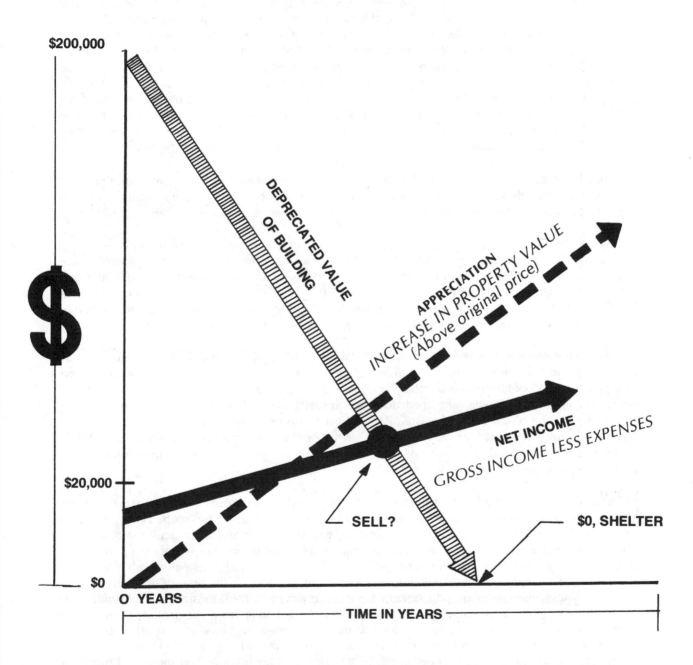

A time will come when your net income is NOT sheltered by depreciation (tax write-off). Prior to that time you should consider trading or selling.

GRM vs. CAP RATE

The 'quick and easy' way to establish the value of a property is with an annual gross rent multiplier (GRM). You must first establish the average GRM for the area of your interest, e.g., a three block radius. Say the GRM for a particular area ranged from 9 times gross to 11 times gross, the average is then 10 times gross annual rents. The GRM for an area is established by **simply dividing the purchase price by the gross annual rent for each property**. You can obtain purchase prices from your broker, city records or you can determine an estimate of GRM's by checking prices and income listed in the newspaper 'for sale' ads. Ideally, you would try to find GRM's for properties of comparable location, size and quality to the property of your interest. It is best **not** to include single family houses in establishing GRM's, as houses are purchased for reasons other than income, and the GRM for a house is usually very high based on rental income.

Within a three block radius you could have houses selling at 20 times gross, a 3 unit building at 13 times gross, a 10 unit building at 10 times gross, and a 200 unit complex selling at 7 times gross. In general, all other things being equal, the **greater** the number of units, the **lower** the GRM.

Let us say the GRM for your area is 10 times gross. In a matter of **two seconds** you can estimate the value of the property by multiplying by 10 times the gross annual income. For example, if the gross income is $23,500, to find the value with a 10 times GRM, simply move the decimal one place to the right to obtain a property value of $235,000. (Many 'experts' use a factor of 100 times the monthly income to obtain the value, this is the equivalent of 8.33 times the annual income, but it only works if the GRM for your area happens to be exactly 8.33.)

The caution with using GRM's is that you may not be dealing with the **actual** gross income, but rather a 'projected' or 'estimated' rental schedule. Be sure to verify the actual gross income on any property you contemplate purchasing. This is done by requesting to examine copies of all leases or rental agreements, and then doing an actual survey of rental housing in the area to establish that the rental schedule is realistic. You may find the rents are very low and that you have a bargain, if the rents can be increased. The other point to keep in mind when using GRM's is that you are dealing with gross income and not net income. Expenses must be analysed with the same caution used to examine rentals.

On a 'broker's statement' (a sheet describing the property) the **expenses usually represent about 25% of the gross income**. In most cases it is accurate as far as it goes, but many times the statement does **not** indicate expenses for management, vacancy factor and in particular the expenses involved in 'deferred maintenance' (needed repairs and renovation) and 'maintenance reserves' (future repairs). Obviously, the amount of repair and renovation a building needs, both now and in the future, can vary widely depending on age and condition, and on the quality of the tenants. A good contractor can be invaluable when it comes to estimating these expenses. A rule of thumb to cover expenses **plus** maintenance reserves is to **subtract 40% from the gross income**. Some lenders go as high as 50% of gross income to estimate expenses. Since almost all of these expenses are tax deductible, and can occur over an extended period, e.g., paint exterior every five years, etc., and can also be compensated by increased rental income and increased property value, the 40% expense bite is not as bad as it first seems.

With these cautions the GRM method of valuation is a most useful tool.

CAPITALIZATION RATE

The Cap Rate is equally valuable compared to the GRM method, but more time and cautions are involved. Since the Cap Rate is expressed as a percentage of the **net** income divided by the value of the property, you simply take these numbers as stated on the property statement and determine the Cap Rate (rate of return) for any particular building, e.g., a $100,000 building with a $10,000 **net** income has a Cap Rate of 10%. By lowering the price paid for a property, the Cap Rate would increase, e.g., a $50,000 building with a net income of $10,000 has a Cap Rate of 20%. Ordinarily, in determining Cap Rates you do **not** include maintenance reserves, so you must be very careful **to compare building expenses equally**. One property statement that lists a $15,000 per year manager, includes **current** taxes and a vacancy and bad debt factor of 4%, of course, is going to have a lower **net** income than a statement that does not consider these factors.

Because the GRM can be determined **without** reference to **expenses** it is 'quick and easy.' With both GRM and Cap Rate you will want to take a hard look at expenses and income. There is no reason why you should not use both methods, or any of the other methods mentioned in this book. Your time is the only limiting factor.

CAP RATE ANALOGY

Capitalization Rate, or Cap Rate, is a real estate appraisal term that is analogous to interest rate.

Example:

If you have a $200,000 loan (principal) and pay $20,000 per year (interest payment), then you are paying a 10% (interest rate) per year.

BUSINESS LOAN		REAL ESTATE
Principal	$200,000	Value of property
Interest payments	$20,000	Net income (rentals)
Interest rate	10%	Cap Rate

Here is a fair analogy and a simple one: remember that the interest rate a banker charges on a loan compares with the Cap Rate a real estate investor requires from a property.

The appraiser or investor must determine the capitalization rate (rate of return) that is desired for a specific property based on comparables, and on the property's potential or lack of potential (degree of risk), to produce a "stream of FUTURE income" (rentals).

By using Cap Rate, one is attempting to determine the present worth ($200,000) of future earnings ($20,000 per year).

RATE OF RETURN

R $=$ CAPITALIZATION RATE

R $=$ RATE OF RETURN ON INVESTMENT

RATE $=$ $\dfrac{\text{NET OPERATING INCOME}}{\text{VALUE OF PROPERTY}}$

R $=$ $\dfrac{I}{V}$

So if:

I $=$ $ 20,000

V $=$ $ 200,000

R $=$ $\dfrac{\$\,20,000}{\$\,200,000}$

R $=$ $\dfrac{2}{20}$ $=$ $\dfrac{1}{10}$ $=$ 0.10 $=$ 10%!

CAPITALIZATION RATE

Fluctuates based on the degree of risk or safety of the investment.

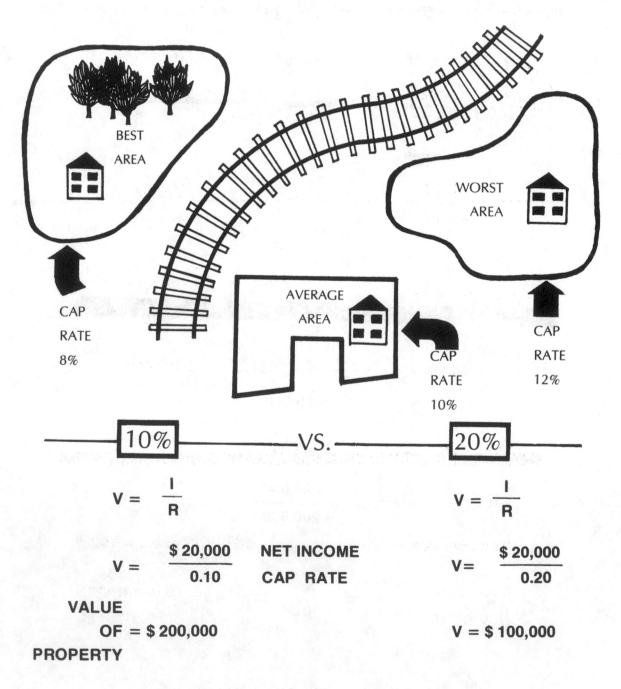

BEST
AREA

WORST
AREA

CAP
RATE
8%

AVERAGE
AREA

CAP
RATE
10%

CAP
RATE
12%

10% —VS.— 20%

$$V = \frac{I}{R}$$

$$V = \frac{\$20{,}000}{0.10}$$ NET INCOME / CAP RATE

VALUE
OF = $200,000
PROPERTY

$$V = \frac{I}{R}$$

$$V = \frac{\$20{,}000}{0.20}$$

V = $100,000

So if the net income remains the same and YOU increase
the Cap Rate because of the greater risk, the VALUE DECREASES!!

CAPITALIZATION RATE

Changing Cap Rate, when net income ($10,000) remains the same, affects Value and Time:

$$Value = \frac{Net\ Income}{Cap\ Rate}$$

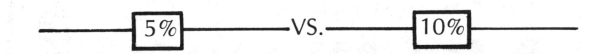

$$V = \frac{\$10,000}{0.05}$$

Value = **$200,000**

$$V = \frac{\$10,000}{0.10}$$

Value = **$100,000**

5% x 20 years = 100%

20 years to return
Value of property

10% x 10 years = 100%

10 years to return
Value of property

NET INCOME

NET INCOME	**=**	CAP RATE X VALUE

I	**=**	**R V**

TO REMEMBER: TRY **IRV**ING

So if:

(Rate)	R	**=**	**10%**
(Value)	V	**=**	**$ 200,000**
(Income)	I	**=**	**0.10 x 200,000**

INCOME   **=**   **$ 20,000!**

VALUE OF PROPERTY

$$\text{VALUE} = \frac{\text{NET OPERATING INCOME}}{\text{CAP RATE}}$$

$$V = \frac{I}{R}$$

So if:

$$I = \$20,000$$

$$R = 10\%$$

$$V = \frac{20,000}{0.10}$$

$$\text{VALUE} = \$200,000!$$

VALUE BY GROSS RENT MULTIPLIER (GRM)

Value of property = Gross Income x GRM

V = G.I. x GRM

So If: V = $20,000 x 8 GRM

Value = $160,000

As with Cap Rate the GRM varies with the quality of the investment.

or to FIND GRM:

$$GRM = \frac{V}{G.I.}$$

So If:

$$GRM = \frac{\$160,000}{\$20,000}$$

GRM = 8!

VALUE BY GRM

The simple and fast way to determine value of income property

Example:

Value = Gross Income (not net) × GRM

GROSS INCOME = $10,000 **PER YEAR**

	GRM	Value
BEST AREA	10 x	$100,000
AVERAGE AREA	8.5x	$85,000
WORST AREA	7x	$70,000

PROPERTY AS A FISH

THE SECOND OPINION

Jonathan M. Rutledge, attorney, when asked to give his opinion on one of the author's contemplated projects, stated, "That is known as how to turn your profits into attorney's fees . . . if it was a fish, I would throw it back." He was probably right. It pays to have a second opinion.

KNOW WHEN TO HOLD
&
KNOW WHEN TO FOLD

One of the most difficult decisions in real estate (and in life) is knowing when to make your move. When do you leave the security of the $20,000 investment or job, for the less secure $40,000 investment; the $40,000 for the $80,000. . .the $500,000 investment for the $1,000,000? The ancient Greeks tell us that happiness is the pursuit of excellence within the range of our capabilities. By this standard, go as high as your capabilities will take you.

Another guide is to let go of the bird in the hand, when, in your other hand, you have the bluebird by the throat.

A PAPER PROFIT

Monies gained through mortgage reduction and property appreciation are not realized until sale. The exception being to take out this equity build up by refinancing, or to obtain an 'equity loan.

CONDOMINIUM CONFUSION

Peter Stocker, a principal with the Pacific Union Co., once mentioned, "When I first heard about condominiums I thought they were related to birth control, and I became very concerned when they asked me to sell used ones."

NEGOTIATING
PRICE OR TERMS (POT)

Unless you are prepared to pay all cash and at the Seller's asking price . . . you will be negotiating Price or Terms.

Negotiating is bargaining to reach agreement.

As a starting point let us say that the Fair Market Value (not necessarily the asking price) of a property equals 100 points . . . and the usual Terms (say 20% down and 80% first loan) equals 100 points.

THEN:
Purchase price = FMV = 100 points

Terms = Usual = <u>100 points</u>

Price + Terms = 200 points

Roy's Rule of Thumb "ROT, POT": If a Seller is firm on Price negotiate the Terms . . . if firm on Terms, then negotiate the Price. If not firm (or unknown) then you can negotiate Price and Terms.

Example:

Instead of: FMV = 100
Terms = 100

a. Try FMV = 100
Terms = 90

b. Or FMV = 110
Terms = 70

c. Or FMV = 90
Terms = 100

Note that:

a. Holds the price and lowers Terms to Buyer's advantage.

b. Increases the Price but asks for more favorable Terms for Buyer, i.e., 10% Down, 10% 2nd loan with interest only, and an 80% First loan.

c. Lowers the Price but Holds the Terms.

You can vary the Price or Terms until you reach a compromise.

Counter-offers can go back and forth as many times as needed, but it is prudent to deliver an acceptable offer as soon as possible.

Please note Letter to Author pgs. 377, 378 & 379.

SPECIAL RULE FOR WORDS ENDING IN 'OR' & 'EE'

'<u>OR</u>' designates <u>O</u>wne<u>R</u>

Assign<u>OR</u>	=	owns thing being assigned
Grant<u>OR</u>	=	owns property being granted
Less<u>OR</u>	=	owns property being leased
Stuck<u>OR</u>	=	person doing sticking

'<u>EE</u>' designates Rec<u>EE</u>ver

Assign<u>EE</u>	=	receives thing being assigned
Grant<u>EE</u>	=	receives title being granted
Less<u>EE</u>	=	receives property being leased
Stuck<u>EE</u>	=	person being stuck

OPTION TO PURCHASE PROPERTY
CONTRACT TO MAKE A CONTRACT

OPTION is a **CONTRACT,** by which the owner, or **OPTIONOR,** gives the right **TO PURCHASE,** or **NOT TO PURCHASE,** to another party or **OPTIONEE.**

The optionee, or **HOLDER** of the option **MUST** act within a set period of time and **MUST** give actual "consideration"; i.e., **ANY** amount **AGREED** on ... say $ l.00.

The option can be assigned, to another party, after consideration is paid.*

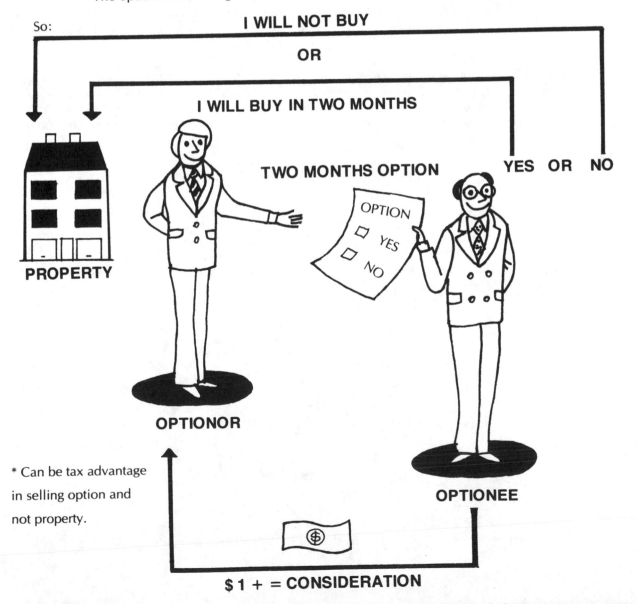

So:

I WILL NOT BUY

OR

I WILL BUY IN TWO MONTHS

TWO MONTHS OPTION

YES OR NO

OPTION
☐ YES
☐ NO

PROPERTY

OPTIONOR

OPTIONEE

* Can be tax advantage in selling option and not property.

$ 1 + = CONSIDERATION

LEASE WITH OPTION TO PURCHASE

A lease-option is simply a combination of two concepts, a conventional lease and a conventional option to purchase. This combination has a synergistic effect (the whole is greater than the sum of the parts).

If you discover a building that is a winner, but do not have an adequate down payment to purchase, then consider a lease-option. With your own management of the property it is possible "to structure the deal" so that the lease payments and expenses are fully covered by the rental income.

By improving the property, using your own money (or preferably your bank's money—a loan), the rental income can be increased, and in turn, increase the property value. The property can be virtually any garden variety; i.e., apartment house, hotel, health spa, golf and tennis club, bar and restaurant, retail store, etc. After the increase in property value due to improved management and judicious upgrading, you can then consider selling your option.

Using the lease-option, your leverage and profit are considerable. A run down apartment house or hotel can be lease-optioned and made ready for sale at up to double the option price. The more run down and problem plagued the property, the easier the terms and the greater the profit. One man's problem is another man's opportunity. It is not uncommon to lease-option a $500,000 property and sell the option for $1,000,000.

ROLLING OPTION

A rolling option is a progressive execution of multiple option agreements. By consummating one option, it automatically establishes your position for the next option, until all are completed.

Instead of eating the whole elephant all at once, you take one bite at a time.

A UNIQUE NO MANAGEMENT POLICY

Would you like to own a residential income property, management free? There is a way. You simply let the tenants manage their own apartments (and their own lives).

For example, if you have a rental unit that is worth $500 per month, contract with the tenant on a price of $475 per month, but the tenant is responsible for all non-structural repairs and maintenance of the unit and all appliances (stove, refrigerator, washing machine, etc.). The lease is written so that any calls to the owner for service entails a $50 service charge and, that the appliances are in the unit at the option of the owner.

This system eliminates almost all calls from tenants regarding maintenance, repairs and management.

It is also useful to consider this system when rent control, or other government intervention restricts the amount of rent allowed.

When the lease is written properly, the tenant is very happy with the lower rent, and the landlord is pleased to have a management free building.

SELL LEASEHOLDS NOT PROPERTY

There are some very creative ways of selling leasehold interests in a building so that both the leaseholder and the owner benefit.

For example, a building that has been converted to condominiums can be sold as individual units, since individual deeds have been created, but rather than sell the units, you can sell leasehold interests in each unit. A $100,000 unit that can be sold as a condo with $20,000 or $30,000 down, may be easier to sell on a short term lease with only $2,000 down. The sale of a leasehold combined with a maintenance by tenant clause, leaves the owner with a management free property. The owner then has the future choice of either re-leasing the units, trading up, or selling.

A RELUCTANT INVESTOR'S LAMENT

*I hesitate to make a list of all the countless deals I've missed—Bonanzas
that were in my grip; I watched them through my fingers slip. The windfalls which I should
have bought were lost because I overthought; I thought of this—I thought of that, I could have
sworn I smelled a rat. And while I thought things over twice another grabbed them at the price.
It seems I always hesitate, then make my mind up much too late. A very cautious one am I, and
that is why I never buy.*

*When tracts rose high on Sixth and Third, the prices asked I felt absurd. Whole
blockfronts—bleak and black with soot, were priced at thirty bucks a foot! I wouldn't even
make a bid. But others did. Yes, others did. When Tucson was cheap desert land I could have
had a heap of sand. When Phoenix was the place to buy, I thought the climate much too dry.*

"Invest in Dallas . . . that's the spot!"
*My sixth sense warned me I should not.
A very prudent one am I, and that's why I never buy.*

DOWNPAYMENT & CASH FLOW

BREAK-EVEN POINT

CASH FLOW = NET INCOME (−) LOAN PAYMENTS

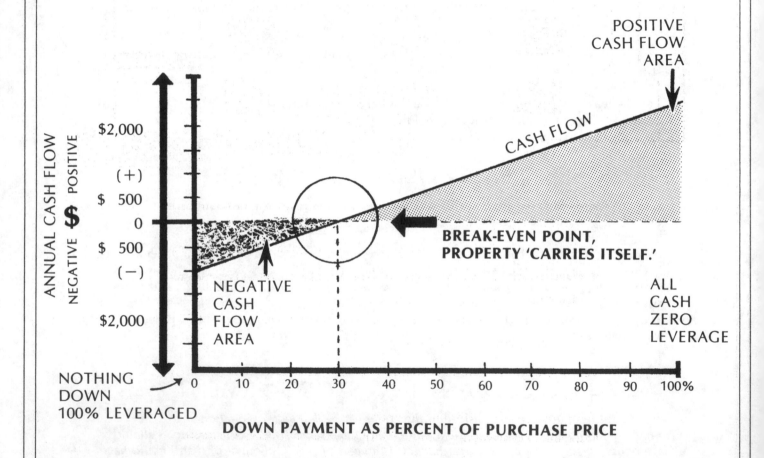

DOWN PAYMENT AS PERCENT OF PURCHASE PRICE

The greater the down payment, the greater the cash flow. Paying all cash for a property results in the maximum cash flow. One hundred percent cash down also represents zero leverage, and the tax write-off on the interest on the loan is lost.

For a property to 'carry itself' (no negative cash flow) the down payment must be great enough (usually in the 30% to 50% range) in order that the loan payments are equal to, or less than, the net income (gross income, less expenses).

IMPROVING PROPERTY AND VALUE

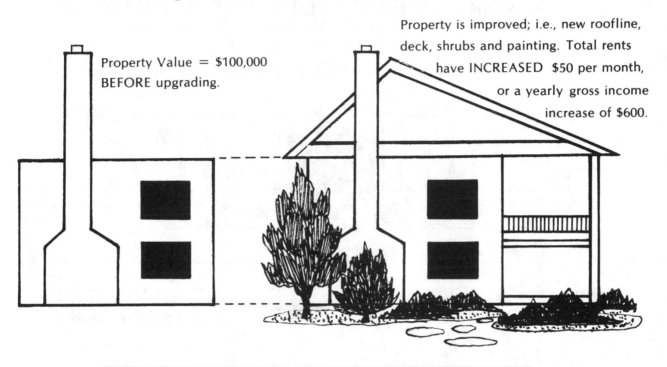

Property Value = $100,000 BEFORE upgrading.

Property is improved; i.e., new roofline, deck, shrubs and painting. Total rents have INCREASED $50 per month, or a yearly gross income increase of $600.

Multiply the INCREASED gross income × the gross rent multiplier, GRM . . .for your area = Property Value Increase.

Example:
$600 gross income increase, *actual or expected*, × 10 GRM = $6,000! Property Value Increase.

Therefore:
Property Value after improvements = $106,000.

So:
Using the rule of thumb of $1 of improvement cost to equal $2 of property VALUE INCREASE. . .you could spend $3,000 on improvements, to obtain a *$6,000 property value increase*. . . capital improvements are added to cost basis of building and depreciated as a tax write off . . . while repairs are deducted as an expense.

Note that even a relatively small increase in gross income ($600) produces a tenfold increase ($6,000) in equity. This is a huge advantage of real estate.

COMMERCIAL OR INDUSTRIAL PROPERTY

TRIPLE NET LEASE (NNN)

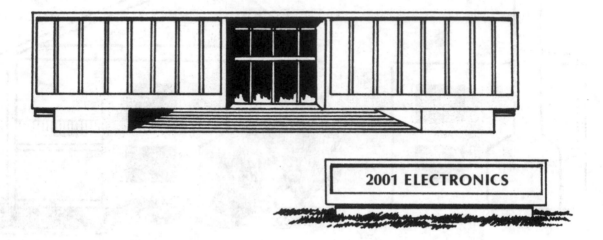

2001 ELECTRONICS

Commercial (business) property or Industrial (manufacturing) property with a long term (10 to 20 year) *'triple net lease'* NNN (percentage return after tenant pays for taxes, insurance, utilities and maintenance) is similar to a corporate bond, since the rental income is lower and the risk is also less with a 'blue chip' company as a lessee.

The main value of income property is the income it produces. You therefore may have to wait, until the present lease expires, to benefit from the appreciated value of the property as reflected in an increase in the rental income.

Be careful of 'special use' buildings. For example, a bowling alley that is not suited to another use could be very difficult to lease when the present lessee leaves.

Please note Letter to Author pgs. 371 & 372.

COMMERCIAL OR INDUSTRIAL PROPERTY

CASH ON CASH

On the other end of the investment spectrum is the short term lease (1 to 5 year) to more than one commercial tenant, as opposed to the long term triple net lease to one class 'A' tenant. Since the leases can be renewed and the rental income increased more frequently, it follows that the property value will also increase accordingly.

Leases may also have an 'escalator clause' based on the Consumer Price Index (CPI). For example, if the CPI increases 10% for the year, then the rent also increases 10%. Sometimes, for retail stores a 'percentage lease' has a proportion of the gross sales go to the landlord.

A rule of thumb for commercial property is to obtain at least a 10% *'cash on cash'* return (annual *net* income return as a percentage of the cash down payment), e.g., a $5,000 net income on a $50,000 down payment is a 10% cash on cash return.

In addition to the usual deductions for depreciation, taxes, loan interest and maintenance, you may qualify for a special tax credit for renovating a building at least 20 years old, or qualify for a rapid write-off of renovation expenses on a designated historic preservation building. For help on a historic building (commercial or residential) contact: National Trust for Historic Preservation, 740 Jackson Place NW, Washington, DC 20006.

UPGRADE TO PROFIT

PRIVATE REDEVELOPMENT FOR FUN AND PROFIT

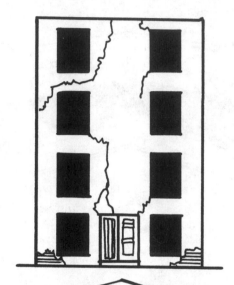

PURCHASE PRICE. . .$250,000

With professional help:

A. REMODEL. . .
   change structure
   inside & out.

B. RESTORE. . .

   return to original
   form & condition.

C. RENOVATE or REPAIR. . .

   improve existing
   inside & out.

REMODEL COSTS. . .$100,000

When properly done a $100,000 remodel cost should increase value about
$200,000, as reflected in the increased income. New total property value is then $450,000

Property *appreciation* based on inflation, for one or two years, and increased equity
build-up, resulting from the amortization of the loan (paydown) $50,000

NEW NET SALES PRICE $500,000

GROSS PROFIT WHEN SOLD ($500,000 less $250,000 original price and less
$100,000 remodel costs) **$150,000**

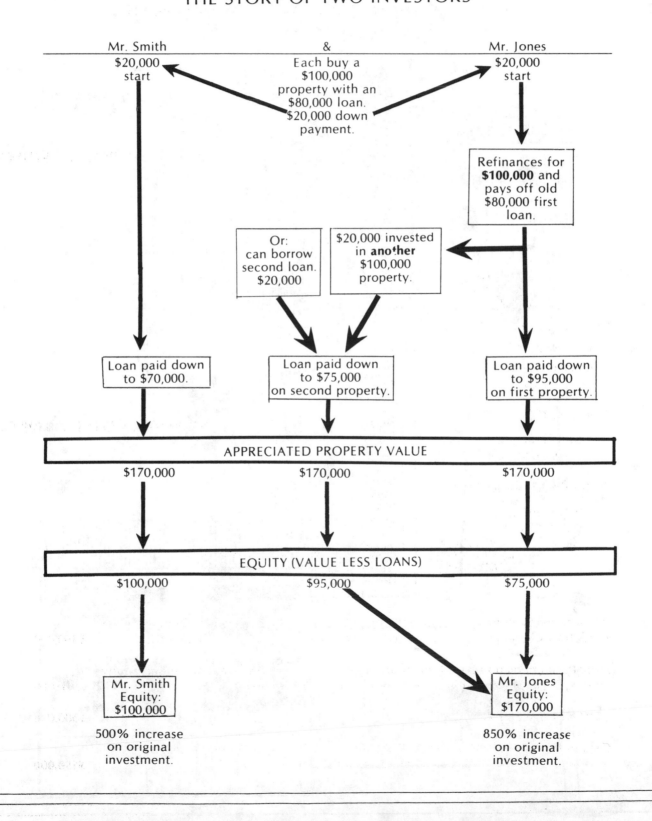

EQUITY PYRAMIDING
THE STORY OF TWO INVESTORS

Mr. Smith
$20,000 start

&
Each buy a $100,000 property with an $80,000 loan. $20,000 down payment.

Mr. Jones
$20,000 start

Refinances for **$100,000** and pays off old $80,000 first loan.

Or: can borrow second loan. $20,000

$20,000 invested in **another** $100,000 property.

Loan paid down to $70,000.

Loan paid down to $75,000 on second property.

Loan paid down to $95,000 on first property.

APPRECIATED PROPERTY VALUE

$170,000 $170,000 $170,000

EQUITY (VALUE LESS LOANS)

$100,000 $95,000 $75,000

Mr. Smith Equity: $100,000

Mr. Jones Equity: $170,000

500% increase on original investment.

850% increase on original investment.

FOUR STEPS TO $1,000,000

CHAPTER II

OWNERSHIP

OWNERSHIP OVERVIEW

Ownership, the basis of all major conflicts on our globe, is a rather important concept based on the men the author has talked with who were spilling their blood for the ownership of a few square yards of mud and sand at Normandy, Bastogne, Tarawa or Iwo Jima, to mention but a few from a long litany of blood-soaked soil.

Why do these place names go down in history, and why did so many volunteer to defend and die for isolated islands and hamlets, never to be seen again? The survivors tell us answers we are familiar with; 'to defend democracy and our way of life,' 'to protect our country from being butchered,' 'because I wanted to do my share,' 'somebody had to do it,'—and then there's one more—'because my friends were being blown away.'

To deny the 'right of ownership' when thousands of victims of their own valor are buried in that soil. . .to protect that right. . .is to mock the dead. The people who returned to Corregidor and took it back—the ones who did not break their backs and lives on the face of the cliffs, who were not shot as they dropped from the sky, or who did not end on the bottom of Manila Bay with a hundred pounds of battle-gear strapped to their bodies—these are the people, that later, the author was priviledged to jump with. I do not recall one man who was not prepared to do it all again. If courage is 'endurance for one moment more,' I would give them an hour.

It does not matter whether the name is from the honored past, whether it is Corregidor, San Francisco or Jackass Flats, the bottom line is that the people were defending ownership. The author has attended perhaps fifty hours of meetings listening to the thoughts of planning departments, zoning commissions, mayor's legal divisions and Boards of Supervisors. To the best of my knowledge the 'right of ownership' never entered their minds. They are all very concerned and aware, as the public is, of a few greedy landlords who ask for inordinate amounts of rent, and have no concern for the poor, handicapped or elderly. Granted that a few landlords should be fined, jailed or worse, but one pig should not wipe out two hundred years of our heritage.

The more that government controls, restricts and prevents our private ownership, the more democracy we lose. It is not overstated, it is not pompous, it is not flag-waving, to state that the right of ownership is democracy and freedom. Our country is private ownership.

BUNDLE OF RIGHTS

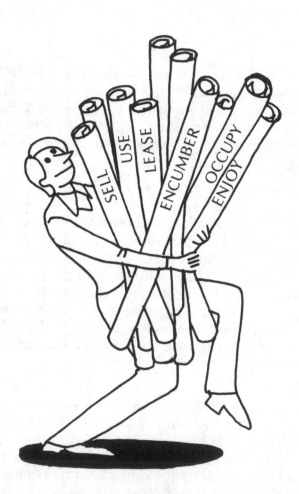

The *bundle of rights* concept comes to us from English law. It includes all rights that attach to the ownership of real property, e.g., the right to own, possess, sell, lease, enjoy, etc. The greatest bundle of rights would attach to *fee simple absolute* ownership. No ownership is unlimited, it is always limited by government regulation and police power, e.g., zoning, taxation, rent control, etc.

OWNERSHIP FLOW CHART

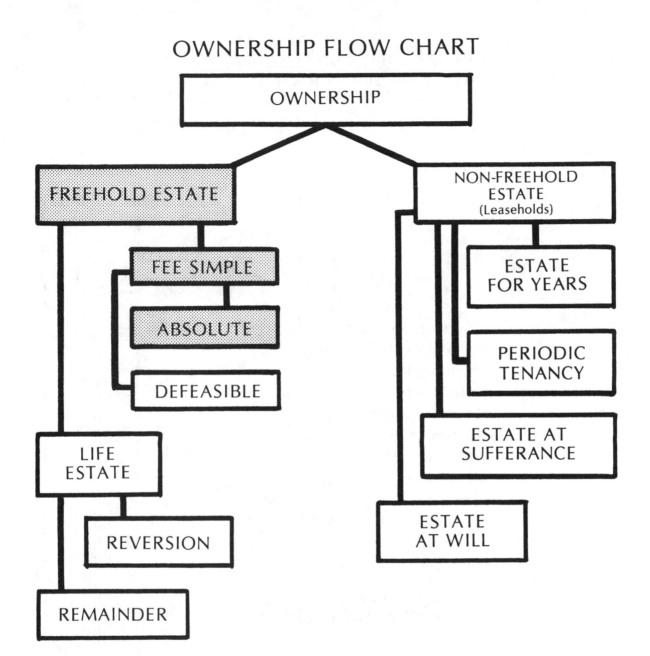

A *freehold estate* is one of unknown duration, as opposed to a *non-freehold estate* (less than freehold) which has a definite termination period.

The highest form of ownership that exists is *fee simple absolute*, which entitles the owner to all rights incident to the property. Ownership is always limited by the government, and police powers.

Fee simple defeasible is limited by some condition, such as no beer to be consumed on the premises, or you lose your fee.

An *estate for years* (lease) is an estate in real property for a definite period of time, e.g., a week, a month or a year. It requires no notice of termination.

A *periodic tenancy* is a real property estate for successive periods, e.g., week to week, month to month or year to year. It requires a notice of termination.

The chart lists the main forms of ownership, but not all.

OWNERSHIP

FRANK LLOYD WRIGHT* ON OWNERSHIP

The style of each building may be much more than ever individual. Therefore the necessity for a new cultural integrity enters: individual sensitivity and personal responsibility are now essential. So comes a man-sized chance to choose a place not only in which to be alive, but in which to live as a distinguished entity, each individual owner genuinely a contributor to the indigenous culture of his time.

* From *A Testament*, 1957

REAL PROPERTY

"From the center of the earth to the upper limits of the sky."
Modern law allows for air navigation, i.e., planes, satellites, etc.

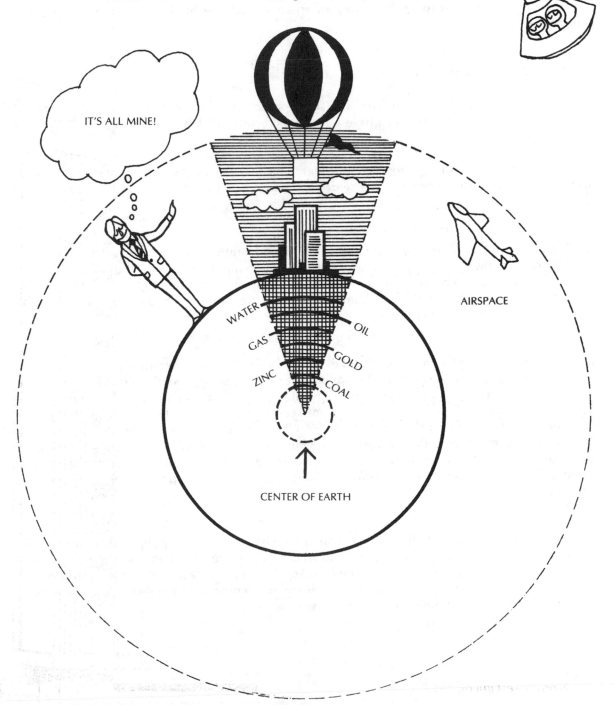

Real property = realty . . . the land and all affixed buildings, trees, etc., and embedded swimming pools, etc., and appurtenant easements, etc. and *that which is immovable*.

CONDOMINIUMS, COOPERATIVES & FINANCING

Condos and cooperatives for tax purposes are treated exactly as houses. If you live in one it *is* your home.

A few other points of interest:

1. Only with the condo do you have 'fee simple absolute' (the greatest 'bundle of rights' of ownership). With a cooperative you have a leasehold estate, usually for 99 years.

2. With both a condo and cooperative apartment you have the 'right of occupancy' for a certain portion of the structure, whether high-rise or town house, you have the right to live in a specific apartment.

3. The main difference between a condominium or cooperative, and a house is that you do *not* own the land, hallways, swimming pool, exterior of the building, or any of the other 'common areas.' Rather, these common areas are owned jointly by all of the other owners in the case of condominiums, usually as 'tenants in common,' (and by the corporation, or lessor in the case of the cooperative).

4. With a condo you obtain an individual deed or mortgage to your specific unit, and it is rather easy to obtain financing. At least as easy to obtain as it is for a home. With a cooperative, on the other hand, it can be very difficult if not impossible to obtain financing. The reason for this is quite easy to explain. Lending institutions want secure collateral for their loans, so that in the event of default on the loan they can readily foreclose on the property, and receive payment on their loan. It is much easier for a bank, or savings and loan company to foreclose on a condominium deed, than it is on a few shares of a leasehold, that represent cooperative ownership. When selling, the owner of a cooperative usually has to 'carry the paper' (create a purchase money loan).

5. With a condo you can sell and lease as you choose, since you have all the rights for your 'air space' of *fee simple.'* With a cooperative you would have shares in a corporation, as in a *stock cooperative*, or you would have a lease (sub-lease) under a master leasehold. The net result is that with a cooperative, either the corporate (or leasehold) committee may decide against your selling, or leasing to your favorite trumpet playing uncle.

CONDOMINIUM AND COMMUNITY APARTMENTS

CONDOMINIUM vs COOPERATIVE OR COMMUNITY

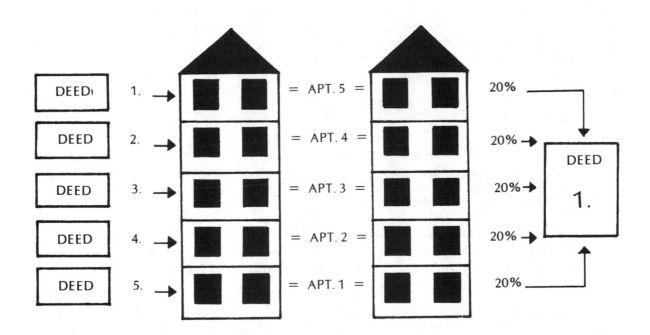

A. One deed for EACH Apt. UNIT.

B. SEPARATE tax bills.

Subdividing the legal ownership of a property from one deed to multiple deeds is to condominiumize.

A. One deed only. Each Apt. unit owning a PERCENTAGE.

B. ONE tax bill that is shared. You could be liable for all.

Either one could be:

A planned development project (*subdivision*), a high-rise, a row house, a town house or have a sharing of common areas; i.e., walks, pool, garden, etc.

CONDOMINIUMS & ARCHITECTURE

A common misconception is that a condominium implies a certain type of architecture, a townhouse, for example. This is not true. A condo can be any style of architecture, or none at all. A condo is a *legal change in the form of ownership*, and it does not matter what the physical structure consists of, as long as it is up to code. You can condominiumize water into boat slips, raw land into small ranches, a cocktail lounge into condo bar stools, a recreational area into condo tennis courts, or barns into horse stables (equestrian condos). To create a condo is simply to increase the number of deeds. The ten unit building with one deed, becomes ten condos with ten deeds and joint ownership of the 'common areas' (halls, garden, pool, tennis court, etc.).

VERTICAL SUBDIVISION

The term 'vertical subdivision' relates to condos because the deed description not only gives length and width, but also height above the ground. If a building is destroyed, the deed giving XY&Z dimensions of the 'air space' is still valid. A condo deed creates ownership of a parcel of space, even if the structure does not exist. When the project is completed. or rebuilt, you own from 'the interior of the exterior perimeter.' This definition includes the windows and doors, so that if the outside half of a window or door is damaged it would be considered a common area, and paid for by all owners. If the inside half of the window is damaged, then it is considered your exclusive property, so try and see to it that only the outside of your glass is scratched.

There *is* a connection between architecture and condominiums—good design and lower prices will sell.

CONDOMINIUMS — A NEW IDEA

Not exactly. The Roman baths were condominiumized over two thousand years ago. From the Latin we learn that *con* is *jointly,* and *dominium* is *property*. A condominium is a joint sovereignty

Four thousand years ago (2,000 B.C.) in Babylon, the owner of a building created a document that allowed him to sell the first floor, and keep the second floor. This was the world's first known condo conversion.

ONE MILLION B.C.

MORTGAGE vs DEED OF TRUST

. . . Both are CONTRACTS by which borrower agrees to pay
back monies borrowed, (*loan*). Lenders need less time to foreclose,
take back, property with Deed of Trust, *120 days*, than with a
Mortgage, 1 year . . . Pay ALL cash and you do not need either.

Parties in Mortgage:

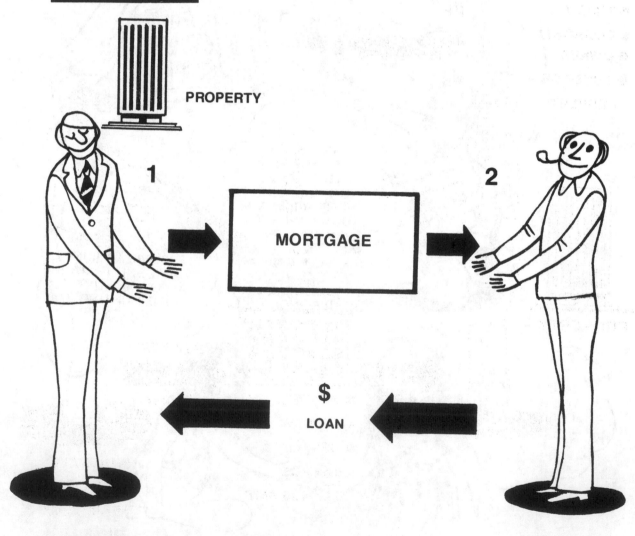

PROPERTY

1

MORTGAGE

2

$
LOAN

MORTGAGOR •
OWNER •
BORROWER •
BUYER OF PROPERTY •

• MORTGAGEE
• LENDER
• HOLDER OF NOTE
AND MORTGAGE

DEED OF TRUST

Parties in Deed of Trust:

- TRUSTOR
- BORROWER
- OWNER
- BUYER OF PROPERTY

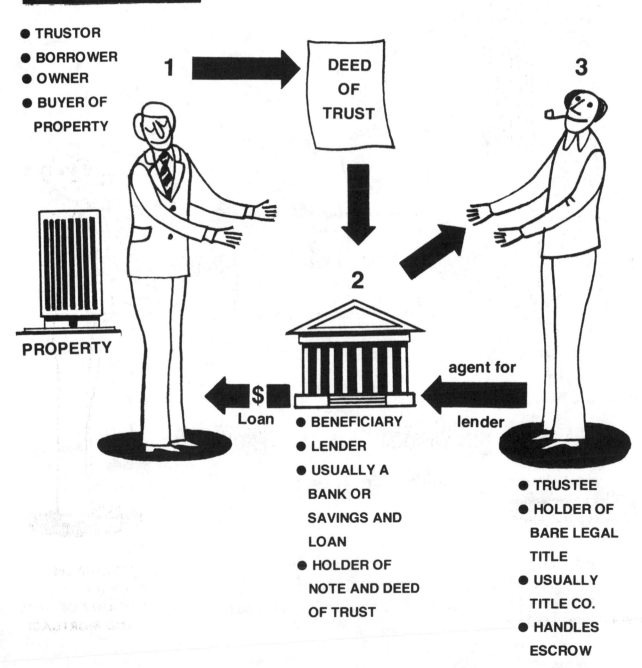

PROPERTY

1

DEED OF TRUST

2

$ Loan

- BENEFICIARY
- LENDER
- USUALLY A BANK OR SAVINGS AND LOAN
- HOLDER OF NOTE AND DEED OF TRUST

3

agent for
lender

- TRUSTEE
- HOLDER OF BARE LEGAL TITLE
- USUALLY TITLE CO.
- HANDLES ESCROW

OWNERSHIP =

REAL PROPERTY SALES CONTRACT

Also known as: Land contract, agreement of sale, conditional sales contract or installment sales contract.

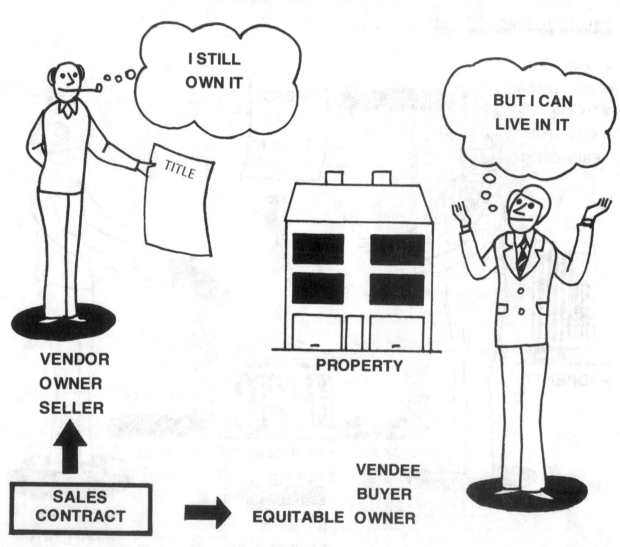

I STILL OWN IT

TITLE

BUT I CAN LIVE IN IT

VENDOR OWNER SELLER

PROPERTY

↑

SALES CONTRACT ➡ **EQUITABLE**

VENDEE BUYER OWNER

Buyer will obtain title only after meeting all contract conditions and paying agreed upon monies.
In **CONCEPT** like a lease with an option to buy.
Can get complicated, be careful.

PROBATE SALE

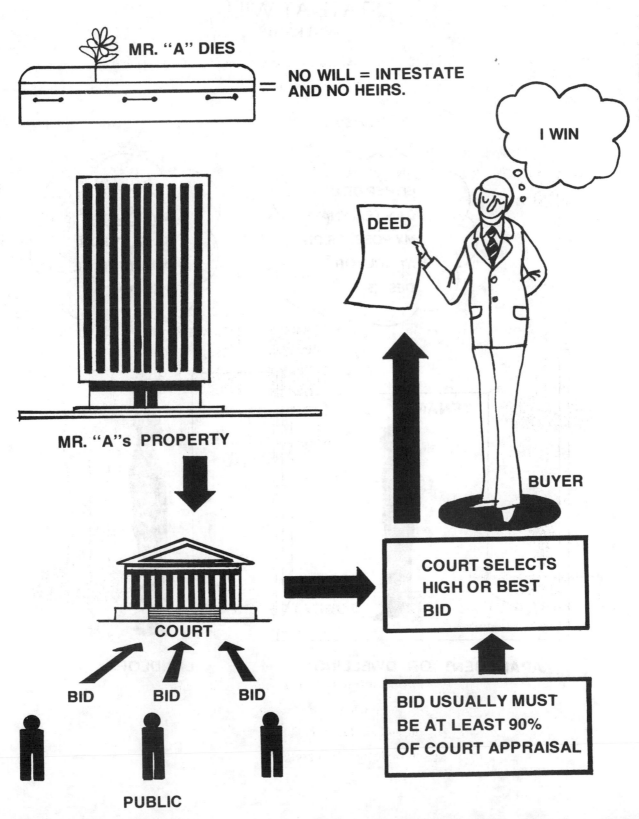

MR. "A" DIES

NO WILL = INTESTATE AND NO HEIRS.

I WIN

DEED

BUYER

MR. "A"s PROPERTY

COURT

BID   BID   BID

PUBLIC

COURT SELECTS HIGH OR BEST BID

BID USUALLY MUST BE AT LEAST 90% OF COURT APPRAISAL

ESTATE AT WILL
OWNERSHIP

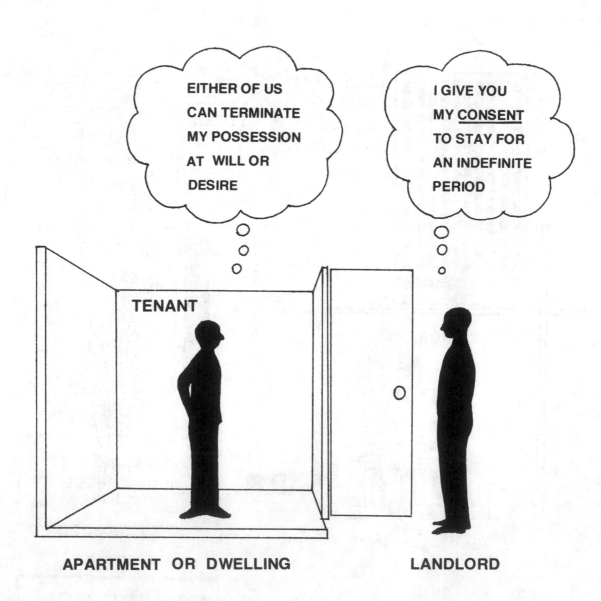

APARTMENT OR DWELLING   LANDLORD

ESTATE AT SUFFERANCE
OWNERSHIP

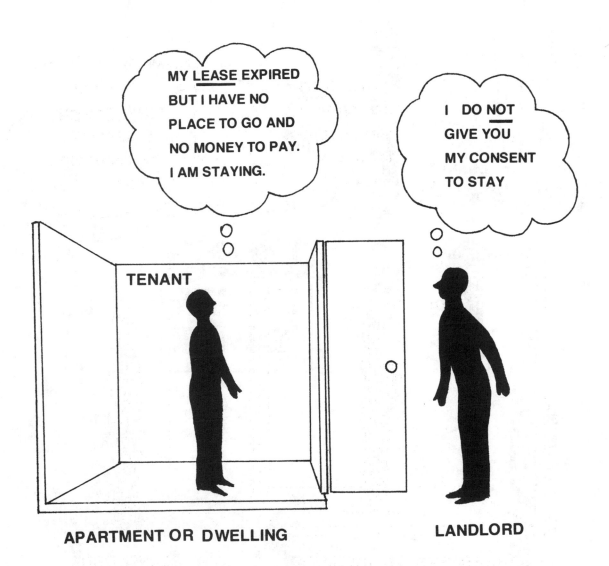

OWNERSHIP II

LIFE ESTATE
OWNERSHIP

DEED

You deed or will...

OR

WILL

Your property to Mr. "B" for the life of Mr. "B" Mr. "B" holds a life estate.

I live here For Now.

GRANTOR

DEED

BACK TO YOU OR HEIRS

ESTATE IN REVERSION

R.I.P.

Mr. B

MR. "B" DIES

• Mr. "B"
• LIFE ESTATE
• GRANTEE

OWNERSHIP

ESTATE IN REMAINDER
OWNERSHIP
YOU DEED OR WILL ...

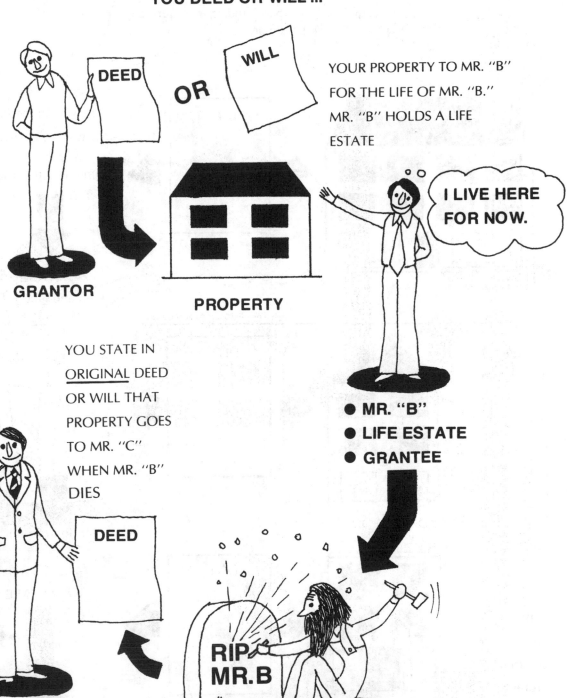

DEED

OR

WILL

YOUR PROPERTY TO MR. "B"
FOR THE LIFE OF MR. "B."
MR. "B" HOLDS A LIFE
ESTATE

GRANTOR

PROPERTY

I LIVE HERE FOR NOW.

- MR. "B"
- LIFE ESTATE
- GRANTEE

YOU STATE IN
ORIGINAL DEED
OR WILL THAT
PROPERTY GOES
TO MR. "C"
WHEN MR. "B"
DIES

DEED

RIP MR.B

- MR. "C"
- ESTATE IN REMAINDER
- GRANTEE

MR. "B" DIES

COMMUNITY PROPERTY
Ownership *

Property acquired by husband and/or wife during marriage
unless acquired as "separate property. **

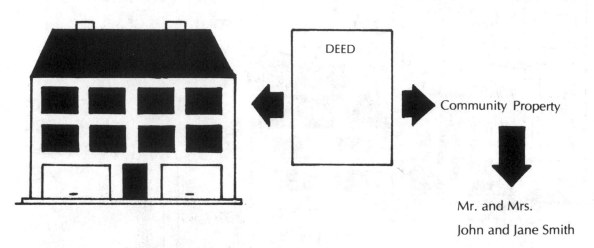

DEED

Community Property

Mr. and Mrs.
John and Jane Smith

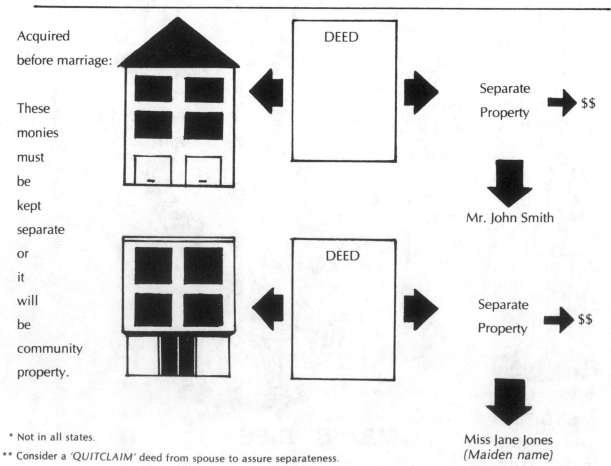

Acquired
before marriage:

These

monies

must

be

kept

separate

or

it

will

be

community

property.

DEED

Separate
Property $$

Mr. John Smith

DEED

Separate
Property $$

Miss Jane Jones
(Maiden name)

* Not in all states.

** Consider a *'QUITCLAIM'* deed from spouse to assure separateness.

TENANCY IN COMMON
OWNERSHIP

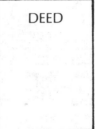

DEED

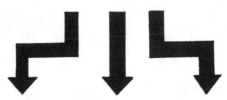

Two or more persons have:

1. Undivided interest, *does not have to be equal*
2. Equal rights of POSSESSION.
3. Without right of survivorship.

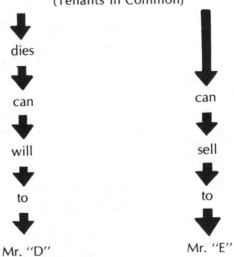

Mr. "A" and Mr. "B" and Mr. "C"
(Tenants in Common)

dies

can

will

to

Mr. "D"

can

sell

to

Mr. "E"

THEN: Mr. "D," Mr. "B" and Mr. "E" are Tenants in Common.

OWNERSHIP =

JOINT TENANCY
Ownership

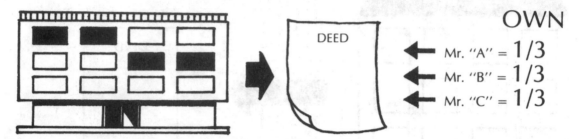

OWN

Mr. "A" = 1/3
Mr. "B" = 1/3
Mr. "C" = 1/3

Four unities:

T 1. Time = Acquired title at same time.

T 2. Title = Acquired title in same deed or will.

I 3. Interest = EQUAL undivided interest.

P 4. Possession = Equal right of possession.

Key = Right of survivorship!!

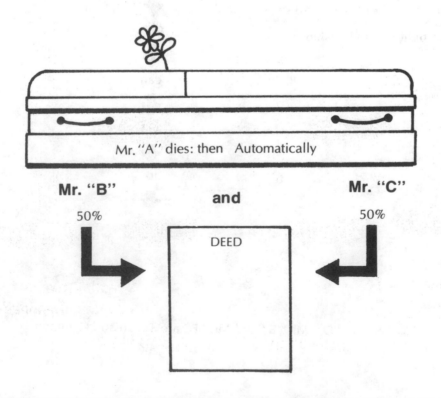

Mr. "A" dies: then   Automatically

Mr. "B"   **and**   **Mr. "C"**

50%   50%

DEED

SALE & LEASEBACK

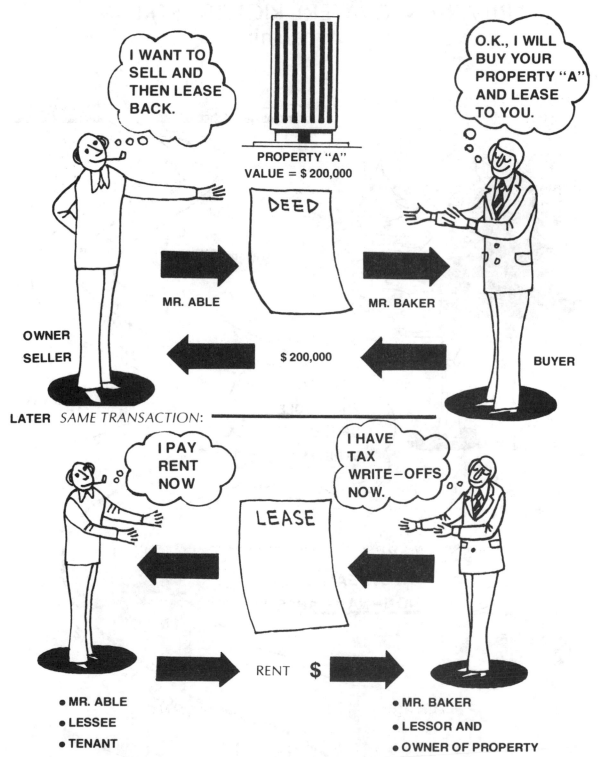

LATER *SAME TRANSACTION:*

Mr. Able has use of $200,000 and possession of property "A."

RIPARIAN (WATER) RIGHTS, STREAM
Ownership

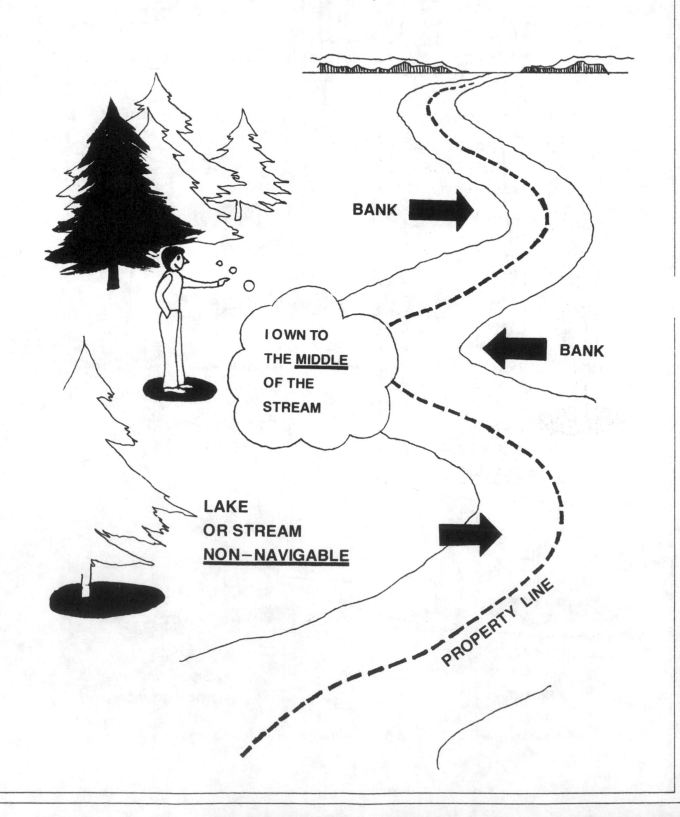

BANK

BANK

I OWN TO THE **MIDDLE** OF THE STREAM

LAKE OR STREAM **NON-NAVIGABLE**

PROPERTY LINE

RIPARIAN (WATER) RIGHTS

RIPARIAN (WATER) RIGHTS, OCEAN

Technically, this page should be headed **Littoral Rights**. Riparian means "River Bank." A riparian owner owns land abutting **flowing** water. If the water is **non-flowing**, e.g., ocean or pond, the owner is a littoral owner.

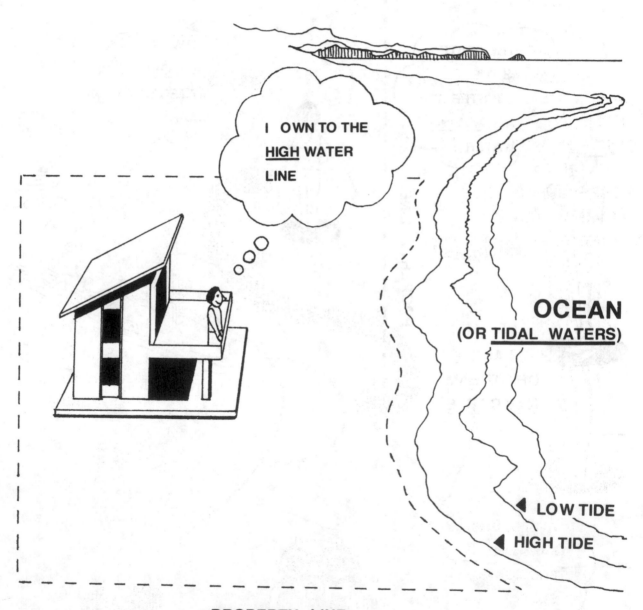

OWNERSHIP   II

RIPARIAN RIGHTS, SURFACE

RIPARIAN RIGHTS, UNDER LYING

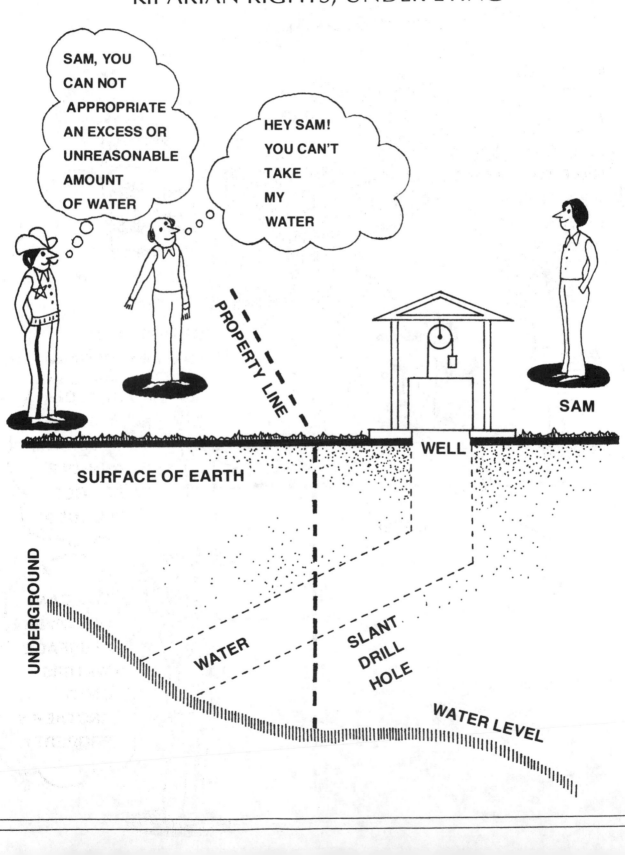

RIGHT OF SUBJACENT SUPPORT

OWNERSHIP

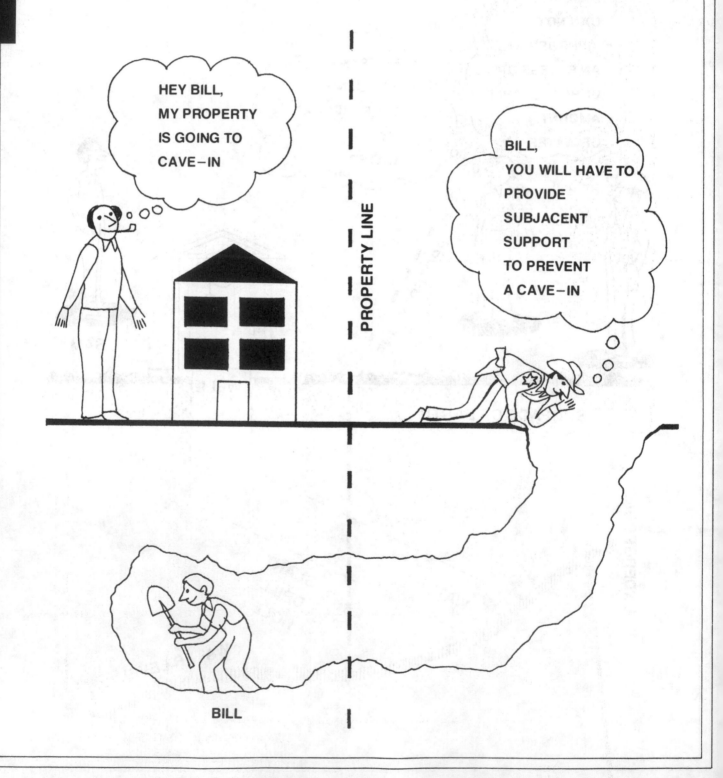

RIGHT OF LATERAL SUPPORT

OWNERSHIP

REIT

<u>R</u>eal <u>E</u>state <u>I</u>nvestment <u>T</u>rust:

    An unincorporated trust or association of at least 100 investors, similar to a corporation except that the investment trust's profits are not usually taxed.

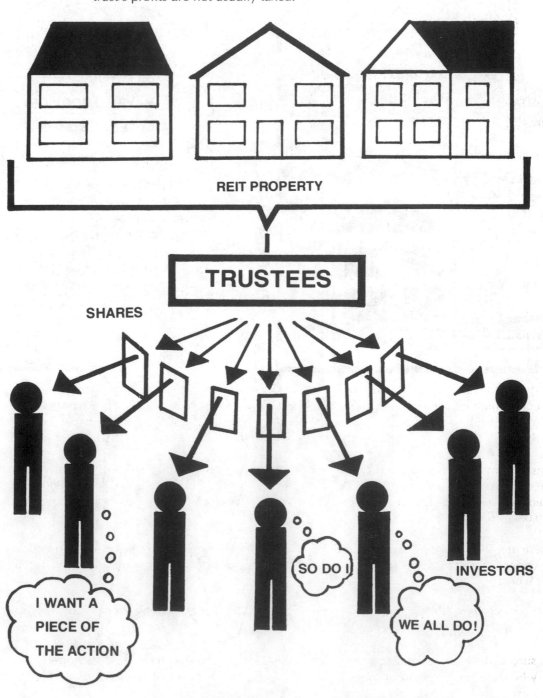

TIME SHARING

With time sharing, you share not only time with others, but also *ownership*. One vacation house, or condominium, for example, could be owned by twelve owners, each using the property for one specific month each year. . .or by twenty-six owners, each using the unit for two specific weeks each year.

This system of sharing the ownership on one unit opens up vacation property to many more people, since you are only required to pay 1/12 or 1/26 of the purchase price. A $120,000 unit to be used one month of the year (in perpetuity, or for the term of the leasehold) would cost only $10,000.

There are all manner of variations on this theme. Once you have purchased, one firm allows you to select from other units in your building, or other cooperating vacation properties throughout the world.

It is an excellent idea whose time seems to have come for those who do not have the means or desire to purchase a 100% interest.

Be sure a professional management team with a 'track record' is handling the property. If not, it may be difficult to round up 25 non-paying owners in the event of foreclosure.

OWNERSHIP & CONTROLS

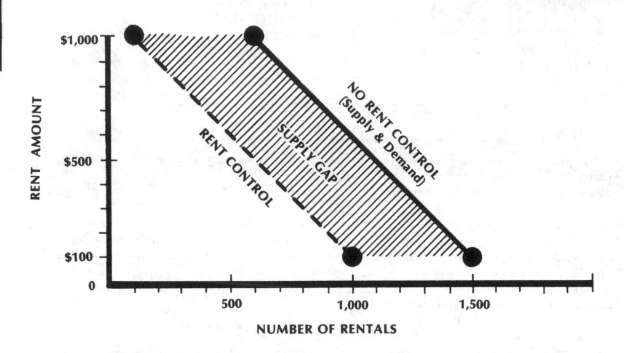

The above chart indicates on the X-axis (horizontal) that the number of units available at the starting rental is about 1,000, under rent control. Without rent control but with the usual supply and demand of the market place, the number of units available would be about 1,500. The difference of 500 units is easily explained by the fact that builders are reluctant to build new units in a city with rent control, since it also controls the value of the units and their profit.

If the 'right to ownership' is to be considered a fundamental basic right in a democratic society, and concern for the financially impoverished—including the elderly and the handicapped—is an equally noble concern, then why not an 'ownership subsidy', so that all who desire can own property? All other things being equal, is it not basic to have the right to own, as well as the right to rent? 'If you subsidize something you get more of it, if you tax something you get less of it.'

A simple government backing of a loan similar to the 'G.I. loan' would create millions of new owners, and a more stable society. For example, an amortized 40 year loan, at 7% per annum, on a 100% financed purchase price of $70,000, is equal to a monthly payment of $435. The government could back such a loan obtained from a local bank or savings and loan company by guaranteeing the difference between the 7% rate, and the current rate. . .say a difference of 4%. This is not a new concept. The government is deeply involved in attempting to provide loans, or security for loans, for the poor to moderate income groups. The Veteran's Administration (VA), Federal Housing Authority (FHA), and the Community Reinvestment Act of 1977 (CRA) to mention but a few are all involved in loans. A phone call to your banker, or the proper agency can bury you in a swarm of paper and application blanks. Be warned that the paper mill of bureaucracy has all of the machinations of a Kafka novel. The author has spent six months obtaining approval from Washington D.C. on a 'G.I. loan' even after all the documentation was presented. Time delayed is a direct function of the number of government agencies involved. Efficiency is rewarded only if profit oriented.

A new, efficient government backing of loans with local decisions appears to be the only answer. In doing this, home ownership would be opened up to the average person. With both a first loan and the ownership subsidy secured by the property, both the lender and the government would be paid off in full when the house (or apartment) was sold, or when the last member of the immediate family either sold the property, or died. Passage of enough time would assure payment in full.

RENTERS & OWNERS

To say that, 'because there are more renters than owners, renters should have more rights,' is not exactly on the mark. There are also more sighted than blind, but we do not remove their guide dogs, even when signs for the sighted state, 'No Dogs Allowed.' We do this 'because it is right.'

From the author's experience of listening to city and county legislators who voted for rent control, the main thrust of the arguments is the protection of the rights of the elderly, and disadvantaged tenants who are suddenly confronted with 'a new landlord who immediately raises all the rents $200 per month for people on a fixed income, who can least afford it.' A compelling and valid grievance. Obviously, there are landlords who are unscrupulous, just as there are doctors, lawyers, car salesmen and presidents.

Is the answer, then, to punish all of the innocent along with the guilty, with oppressive legislation? I don't think so. Why not attack the specific problems directly? If there are not enough apartments, then build more. If the laws in the books can not control the errant landlord, then enact specific laws to control each specific problem. How? Simple. If the problem is trauma to the tenant because of an inability to pay a rent increase, or lack of time and money to find new housing, then one solution would be to have a minimum of three months notice before any rent increase could go into effect. Further, if a tenant chooses to leave because of the rent increase, then that tenant would be entitled to a cash payment of ten percent of all monies that had been paid in rent, e.g., if the tenant had paid in $40,000 over the rental period, then upon leaving the apartment due to a rent increase (above the cost of living increase), the tenant would be entitled to $4,000. If this is not the exact answer to the problem, at least it is an approach. Better to have laws control specific abuses, than to eliminate the 'free market place.'

The objectives of the San Francisco master plan that might well be a guide for other cities, are as follows:

(1) Improve the choice, quality and number of housing units especially for low and moderate income families.
(2) Prevent major displacements of people and facilitate inhabitant ownership.

The goals are impressive, the accomplishments have yet to be revealed.

If you want more slices, you bake a bigger pie . . . you don't try to shut down the bakery.

WHICH ONE WILL LAST FOREVER?

COLD DRINK	TEN MINUTES	BOAT	THIRTY YEARS
T.V.	SEVEN YEARS	CAR	TEN YEARS
	MAN	SEVENTY-TWO YEARS	

Only the land lasts forever. A rather nice gift for your heirs a thousand, or million years from now.
Even under the water is the land.

UNDER ALL IS THE LAND.

CHAPTER
III
SIMPLE
ARITHMETIC

SIMPLE ARITHMETIC OVERVIEW

Numbers are the name of the game. You can not be successful in real estate investing without knowing how to work with numbers. You *must* use them when speaking of purchase prices, income streams, expenses, outflows, cash flows, cap rates, gross rent multipliers, square and cubic footages, interest rates, rates of return, loan amounts, occupancy rates, traffic counts, head counts, distances, architectural measurements, inventories, assets, liabilities, liquid reserves, non-liquid reserves, cost to loan ratios, tax holding periods, permit qualifying periods, life expectancy periods for humans and buildings, legal fees, accounting fees, permit fees, insurance fees, estate fees, cash deposits, personal income now and future, cost of living indices, retirement and pension fund incomes and a myriad of others.

The easier you can work with numbers the more efficient and productive you become. Unfortunately, you can't just say the price is "high" or "low" . . . it must eventually be given a specific number.

In this chapter we look briefly at a few simple examples of working with numbers.

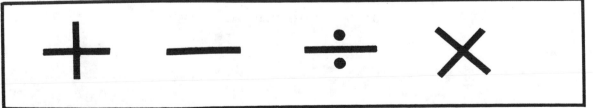

PERCENTAGES, DECIMALS & FRACTIONS

SIMPLE
ARITHMETIC

III

Percentage	Decimal	Fraction
100%	1.00	1/1
66 2/3%	0.6667	2/3
50%	0.50	1/2
33 1/3%	0.333	1/3
16 2/3%	0.1667	1/6
12 1/2%	0.125	1/8
6 2/3%	0.0667	1/15

$$5\% \ = \ 5/100 \ = \ 0.05$$

$$0.5\% \ = \ 1/2 \ \text{of} \ 1\% \ = \ 0.5/100 \ = \ 0.005$$

$$0.05\% \ = \ 0.05/100 \ = \ 0.0005$$

THE NEARNESS OF ONE MILLION

You may not be as far away from a million dollars as you think. Starting with a $1,000 equity investment, and the big advantage of compounding, try to double your money as fast as possible. A **14%** return on an investment compounded will double in a little over five years. If you add to the principal it will happen sooner.

For example:

MULTIPLE	EQUITY
START	$ 1,000
FIRST	2,000
SECOND	4,000
THIRD	8,000
FOURTH	16,000
FIFTH	32,000
SIXTH	64,000
SEVENTH	128,000
EIGHTH	256,000
NINTH	512,000
TENTH	$1,024,000

DETERMINING GROSS PRICE
FROM A NET PRICE

To determine the gross price when adding a commission to a net price, simply *subtract* the commission percent from 100%, and *divide* into the net price.

$$\frac{\text{NET PRICE}}{100\% \, (-) \, \text{COMMISSION \%}} = \text{GROSS PRICE}$$

EXAMPLE:

$$\frac{\$100,000}{100\% - 6\%} = \text{GROSS PRICE}$$

$$\frac{\$100,000}{94\%} = \$106,383 \text{ GROSS PRICE}$$

DEBT SERVICE RATIO

The *net income* divided by
the *debt service* equals the
Debt Service Ratio.

Debt Service Ratio   = $\dfrac{\text{NET INCOME (annual)}}{\text{DEBT SERVICE (annual)}}$
(mortgage payments)

EXAMPLE:

$\dfrac{\$125,000\ net\ income}{\$100,000\ debt\ service}$ = 1.25 debt service ratio
(ahead of the game)

$\dfrac{\$100,000\ net\ income}{\$100,000\ debt\ service}$ = 1.00 debt service ratio
(exactly even)

INTEREST DIFFERENTIAL

If loan X is for $50,000 at 10% interest, and loan Y is for $50,000 at 1% per month interest (12%), then the *interest differential* is 2% (assume loan due dates are the same).

In dollars 2% of $50,000 equals a difference in interest the first year of exactly $1,000. If both loans are *interest only* loans, then the difference continues at $1,000 per year until paid off.

The author has seen deals blow up because of a 1% extra interest difference. In the case of loans X and Y, would it be wise to walk away because of $500 per year? Probably not, if inflation is increasing the value of the property by $5,000 per year.

RULE OF 72, DOUBLE YOUR MONEY

To determine the number of years required to double your money when the interest rate is being compounded yearly, e.g., bank account, certificate of deposit, or real estate, simply divide the number 72 by the interest rate per annum.

$$\frac{72}{\text{INTEREST RATE PER YEAR}} = \text{NUMBER OF YEARS TO DOUBLE INVESTMENT}$$

$$\frac{72}{4\,(\%)} = 18 \text{ YEARS} \qquad\qquad \frac{72}{9\,(\%)} = 8 \text{ YEARS}$$

$$\frac{72}{8\,(\%)} = 9 \text{ YEARS} \qquad\qquad \frac{72}{12\,(\%)} = 6 \text{ YEARS}$$

The reverse is also true, namely, you can divide the number of years to double into 72, to determine the interest rate. For example, 72 divided by eight years equals nine percent.

EQUITY BUILD-UP

APPROXIMATE WITHOUT TABLES

To determine the *equity build-up* (principal pay-down) on an $80,000 loan for the first year, proceed as follows:

LOAN	=	$80,000
INTEREST	=	10%
TERM OF AMORTIZED LOAN	=	30 YEARS
MONTHLY PAYMENT	=	$702

$702 MO. × 12 MO.	=	$ 8,424	PER YEAR
$80,000 × 10%	=	8,000	INTEREST PER YEAR
EQUITY BUILD-UP	=	424	PER YEAR
$80,000 (−) $424	=	$79,576	LOAN BALANCE END OF FIRST YEAR

TO MEASURE THE EARTH WITH A SHADOW

NOTHING CAN REMAIN IMMENSE IF IT CAN BE MEASURED.

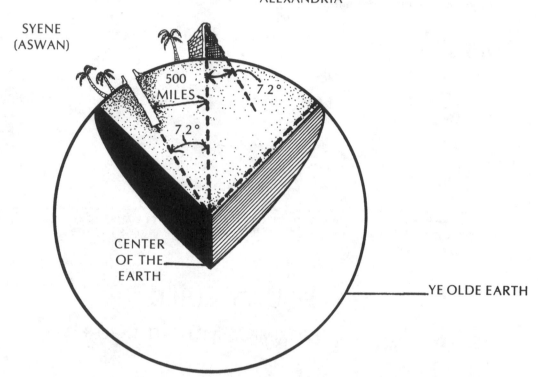

Eratosthenes, a Greek poet, was the head librarian in Alexandria. He noticed that at high noon during the summer solstice (the sun's Zenith), the sun shone directly into a well at Syene (now Aswan). He reasoned that because of the curvature of the earth, the sun would not be shining directly down in Alexandria located five hundred miles to the north.

He waited a year until the next solstice, and then measured the shadow in Alexandria cast by a pole absolutely plumb (at high noon). The shadow cast at an angle of 7.2°. From simple mathematics he knew that a line crossing two parallel lines made corresponding angles, thus the angle from Syene to the center of the earth and back to Alexandria was also 7.2°. He knew that 7.2° represented 500 miles, and that the full circumference of the earth represented 360°, or 50 times more than 7.2°. He estimated the circumference of the earth at 50 times the 500 mile distance, or 25,000 miles.

Modern science, using sophisticated electronic and photographic equipment, tells us that the equatorial (latitudinal) circumference is 24,904 miles, and the meridional (longitudinal) circumference is 24,860 miles.

Eratosthenes didn't do too badly considering his only tools were his brain and a stick. Also, he did it over 2,000 years ago.

Ancient man observed that it took about 30 days for the moon to travel around the earth (a 'moonth'). They also noticed it took 12 months for the sun to reach its zenith (solstice), as well as certain stars. The 12 months, or 360 days became the basis for our year, and also the reason we use 360 degrees in a full circle.

WHERE IN THE WORLD ARE WE?

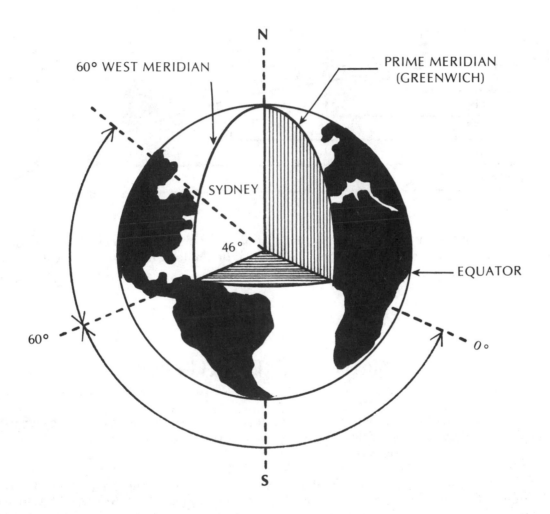

Let's say you are standing in the middle of Sydney, Canada and wanted to describe where you are in terms of world location. You could start by locating the Prime Meridian that runs through Greenwich, England. Meridians are the great circles running north and south through the center of the earth. Where the Prime Meridian intersects the equator is the starting point, or 0° for measuring east or west around the equator. Ancient man spoke of 'medius dies,' or middle of the day, when the sun was directly overhead. *Medius dies* eventually became meridian. If you go in an arc in a westerly direction 60° from the Prime Meridian you arrive at the 60° West meridian at the point it crosses the equator. If you now proceed due north on this meridian for 46° you will arrive at Sydney, Canada. Its location on earth is 46° N, 60°W.

THE TERRITORY CURVES

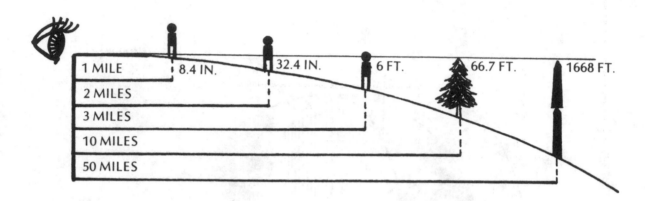

The curvature of the earth is indicated in the illustration. At one mile the curve drops below the level by 8.4 inches, at three miles it drops 6 feet, and at fifty miles it represents a curvature with a drop of 1,668 feet.

KNOW THE TERRITORY

Our earth is about 60% water and 40% land. Of this 40%, less than half is in private ownership, and only a small portion is for sale. On any one day perhaps 1% of the earth is available to buy, sell or trade. That is the territory.

Of this 1% the most practical area to explore is that area within a walking radius of your home. As time progresses, knowledge and inclination can lead to further corners of the earth. With the help of firms such as the American Real Estate Exchange (AMREX), or Previews, the investment world is brought to your doorstep via mail, phone and teletype.

ACRES TO LOTS

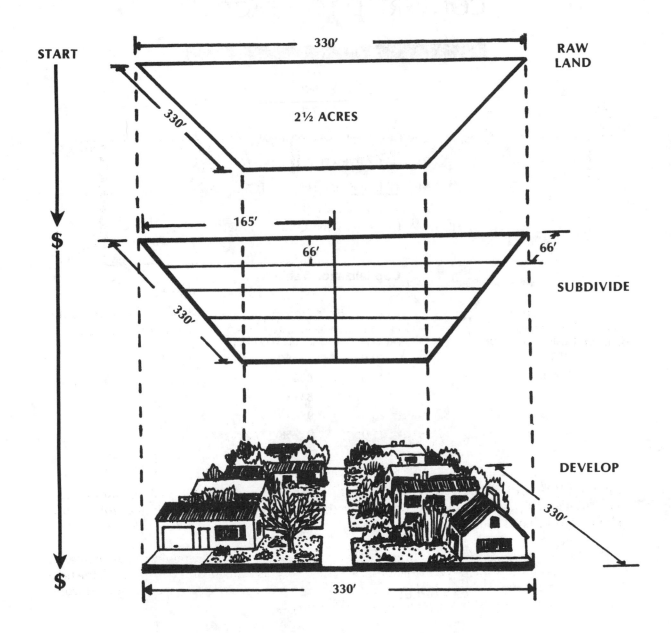

Starting with a 2½ acre parcel of land which is 330 feet square, subdivide the raw land into ten quarter acre lots, each lot being 165 feet long and 66 feet wide.

Then develop the ten quarter acre lots with ten houses.

If the raw acreage cost $20,000 and the houses sold for $102,000 each, the total is $1,020,000. The gross profit is one million dollars.

CAPITALIZATION RATE
CONVERTED TO A FACTOR

$$VALUE = \frac{NET\ INCOME}{CAP\ RATE}$$

DIVIDING THE NET INCOME

BY THE CAP RATE IS EQUAL TO

<u>MULTIPLYING</u> BY THE FACTOR.

THUS: VALUE = NET INCOME × FACTOR

Capitalization Table

RATE OF CAPITALIZATION	FACTOR	RATE OF CAPITALIZATION	FACTOR
2%	50.0	7½%	13.3
2½%	40.0	8%	12.5
3%	33.3	8½%	11.7
3½	28.5	9%	11.1
4%	25.0	9½%	10.5
4½%	22.2	10%	10.0
5%	20.0	10½%	9.52
5½%	18.1	11%	9.09
6%	16.6	11½%	8.69
6½%	15.3	12%	8.33
7%	14.2		

EXAMPLE:

$$VALUE = \frac{\$20,000}{8\%} = \$250,000$$

or

VALUE = $ 20,000 X 12.5 = $ 250,000

NOTE: $\frac{1}{.08} = 12.5$

RETURN ON INVESTMENT

Purchase Price = $ 200,000

Cash Down =   20,000

Assume that you have no net income after including selling expenses.

So: Gross Income = Debt Service and Expenses

5 YEARS LATER YOU SELL

Selling Price = $300,000

Purchase Price =   200,000

Profit 5 Years = $100,000

100,000 Profit
——————————— = 500% Profit
20,000 Investment

500%/5 Years = 100%/Year

Return ON Investment = $ 20,000/Year Profit

Please note Letter to Author, On Calculators, pg. 376.

SIMPLE AND COMPOUND INTEREST COMPARED

SIMPLE INTEREST...Common in Real Estate

$100,000 @ 10% year.

1st year = $10,000 interest

2nd year = $10,000 interest

3rd year = $10,000 interest

At the end of 3 years you have paid $30,000 in interest.

COMPOUND INTEREST

$100,000 @ 10% year.

1st year = $10,000 interest

$ 100,000		
10,000	1st year	= $10,000 interest
$110,000		
11,000	2nd year	= $11,000 interest
$121,000	3rd year	= $12,100 interest
	In 3 years	= $33,100 interest

STRAIGHT NOTE ANALYSIS

If you owe $20,000 on a NOTE (*loan*) @ 9% annual interest due in 5 years, then SIMPLE interest is $1,800 per year.

So: **$9,000 = TOTAL INTEREST**

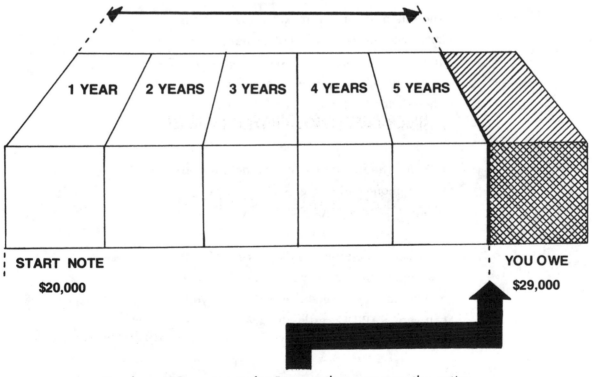

You have NO payments for 5 years, then you owe the entire balance + interest (a big 'balloon payment').

Be sure to check laws, some straight notes are illegal.

HOW TO ESTIMATE YOUR
REAL ESTATE TAXES

1.

$$\frac{FMV \times .80 \times 11.70}{4 \qquad \times 100} = R.\ E.\ TAXES$$

$$FMV \times .0234 = R.E.\ TAXES$$
$$SO:\ FMV \times 2.34\%* = R.E.\ TAXES$$

The sale price or fair market value (FMV) ×
80% (The assessor usually does not use
100% of sales price) . . . The percent used
can be obtained from your local assessor. . .
Then divide by 4 = ASSESSED VALUE.
ASSESSED VALUE × $\underline{\$11.70}$ (The tax
$\qquad\qquad\qquad\qquad 100$

rate per hundred dollars can be determined
with a phone call to the assessor's office.)
= REAL ESTATE TAXES PER YEAR.

* NOTE: By determining the percent of FMV
that equals the estimated R.E. TAXES per
annum based on the above outline . . . you
can very <u>RAPIDLY</u> estimate taxes for <u>ANY</u>
BUILDING.

EXAMPLE:
$100,000 (FMV) × 2.34% = $2,340 R.E. TAXES

2. NOTE: Proposition 13 (JARVIS - GANN)
in California requires the assessor to
take 1% of FMV, e.g., $100,000 FMV = $1,000 Real Estate Tax.

USING ASSESSED VALUE RATIOS

Fair Market Value = $200,000

Assessed Value = $50,000

Assessed Value = 25% of FMV. Is assessor's technique. FMV used by assessor is usually **LOWER** than actual.

STATED ON TAX STATEMENT

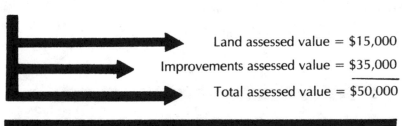

Land assessed value = $15,000

Improvements assessed value = $35,000

Total assessed value = $50,000

So:

Your actual Purchase Price = $220,000

$$\frac{\text{Improvements assessed value}}{\text{Total assessed value}} = \frac{35,000}{50,000} = \frac{7}{10}$$

Improvements therefore = 70% of value.

Internal Revenue will accept this ratio.

0.70 × $220,000 Purchase Price = $154,000

$154,000 = Building Basis for depreciation!

LOAN POINTS & INTEREST

A point is **1%** of the amount of the loan, paid to the lender, in order to obtain the loan and is tax deductable. A one time charge.

> 1 Point = Loan Expense = 1% = 0.01

So:

> 1 Point on $ 100,000 Loan = $ 1,000

Or:

> 1/4 Point on $ 100,000 Loan = $ 250
> 0.0025 (watch the decimal).

As a lender's rule of thumb, to LOWER the INTEREST for the life of a new loan by **1%** would cost about 8 points (*1 point* × *8 years banker's standard*).

So:

> To lower a loan of $ 100,000 from 10% per annum to 9% would cost $ 8,000.

Or:

> To reduce the interest from 10% to 9 3/4% = $ 2,000.

NOTE: you may wish to pay cash up front to reduce the INTEREST rate, if you wish to keep the property.

TO MEASURE A POND

From schoolboy plane geometry we know that 'in any triangle a line which is parallel to a side, divides the other two sides proportionately,'

IF AB IS THE UNKNOWN AND THE OTHER LINES CAN BE MEASURED THEN THE PROPORTION IS STATED:

IF CD IS THE UNKNOWN, USING THE SAME PRINCIPLE EXPRESSED AS 'SIMILAR TRIANGLES' IS:

AB IS TO BD
AS
AC IS TO CE
OR

$$\frac{AB}{BD} = \frac{AC}{CE}$$

AND SOLVE FOR AB.

CE IS ½ EB
DE IS ½ EA
SOLVE FOR CD
CD IS ½ AB.

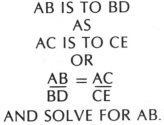

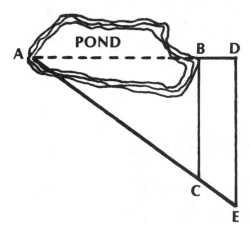

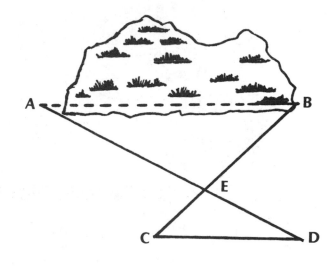

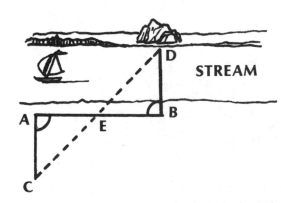

MEASURE A STREAM BY CREATING TWO EQUILATERAL TRIANGLES

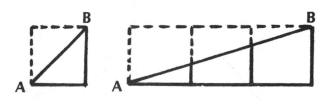

IF YOU HAVE EITHER A SQUARE, OR A RECTANGLE (OF LAND) AND DRAW A DIAGONAL LINE SUCH AS **AB**, THE AREAS IN THE SQUARE AND THE RECTANGLE ARE EACH DIVIDED EXACTLY EQUAL.

AE IS TO EB
AS
AC IS TO BD

AE = EB
AC = BD

CHAPTER
IV
CREATIVE FINANCING
AND
MONEY MATTERS

CREATIVE FINANCING
&
MONEY MATTERS OVERVIEW

Money is like fertilizer, you have to spread it around to have it do any good. In this chapter we analyze how to use as little fertilizer as possible to obtain maximum growth.

Once the basic concepts of investing are mastered, you are ready to explore the mysteries of high finance. The learning curve on financing seems limitless. There are a staggering number of ways to finance property—one of the keys (not including the key to Fort Knox) is 'to use other people's money.' The following are a few methods of raising or conserving cash:

- borrow the salesman's commission on a one year note
- borrow the funds from a friend or relative
- form a syndication with two or more persons then pool resources and go after a larger project
- wrap the existing financing with a new loan
- refinance for a much larger amount and wipe out the existing financing
- lease now and purchase later
- use an option with the right to purchase the property, or to assign the option
- buy land (with a low down payment) with the owner of the land to 'subordinate' (take a secondary position) to a construction loan, and then sell or assign the package to a third party
- have a friend place a deposit equal to your loan (compensating balance)

in the lender's bank to help obtain your loan.
- create first or second notes on one or more properties
- obtain a loan from your stockbroker using your own stocks and bonds as collateral, a non-purpose loan
- use a 'contract of sale,' so that you do not have to deliver a large down payment or disturb the existing loan
- use one or more lesser valued properties as the down payment on a greater valued property (a trade)
- structure a 'progressive sale' (the purchase of one portion of a property gives you the right to purchase one or more other properties)
- assume all existing loans (with minimum, or no cash down)
- use something other than cash as a down payment, e.g., coins, stocks and bonds, antiques, boat, car or plane.

One reason financing appears so difficult is because of technical jargon. Once you plow through the legal-speak, you are on your way to your own personal creative financing. As an example of obfuscation, armed service manuals refer to: aerodynamic personnel decelerator, combat emplacement evacuator and impact attenuation device. They could just have easily stated: parachute, shovel, and an oil drum used as a barrier.

After determining the system needed to obtain the money for investment, the next step is to determine where to get it. As Willie Sutton said when asked why he robbed banks, "Because that's where the money is." You should first try your personal banker and real estate broker for their thoughts. The usual sources of funding are banks and savings and loan institutions. The banker's dictum is, 'If you can prove you do not need the money, we will approve the loan.'

One of the most effective techniques the author has used to obtain loans is to prepare a comprehensive 'loan package.' This package consists of copies of all documents needed to approve a loan, such as: a cover page; a letter explaining the project and purpose of the loan; photos of the property and architectural renderings (in full color and reduced to 8½" x 11"); the original purchase agreement with addendums; government inspection reports; preliminary title-report; a detailed property statement, present and projected rental and sales pricing; comparable appraisal reports; grant deed (or mortgage) and all escrow papers if the property has already been purchased; a breakdown of all work to be completed with contractor's estimates; a personal financial statement of assets, liabilities and net worth; income tax returns for the past two years; and all supporting documents including appraisal reports listing stocks, bonds and other fixed and liquid assets. This entire package, with all pages reduced to 8½" x 11" format, is then bound (velo-bind or other) as a book. Three bankers have stated that this loan package was the most complete and organized they had seen.

A line from an Indian fable, the Panchatantra (circa 326 B.C.), translated from Sanskrit, sums it up rather nicely, "*Wild elephants are caught by tame. With money it is just the same.*"

HAPPINESS IS THE FINAL PAYMENT ON YOUR LOAN

(AT LEAST ON ONE PROPERTY AND LEVERAGE THE OTHERS)

IV
CREATIVE
FINANCING

LENDER SECURITY & FORMULAS

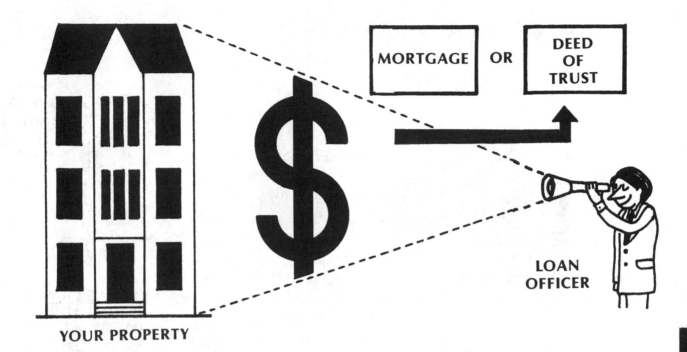

YOUR PROPERTY

MORTGAGE OR DEED OF TRUST

LOAN OFFICER

Unlike a personal loan, a mortgage (Deed of Trust) loan is granted PRIMARILY on the value of the property rather than on the reliability of the application.

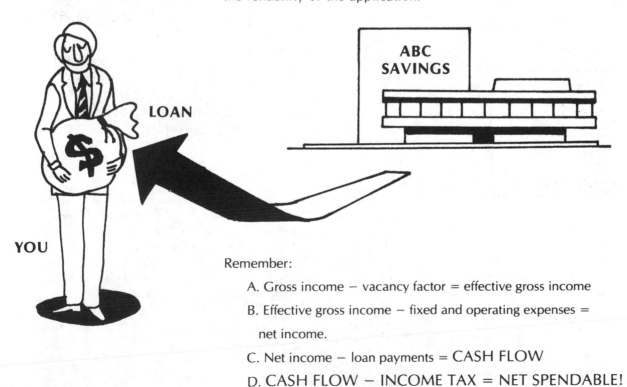

YOU

LOAN

ABC SAVINGS

Remember:

A. Gross income − vacancy factor = effective gross income

B. Effective gross income − fixed and operating expenses = net income.

C. Net income − loan payments = CASH FLOW

D. CASH FLOW − INCOME TAX = NET SPENDABLE!

IV CREATIVE FINANCING

REVERSE ANNUITY MORTGAGE . . . RAM

The reverse annuity mortgage was designed to aid the fixed income elderly who own their own home free and clear, or have a substantial equity. Rather than selling their home to tap the equity, a lending institution, or in some cases an individual lender can create a RAM. There are all manner of combinations, but the essence of a RAM is that the lender will create an annuity (payment) that will be paid monthly to the owners of the home. The annuity can be for life, or some fixed period. The lender in turn receives payment for the annuity by sale of the property at a future date, or by sale after the death of the owners (or, the lender could be cashed out).

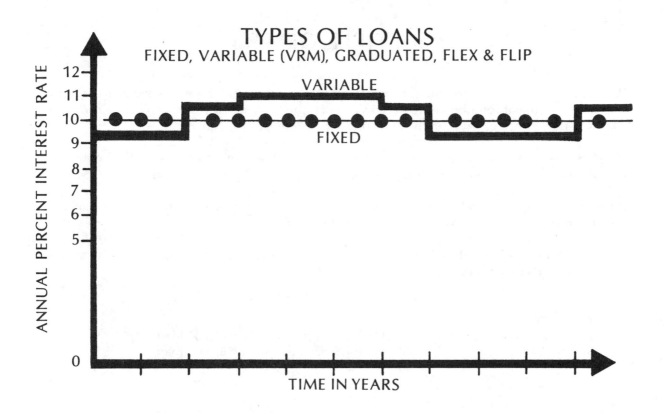

TYPES OF LOANS
FIXED, VARIABLE (VRM), GRADUATED, FLEX & FLIP

VARIABLE

FIXED

ANNUAL PERCENT INTEREST RATE

TIME IN YEARS

For many generations there was only one type of loan, the *fixed loan*, a fixed annual percent interest for the life of the loan. The monthly loan payments were 'level' (same amount each month), and the loan was fully amortized (paid off) at term, e.g., a $500 per month payment (including principal and interest) at 10% per annum, and paid in full in 30 years. With double digit inflation, 6% to 10% interest on fixed interest loans was not particularly appealing to lenders, so they have given us a profusion of new types of loans to consider (they still insist on being paid). A few of the more common types of loans are as follows:

1. *Variable Rate Mortgage* (VRM), also know as *Variable Interest Rate* (VIR). As the name implies, the interest rate varies as inflation increases. Fortunately, they usually have an upper limit increase not to exceed 3% (or less) over the original starting interest rate. Increases are usually limited to ¼ % per year, and have no bottom limit, so if inflation rates decrease, you could end up with a 4% per annum loan (not likely). It is not all bad news. There is a great advantage with a VRM, in that the lenders have no qualms about having a new buyer (with good credit) assume (take over) the loan, since the lender knows the rate is not fixed, but can go up if need be with the new buyer. The ability of a buyer to assume the existing loan is of great aid in completing the sale.

2. *Graduated Payment Mortgage (GPM)*. With a *graduated payment mortgage*, the monthly payments start out at a low level and gradually increase (say, 3% a year) until they rise just above the level at which a conventional mortgage would have been written. Thus, the GPM should be particularly attractive to young families buying their first home, or to people who plan to live in the home less than ten years.

3. *Flexible Loan Insurance Program* (FLIP). The FLIP loan is a fully-amortizing, graduated payment mortgage that treats the down payment in a unique way. Instead of the down payment used as equity in the building, a major portion (say 80%) is deposited in a pledged savings account to serve as additional collateral for the lender, and as the source of supplemental payments for the borrower during the first few years of the loan.

The lender can advance up to 100% of the purchase price, and each month, the lender withdraws a set amount from the savings account and adds it to the borrower's reduced payment to make a full normal loan payment.

As long as inflation and rising prices are with us, we can look to additional *Alternative Mortgage Instruments* (AMI) to help more people to have their piece of the action.

MULTIPLE OFFERS

When purchasing a property, more than one offer to purchase can be presented at once. Note that it is not ethical for a broker to present a lower offer to a seller, when he has a signed offer that is better. Ethics dictate that he must present all offers to the seller.

Multiple offers are especially useful when the seller's needs are unknown. The odds on obtaining a deal improve when you offer multiple choices, but do not make it confusing.

When other potential purchasers are involved, remember that if there is a counter-offer, and it is not stated otherwise, the first signed counter-offer returned wins.

Examples below are offers to submit simultaneously on the same property. All it takes is the time to type two extra pieces of paper.

1. $95,000   All cash.
2. $100,000 $25,000 down payment and a $75,000 loan.
3. $105,000 $10,000 down payment and a $95,000 loan.

USING FIRST & SECOND NOTES AS CASH

When purchasing a property, first and second notes can be used as the equivalent of cash. Notes which you own can be made more attractive when accompanied by actual cash, or other consideration. For example, "down payment to be $40,000 in the form of $20,000 cash and a $20,000 second note." The author once used a second note and a custom sport car as the total down payment.

The advantage of using notes as a down payment is that you receive 100% of the value of the note. If you converted the note directly to cash by selling it, you would most likely have to sell the note for less than the principal balance, i.e., "discount the note."

A rule of thumb for selling a note, is to estimate 5% per year discount, for each remaining year to maturity, with a minimum, usually, of 10% discount.

The amount of discount depends on the interest rate, the number of years remaining, the payout amounts and the "seasoning of the note," i.e., the history of payments. The property equity that secures the note is also important.

CREATE MONEY

A very quick & easy way to obtain a down payment for a property you would like to purchase is to *create a second note from the equity in a property that you own.*

SOMETIMES THREE LOANS

Under certain circumstances it is better to create two or more loans rather than one from a bank or savings and loan firm.

This is particularly true if you know the holder of a second or third loan would like to cash out in the future.

Example:

Say you could obtain a bank first loan of $150,000

It may be better to create three loans:

First loan (bank) . . . .$ 80,000
Second loan (private) 40,000
Third loan (private) 30,000

TOTAL = $150,000

THE BUYER

If the second and third notes are written for interest only the payments are held down, and as a buyer you have the option, at your convenience, of paying off the second and third. By paying off the second and third or a total of $70,000 for a discounted cash value of, say, $60,000, you have effectively reduced the price by $10,000. The savings are more substantial the higher the loan amounts.

THE SELLER

From a seller's point of view, having two notes as opposed to one large note, means more flexibility. The two notes can each be used as down payments on two different properties.

CONCLUSION

Don't be afraid of a third note or of creating one, as long as the equity, and the numbers make sense.

DELAYED DOWN PAYMENT

Many times a buyer can make a more attractive offer to the seller by increasing the amount of the down payment, even if you do not have the cash immediately available, but will have it at a later date.

Example:

Down payment of $30,000 cash with $20,000 cash to be placed in escrow within ten days upon acceptance of this offer, and *$10,000 cash payable within 120 days from close of escrow.*

DOLLARS TO KEEP

Unless you enjoy paying more than your fair share of taxes, the dollars you keep are more important than the dollars you make. For example, it is better to keep $70,000 out of an income of $80,000, than to keep $50,000 out of an income of $100,000.

To have a million, and owe two million is to be a <u>negative millionaire</u>.

BORROWED MONEY

Bankers use real estate loans to gather individual income. With about eighty percent financing all net rentals go to the bank. A fisherman uses nets to catch fish, a landlord uses apartments to gather some of the tenants' income (he gives the value of occupancy in return). The bank gives loans to get the owner's income.

For borrowing to be worthwhile, one must *do something* with the borrowed money that *brings a greater return than the cost of the loan*. Borrowed money may be tax free, but it is a debt, and must be returned with interest.

TYPES OF MILLIONAIRES

Absence of a future expense is better than the presence of a future income. Better to have a price paid in the past with the benefits yet in the future.

One definition of wealth is to already have outright ownership of everything you will ever need.

Far better to be a *net worth* millionaire, than an *asset* millionaire.

SUBLEASED APARTMENTS
AS AN INVESTMENT OPPORTUNITY

In Europe, Hawaii, California and elsewhere, many apartments are leased for long terms—as much as ninety-nine years. In some cities of the United States there may be a market for fully furnished luxury apartments. A small investor might lease such an apartment with *'the right to sublet'* and then furnish and decorate it. The apartment *might* be rented to a reliable tenant for enough more than the original lease to provide a profit. This method may provide a supplementary income for very little cash investment. This may be a useful idea for the right person with taste and little more than one month's rent to invest.

BUY FOR CASH, SELL FOR CREDIT

Some very consistently successful real estate operators use this principle extensively.

There are many more people with $10,000 cash available to them on a given day than there are people with $100,000. Frequently a substantial profit may be gained by buying a property for cash (perhaps borrowed cash) and then selling to another person at a higher price with a lower cash down payment, taking back the remainder of the purchase price as a second mortgage.

For example, you could negotiate an all cash purchase price of $80,000 for a building and sell for $100,000 with a low down payment of $10,000. You would then have a choice of having the buyer obtain an 80% first loan ($80,000) and carrying a second loan yourself for $10,000. Or, you could carry the entire first loan of $90,000.

MILLIONAIRES HAVE TO LIVE SOMEWHERE TOO

Eric Berne, the noted psychiatrist, once said, "The sooner you make new friends, the sooner you will have old ones." A well-built house has a useful life of hundreds of years. Many lower income people now live in buildings originally built by and for the wealthy. Some concerned people deplore the construction of new luxury housing.

However, *the true social cost of housing is mainly dependent on the length of the useful life of the structure, and this depends on the quality.*

Better the rich to build new housing, than to displace the poor. Today's well-built house of the rich could well be the poor man's home of the future. . .as it has been for generations past.

CREATIVE FINANCING IV

DOUBLE ESCROW

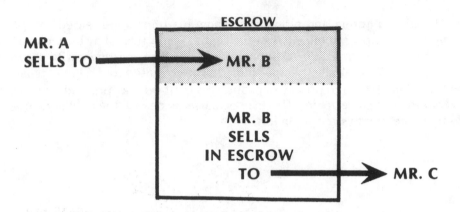

ESCROW

MR. A
SELLS TO → MR. B

MR. B
SELLS
IN ESCROW
TO → MR. C

Mr. B purchased from Mr. A. Mr. B *owned the property for an instant in escrow.* Mr. B sold the property to Mr. C in escrow. This is an example of *double escrow.*

If Mr. B purchased the property for $100,000 and sold in escrow to Mr. C for $150,000, he had a gain of $50,000 with *no cash*, other than the down payment and loans placed in escrow to complete the sale. An instant later Mr. B had the money from Mr. C.

If Mr. B borrows the funds from a bank for the one day needed to close escrow, he has *none of his own money in the deal*, and has made $50,000.

If Mr. B was a real estate agent, and did not disclose the sale to Mr. A, he could be subject to charges of "hidden profits," or fraud.

USURY

Usury is charging interest in excess of a certain amount specified by law. Unfortunately the law does not keep pace with inflation, and in most states the interest rate considered usurious is not even as high as the rate the banks charge their most favored customers (prime rate). Lenders who abide by the law then go to other states that have higher legal interest rates. The net result is that the law designed to protect the borrower from loan sharks, merely forces money out of circulation for a given area, and the consumer has less money available to borrow,

Yesterday's loan shark interest, is today's goldfish rate.

"WRAP-AROUND" LOAN

(AIDT)

A 'wrap-around' or 'all-inclusive' Deed of Trust is used by
a seller ... so as NOT to change the existing financing.

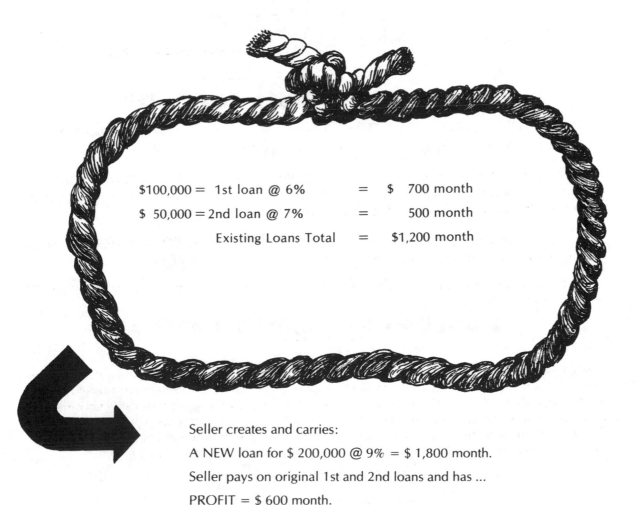

$100,000 = 1st loan @ 6%   = $ 700 month

$ 50,000 = 2nd loan @ 7%   =   500 month

Existing Loans Total   = $1,200 month

Seller creates and carries:

A NEW loan for $ 200,000 @ 9% = $ 1,800 month.

Seller pays on original 1st and 2nd loans and has ...

PROFIT = $ 600 month.

INTEREST & REFINANCE

Remember that 1½% interest per month is **18%** interest per year.

A $10,000 loan @ 1½% per month will cost you . . .

$$\begin{array}{r} \$10,000 \\ \underline{.18} \\ \$1,800 \end{array} \quad \text{interest per year!}$$

TRY TO AVOID HIGH INTEREST!

Credit card loans, et al . . .

Obtaining a loan or an investment can be very 'easy' and 'friendly.' Be sure it is just as easy to pay off the loan or dispose *(liquidity)* of the investment.

Always consider a lower interest REFINANCE of your property, *consolidate loans*, thus raise the PRINCIPAL amount enough to cover the extra money you require.

PASSBOOK LOAN

How to obtain a 1% per year loan:

First: Place $5,000 in a 6 year savings account @ 8% per annum.

Then: Borrows $4,000 @ 9% using the $5,000 as collateral.

Result: The cost of the loan is 1% and you have established credit.

INVESTING IN 2nd DEEDS OF TRUST OR MORTGAGES

Your investment security is primarily in the property you lend on, and secondarily in the credit of the borrower.

A. $100,000 = Property value
70,000 = Equity **the more the better**
20,000 = Balance of 1st loan
10,000 = YOUR 2nd loan

Borrower has AAA credit. Based on above, your loan @ 10%, $ 200 month, 5 year pay–off, looks o.k.!

B. If on the above the equity is $10,000 and the balance on the 1st loan is $80,000, your loan is shaky.

When purchasing a second Deed of Trust, **or mortgage,** or on "paying off" a second Deed of Trust PRIOR to the due date, you may be able to "discount the note," **reduce the principal.** A 10% to 15% discount is not uncommon.

A RULE OF THUMB IS TO HAVE AN EQUITY AT LEAST TWICE AS LARGE AS YOUR LOAN.

THE HISTORY OF FMV

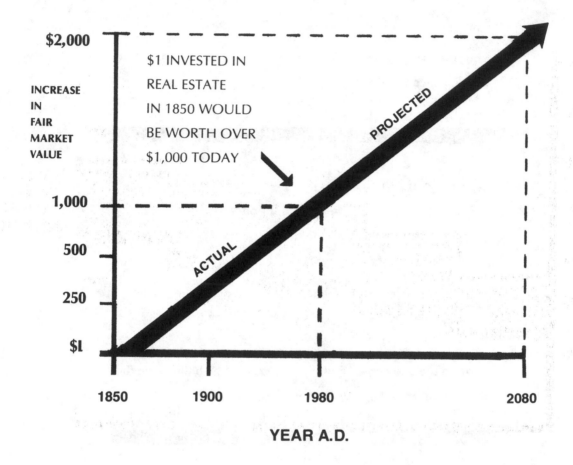

REAL ESTATE (LAND & IMPROVEMENTS) HAS BEEN INCREASING IN FAIR MARKET VALUE AT THE RATE OF ABOUT 5% A YEAR, COMPOUNDED SINCE THE YEAR 1850.

HISTORY DEMONSTRATES THAT REAL ESTATE PRICES KEEP PACE WITH INFLATION.

$1,000 INVESTED IN 1850 REAL ESTATE WOULD BE EQUAL TO OVER $1,000,000 TODAY.

REAL ESTATE INFLATION GRAPH

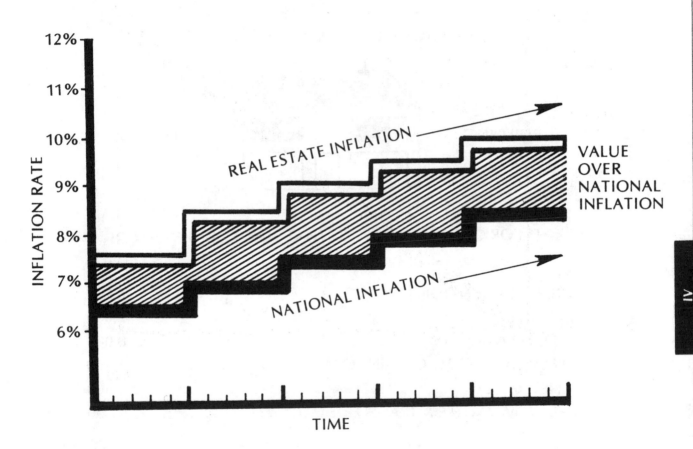

Our leading economists seem to agree that as our national inflation rate (based on the CPI) increases, the real estate inflation rate also increases, and usually averages a few percent higher, i.e., when the national rate is 10% the real estate rate is about 12%. History tends to back up this position, history from the dawn of the Phonecians.

The author is familiar with property that increased in value, for a short period, over 10% on a *daily* basis. Such property is usually the very best available (perhaps, in the world) with names like Kauai, Maui, Carmel, Marina del Rey, Newport Beach, Palm Beach, et al.

IV
CREATIVE
FINANCING

INVESTING Vs SPECULATING

YOU PURCHASE   A   **$ 100,000**

BUILDING   AND RETAIN

IT FOR ONE YEAR. DURING THAT YEAR YOU SPEND FOR:

REPAIR & REMODELLING	$ 10,000
TAXES	2,000
LOAN PAYMENTS	8,000
LOAN POINTS TO OBTAIN LOAN	1,500
INSURANCE	500
ESCROW & TITLE & TRANSFER TAX	1,000

TOTAL OUT−OF−POCKET = $ 23,000

SAY INFLATION IS AT 7 % PER ANNUM   7,000
(And you purchased to at least stay even with inflation.)

TOTAL = $ 30,000

YOU THEN SELL THE BUILDING FOR $135,000

ALSO YOU HAVE NOT PAID CAPITAL GAINS TAX YET.

Q. ARE YOU A SPECULATOR OR AN INVESTOR?

A. ....IS IN THE EYES OF THE BEHOLDER !!

IV
CREATIVE
FINANCING

INCOME & NUMBER OF UNITS

MORE
UNITS

MORE
RENTALS
TO
MANAGE

MORE
APPLIANCES

MORE
PLUMBING

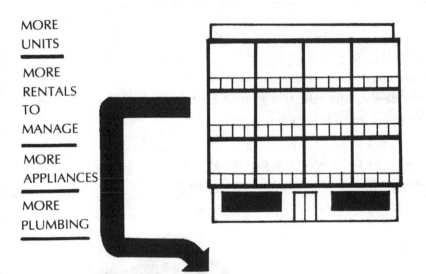

16 Units
_____

16 Bedrooms
16 Baths
16 Refrigerators
16 Stoves
_____

Rental: 1 Unit = $100 Month

SAME: GROSS INCOME = $1,600 MONTH

LESS
UNITS

HIGHER
RENTALS

MAY BE
HARDER
TO
RENT

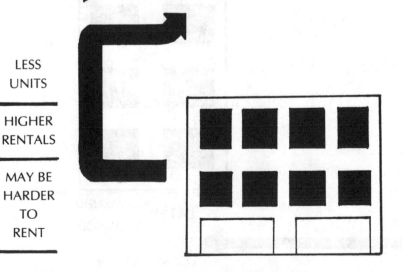

8 Units
_____

16 Bedrooms
8 Baths
8 Refrigerators
8 Stoves
_____

Rental: 1 Unit = $200 Month

INFLATION & INTEREST RATES

$1   VS $1

$1 = $1
"HARD DOLLARS"

LATER = 70 CENTS
"CHEAP DOLLARS"

The *belief* that there is going to be inflation can keep interest rates HIGH, because lenders will be reluctant to lend money that will come back to them worth less than it is now.

The purchaser of property, by using leverage, can usually compensate for high interest because of the greater increase in the value of the property, i.e., *appreciation*.

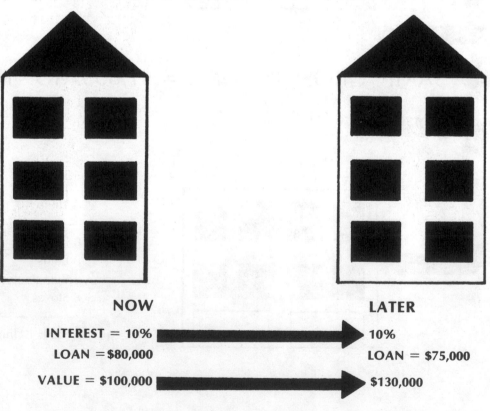

NOW	LATER
INTEREST = 10% →	10%
LOAN = $80,000	LOAN = $75,000
VALUE = $100,000 →	$130,000

Value of property increases, annually above inflation and interest rate.
as dollar shrivels like cheap bacon.

PRINCIPLE OF INCREASING & DECREASING RETURNS

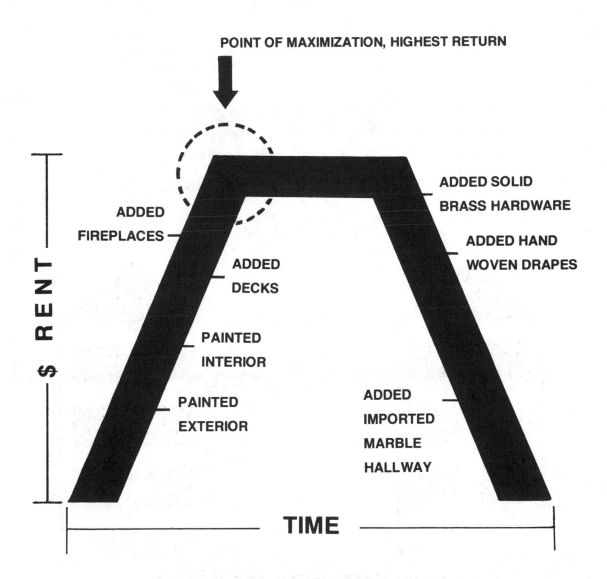

POINT OF MAXIMIZATION, HIGHEST RETURN

ADDED FIREPLACES

ADDED DECKS

PAINTED INTERIOR

PAINTED EXTERIOR

ADDED SOLID BRASS HARDWARE

ADDED HAND WOVEN DRAPES

ADDED IMPORTED MARBLE HALLWAY

$ RENT

TIME

Continued improvement of property will finally reach a point...beyond which you can not raise the rents.

A rough rule, is to have an increase of $2 in property value, for every $1 spent; e,g., $2,000 improvement = $4,000 value.

IV
CREATIVE FINANCING

SUPPLY, DEMAND & EQUILIBRIUM

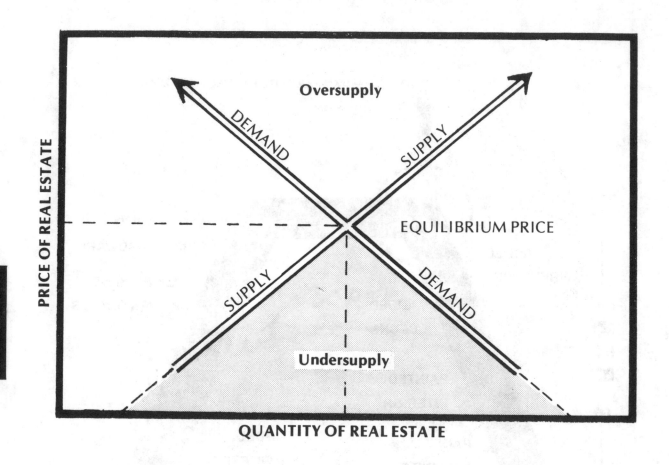

As the prices rise for real estate or other commodities, the number of people who can afford it diminishes. A price will finally be reached whereby only a handful have the means to purchase. A large supply of expensive property, demanded by a few, is an oversupply.

An ideal situation is to establish a price of housing, and a supply of housing, that exactly meets the demand. This is an *equilibrium price*.

NO MAN IS AN ISLAND

THE CIRCULAR FLOW OF ECONOMIC ACTIVITY

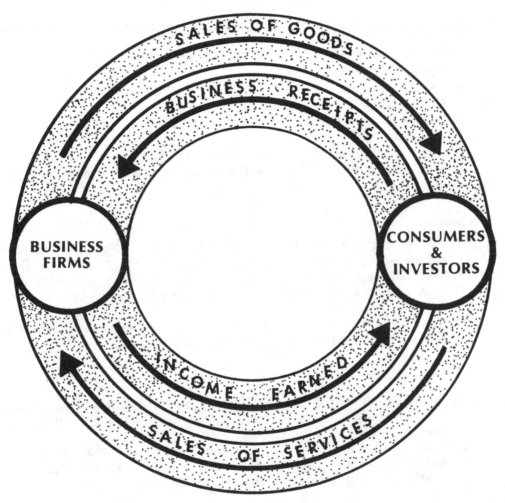

Unlike primitive man who produced everything he needed, modern man, for his goods (with the exception of hermits), depends on millions of people he will never know. Take your own home and everything in it, and try to trace every person who was involved in any way with bringing it to your doorstep. The numbers involved are so great that they are uncountable.

Business firms produce products, be they toothpicks or highrises. These goods are sold to consumers and investors, who in turn are involved with selling their services to business, as employees, or other wage earners. The consumers and investors selling their services to business receive an earned income, which they then proceed to spend on the products of business.

One of the most expensive products in this endless circle of activity is the purchase of housing. The purpose of this page is not to imply that understanding one simplified diagram explains our economy, but rather to show that this circular treadmill of activity is what every real estate investor steps on. Enough individual sales do change our economy, and for the better.

No sales, no economy.

M1, M2, M3 — LOANS

MI: **Is the most basic measure of the money supply. It includes:**
- **A.** Currency and coin in circulation
- **B.** Travelers' Checks
- **C.** Demand deposit balances in checking accounts
- **D.** Balances in Negotiable order of Withdrawal (NOW) and Super-NOW accounts
- **E.** Balances in Automatic Transfer Services (ATS) accounts
- **F.** Balances in credit union share draft accounts, thrift accounts, and mutual savings banks

M2: **Is MI plus:**
- **A.** Savings and time deposits *less* than $100,000 at all depository institutions, including Money Market Deposit Accounts (MMDA)
- **B.** Overnight Repurchase agreements (RP) issued by all commercial banks.
- **C.** Overnight Eurodollars issued to U.S. residents by foreign branches of U.S. banks worldwide.
- **D.** Balances in both taxable and tax-exempt general purpose Money Market Mutual Funds (MMMF) held by the public and small businesses.

M3: **Is M2 Plus:**
- **A.** Large time deposits of *over* $100,000 at all depository institutions.
- **B.** Repurchase agreements (RP) with maturities longer than one day at all commercial banks and thrift institutions.
- **C.** Eurodollars held by U.S. residents with maturities longer than one day.
- **D.** Balances in both taxable and tax-exempt Money Market Mutual Funds (MMMF) held by large institutions and corporations.

LOANS: **M3 is of particular importance to the individual borrower, since the more money in savings deposits, the more money available for real estate and other loans.**

Velocity of Circulation of Money: The rate at which money circulates in the economy, as measured by the number of times during a year the same dollar becomes someone else's income.

Calculated by dividing Gross National Product (GNP—the nation's total production of goods and services) by the money supply.

The above information is culled from information by the Board of Governors of the *Federal Reserve System, Washington, D.C. 20551.*

For one of the most interesting, dynamic and informative audio-visual monetary exhibits ever assembled, you may wish to visit the *Federal Reserve Bank of San Francisco at 101 Market Street.*

LIQUID ASSETS vs DISASTER

The late William Zeckendorf was a towering giant of investment brains and guts. . .a wheeler-dealer in the best sense, who could take an idea out of his own head and create beauty, enjoyment, and millions of dollars with a simple phone call. If placed in history at the right time he would have been the man to negotiate the original deals for Manhattan, the Louisiana Purchase and Alaska.

He negotiated placing all of the countries of the world into their United Nations home, as most of us would negotiate for a pair of shoes.

His Arnhem, his 'bridge too far' was to extend his credit too far. He was 'called' on a loan and his empire crashed. This does not diminish this burning meteor of the real estate world, it only makes for a very sad ending to his guiding light.

If there is one man who stands above all others, who stands to investing for the daring, the creative, and the brilliant, then this is that man.

The lesson learned is to *be mindful of loan due dates*. No matter how brilliant you are, the unexpected can happen (and usually does). *Liquid assets* (cash or assets that can be immediately converted to cash, e.g., stocks, bonds, gold coins, etc.) are a vital part of any investment portfolio.

The rule of thumb is to
have liquid assets available in an amount
equal to payments on all loans for six months.

FINANCIAL STATEMENT ANALYSIS
BALANCE SHEET

Assets − Liabilities = Net Worth

$$A - L = NW \quad \text{So: } A = NW + L$$

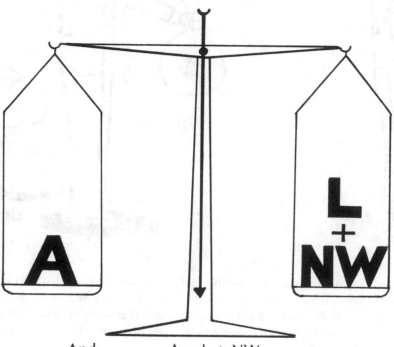

And: $A = L + NW$

$$\$190{,}000 = \$120{,}000 + \$70{,}000$$

Or: $NW = A - L$

$$\$70{,}000 = \$190{,}000 - \$120{,}000$$

Oi: $L = A - NW$

$$\$120{,}000 = \$190{,}000 - \$70{,}000$$

YOUR PERSONAL FINANCIAL STATEMENT SIMPLIFIED

(Required for a Loan Application)

BALANCE SHEET

ASSETS:

Cash on Hand	$ 1,000
Cash in Bank	4,000
Auto	5,000
Cash Value of Life Insurance	10,000
Real Estate:	
Property "A"	100,000
Property "B"	50,000
Stocks and Bonds	5,000
Trust Deeds	2,000
Other:	
Household Furniture	6,000
Personal Property	7,000

TOTAL ASSETS = $ 190,000

LIABILITIES:

Personal Loans	$ 15,000
Auto	2,000
Total Real Estate Indebtedness	100,000
Other:	
Furniture, etc	3,000

TOTAL LIABILITIES = $120,000

TOTAL NET WORTH = $ 70,000

A — L = NW, why not calculate your own net worth?

YOUR PERSONAL FINANCIAL STATEMENT
(REQUIRED FOR A LOAN APPLICATION)

MONTHLY INCOME AND EXPENSES

MONTHLY INCOME:

Gross Salary or Wages	$ 1,300
Rental Income:	
Property "A"	$1,000
Property "B"	700
Interest Income	100
Trust Deed Income	100

TOTAL MONTHLY INCOME = $3,200

MONTHLY EXPENSES:

Rental Now Paid	none
Real Estate Loans:	
Property "A"	1,000
Property "B"	500
Auto	200
Furniture	100
Personal Loans	200
Alimony	0
Other:	100

TOTAL MONTHLY EXPENSES = $2,100

YOUR PROFIT AND LOSS STATEMENT

IF SELF—EMPLOYED...
Required for a loan application.

Gross Sales	$100,000
Less Cost of Goods SOLD	40,000
GROSS PROFIT =	$ 60,000

Less EXPENSES:

Payroll	$ 20,000
Advertising	3,000
Insurance	1,000
Taxes	2,000
Repairs and Maintenance	2,000
Supplies	1,000
Rent 3% of Gross Sales	3,000
Other:	3,000
TOTAL EXPENSES =	$ 35,000

NET PROFIT = $ 25,000

PURCHASING AN APARTMENT FOR CONDOMINIUM CONVERSION

If you are considering converting an apartment building into condominiums, a rule of thumb for estimating the final per unit selling price is to take the existing price if sold as a conventional apartment building and multiply by 1.5 (150%), then divide this number by the total number of units. The result is the average selling price for each condominium unit. This factor allows for normal expenses of conversion and sales.

EXAMPLE:

An 8 unit apartment building
with a value of $400,000
The value per unit, therefore, is   50,000

$400,000 × 1.5 factor   =   600,000

estimated average selling price per unit . . .

$$\frac{\$600,000}{8} = \$75,000$$

The 50% increase would be
roughed out at 35% overhead plus 15% profit.

MONEY IS NOT WEALTH

At present money only serves as a medium of exchange, but not very well as a store of value. As inflation continues it is less and less efficient as a medium of exchange, in that certain value, such as a house, requires more and more money to represent it in an exchange. With taxation and brokerage commissions based on the nominal price in dollars and not on the income, or subjective benefits of ownership, higher prices lead to a rapid erosion of owner's equity, and it is possible in our inflationary times to make money while getting poorer, and to get wealthy while spending more money than you make. It is, for example, possible to create real wealth by improving one's property with borrowed money. The only problem is making the payments. It is easy to become overextended and to experience great losses. It is important to have clear investment goals in mind, and to have a *reasonable* and *flexible* plan for their achievement.

As George David M.D., syndicator and financial wizard, listed in Who's Who of Finance has commented to the author:

"Wealth is large results from small efforts.
Poverty is small results from large efforts
Capital is the means to achieve desired results."

DON'T SPECULATE WITH YOUR KIDNEYS

(OR YOUR HOME)

If you sell something you need for your own use, but can not replace it, you have not made a real profit regardless of how much money you made. Whether you are better or worse off than before depends on what you buy with the money you received, and not on how much money you received. In a time of inflation, money declines in value as prices increase. If a person buys a house for $10,000 and sells it 10 years later for $100,000 he may, or may not have made a true economic profit. If he takes the money from the sale and spends it on personal consumption, he has decreased his wealth.

Many people make unprofitable trades. It should be observed that any sale has substantial expenses involved, and unless a real profit is present to offset these costs, the more transactions a person makes, the more he loses. In the stock market this is called 'churning' and is said to be done by some unscrupulous brokers to collect more commissions. This point may be made forcefully in the following way. Let us assume that there is a market for donor kidneys. Let us assume that the price for donor kidneys increases. Do you, as the possessor of two kidneys consider yourself to be the richer? Of course not. The same concept applies to a home. Borrowed money can be used creatively to produce more wealth but in inflationary times many people overconsume because of the availability of borrowed money.

REFINANCING GRAPH

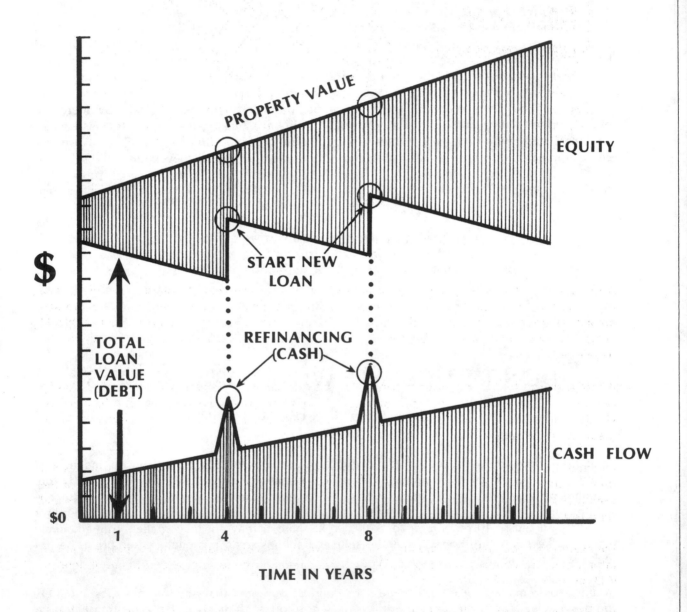

As the property value increases, your property equity increases. In this example, new larger loans are obtained in the fourth and eighth years, based on the increased value of the property. The 'tax-free' cash obtained from these new loans can be used to start other 'investment pyramids.'

Keep in mind that the larger loans represent more debt (more leverage), higher loan payments, and in time less tax shelter when the depreciated building value reaches zero.

SWING, BRIDGE & GAP LOANS

THIRD PARTY COMPENSATING BALANCES

A swing loan is temporary financing, usually six months to one year. A common use of a swing loan is to pay off an existing loan on a property, and thus give the developer time to secure **permanent takeout financing**, e.g., individuals purchasing condominiums obtain permanent (20 to 30 year) 'takeout loans' and a number of these individual loans added together pay off the developer's swing loan.

A **bridge or gap loan** is similar to a swing loan, but is usually the **difference** between the underlying financing and the total dollars required. It is suggested that when dealing with bankers the words 'bridge loan' be used, as the author has determined that most bankers don't like to associate their bank's image with the word 'swing.'

One method of obtaining a swing loan from a lender is particularly interesting and involves not only securing the loan with the property, but **also depositing an amount up to the value of the loan** (compensating balance, a 'linked deposit'). Lenders are very partial to large deposits and tend to favor such borrowers.

For example, if you need a six month $1,000,000 swing loan, you secure it with the property as collateral and also deposit up to $1,000,000 with the banker in the form of a 'certificate of deposit' (CD) or 'money market' deposit.

In the event you do not have $1,000,000 in cash to deposit, the trick is to locate an **investment banker** that will **deposit** the $1,000,000 **in the bank of your choice** and in **their** name. The investment banker's deposit in their name is, of course, a very safe investment and they receive the benefit of all earned interest, plus a fee to you of a few points (percent) for their service.

The swing loan fee is in the range of 2 to 4 percent over the **prime rate** (the minimum interest charged by a bank to its best customer).

The net result of the transaction is that for a few points **you obtain a $1,000,000 loan and have used none of your own money**.

INTERNAL RATE OF RETURN (IRR) OVERVIEW

If the reader understands that $20,000 cash received now is better than $20,000 received at the rate of $1,000 per year over a period of 20 years, then the reader understands the essence of present dollar value, future value, discounted dollars, discounted cash flow (DCF) and internal rate of return (IRR), although the thoughts may never have been expressed in those terms.

Engineers with mathematical formulas can 'prove' that the bumblebee's body is too heavy for its wingspan and therefore can not fly. The bee, not knowing these equations, continues to fly. Do not be overwhelmed by algebraic equations as long as your arm used to determine the Internal Rate of Return (IRR). Many millionaire investors and others well versed in the real world of investing have absolutely no idea of how to explain the mathematics of IRR, or of a Discounted Cash Flow (DCF) math-model.

Reams of computer print-out, bound in Morrocan leather, tanned with sumac and gold embossed with your name do not make the information more accurate, only more impressive. Remember the computer dictum 'Garbage in, Garbage out' (GIGO), or, if you prefer, roses in, roses out.

IRR, DCF math-modeling and other advanced techniques to determine what is happening to your money have a definite use. One friend makes his living explaining syndicating and IRR to investors. . .his knowledge of mathematics is particularly useful to him. For the rest of us mortals, if you understand a simple GRM (gross rent multiplier), a simple Cap Rate, a simple Market Value Appraisal, and a simple property statement including your best projections of 'future income stream'. . .you are in rather good shape—even if you don't build your own computer math model.

The author's view of advanced IRR techniques is that you are trying to predict the unknowable and explain the ineffable, but don't let one man's opinion stop you. If you are comfortable with your factual input, then go to it.

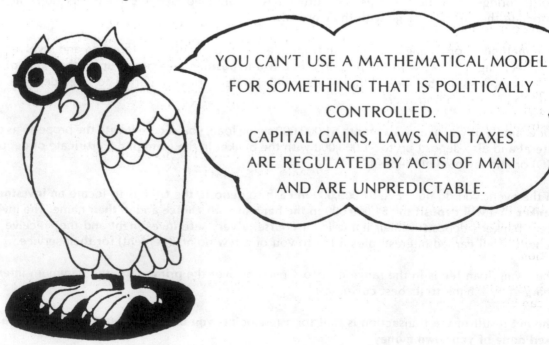

YOU CAN'T USE A MATHEMATICAL MODEL FOR SOMETHING THAT IS POLITICALLY CONTROLLED.
CAPITAL GAINS, LAWS AND TAXES ARE REGULATED BY ACTS OF MAN AND ARE UNPREDICTABLE.

DISCOUNTED CASH FLOW OVERVIEW

CONCEPT OF THE DISCOUNTED DOLLAR

Readers who have reached this far into the book are to be commended for their perseverance. The exception being those whose crayon boxes are open, thinking this was a coloring book.

It is the author's opinion that the most involved subject in real estate is the concept of *Discounted Cash Flows* as they relate to *Internal Rate of Return.*. More garbage and less knowledge seems to be the order of the day. The author believes it is possible to explain these concepts 'quick & easy', and that the readers will understand them perfectly. Here goes.

CAKE TODAY, OR CAKE TOMORROW—LORD KEYNES

One dollar *now* is worth one dollar now. It had a different value a year ago and it will have a different value a year from now. Most of us are familiar with the term 'compound interest'—one dollar at a 10% interest rate per annum is equal to $1.10 at the end of the first year, $1.21 at the end of the second year, and continues compounding as long as the original dollar is invested. The $1 compounded for approximately 48 years at 10% is equal to $100, or, one cent is equal to one dollar.

This simple concept of one cent compounded to one dollar, that most of us would know intuitively, is the principle of the 'time value doctrine of money.'

DISCOUNTED CASH FLOW EXPLAINED

Now that one cent becoming one dollar is clear, let us consider one dollar we do not have, but we *will* receive at a future time. Let us say that we are to be paid $1 in 48 years, and that the interest rate opportunity cost (loss of interest) for the period that we do not have the dollar is 10% per annum. What is the dollar worth today? The dollar we will not receive for 48 years is worth exactly one cent if we choose to accept payment today. The present value of the dollar today is one cent *today*. One cent is the *discounted cash value of one dollar, discounted at the rate of 10% per annum*. That's it. You never have to take a back seat again when the terms *present value* of the dollar and *discounted cash value* are mentioned. DISCOUNTED CASH FLOW is simply the 'income stream' of discounted cash values.

DISCOUNTED CASH FLOW IS THE EXACT REVERSE OF COMPOUND INTEREST

How do you calculate the Compound Interest, or it's reciprocal DCF? Simple, you look up the appropriate intrest rate and dollar value for each. The Compound Interest tables and the Present Value of $1 tables (Inwood Tables) are available in any bookstore having a large real estate section.

If you have a problem, just check with your accountant. The final analysis is in concept, that 1¢ can become $1, and that $1 can be worth 1¢.

PRESENT VALUE & DISCOUNTED DOLLARS

INTERNAL RATE OF RETURN (IRR)
& DISCOUNTED CASH FLOW (DCF)

Internal Rate of Return may be labeled as any of the following:

- The after-tax equity yield rate
- The before-tax equity yield rate
- The math-model interest rate
- The property discount rate
- The discounted cash flow analysis calculated as an IRR

IRR is the *aniticipated* yield. For the actual IRR you would have to wait until the holding period ended, and the property was sold. Not knowing the actual answers for a holding period of five, ten or twenty years does not help you now. So you must take your best guess.

What the hell does all of this mean? The jargon and math are enough to humble an Einstein.

By calculating the IRR you will know that dollars received later are not as valuable as dollars received now. But wouldn't you know that without calculating the IRR? Doing the fancy calculations, either with paper and pencil, or a computer, will *not* change the objective facts. But it may give insight into realizing that the return on the investment is not quite as great as anticipated.

A simple CAP RATE of 10% may, with mathmatical gyrations, turn into an IRR of 9.2%. A drop in the return based on the IRR of 1% represents a drop of $1,000 on a $100,000 property; $10,000 on $1,000,000; or $100,000 on $100,000,000.

The conclusion seems self-evident. On smaller properties, calculating the IRR is not as significant as it is on larger properties.

To determine the IRR on a project you must as accurately as possible, project over the holding period of up to twenty years, the following:

- The future rate of return on dollars taken out of the project, and reinvested in short term money market certificates.
- The income tax rate of your future output.
- The inflation rate and Consumer Price Index that will have a direct bearing of the property expenses and the future rental income stream.

The answers can be stated with certainty, "nobody knows." The more accurately you guess, the more accurate the IRR.

CONCLUSION

IRR is a more accurate way of expressing the rate of return on a property by taking into account the fact that you are not receiving all of your money now, but rather as a future income stream. This future income stream can be calculated mathematically and is known as the discounted cash flow (DCF). IRR and DCF are different sides of the same coin. IRR is the *rate* of return on the investment. DCF is the *monies* received on that investment. In concept, not all that complicated.

PRESENT VALUE OF $1

DISCOUNTED CASH VALUE

	5.0%	6.0%	8.0%	**10.0%**	12.5%	15.0%	17.5%	20.0%
1	.952	.943	.926	.909	.889	.870	.851	.833
2	.907	.890	.857	.826	.790	.756	.724	.694
3	.864	.840	.794	.751	.702	.658	.616	.579
4	.823	.792	.735	.683	.624	.572	.525	.482
5	.784	.747	.681	.621	.555	.497	.446	.402
6	.746	.705	.630	.564	.493	.432	.380	.335
7	.711	.665	.584	.513	.438	.376	.323	.279
8	.677	.627	.540	.467	.390	.327	.275	.233
9	.645	.592	.500	.424	.346	.284	.234	.194
10	.614	.558	.463	.386	.308	.247	.199	.162
11	.585	.527	.429	.321	.274	.215	.170	.135
12	.557	.497	.397	.319	.243	.187	.144	.112
13	.530	.469	.368	**.290**	.216	.163	.123	.093
14	.505	.442	.340	.263	.192	.141	.105	.078
15	.481	.417	.315	.239	.170	.123	.089	.065
16	.448	.394	.292	.218	.152	.107	.076	.054
17	.436	.371	.270	.198	.135	.093	.064	.045
18	.416	.350	.250	.180	.120	.081	.055	.038
19	.396	.331	.232	.164	.107	.070	.047	.031
20	.377	.312	.215	.149	.095	.061	.040	.026
21	.359	.294	.199	.135	.084	.053	.034	.022
22	.342	.278	.184	.123	.075	.046	.029	.018
23	.326	.262	.170	.112	.067	.040	.025	.015
24	.310	.247	.158	.102	.059	.035	.021	.013
25	.295	.233	.146	.092	.053	.030	.018	.010
26	.281	.220	.135	.084	.047	.026	.015	.009
27	.268	.207	.125	.076	.042	.023	.013	.007
28	.255	.196	.116	.069	.037	.020	.011	.006
29	.243	.185	.107	.063	.033	.017	.009	.005
30	.231	.174	.099	.057	.029	.015	.008	.004

TIME IN YEARS

Example: What is the present value of $1, that could be invested at 10% interest, and that you will not receive for 13 years?

To find the answer, simply go to the 10% column and then go down the column to the 13 year row, and then across to the answer, 29 cents.

DISCOUNTING SECOND NOTES (DEEDS OR MORTGAGES)

This concept can also be used for determining the amount to discount second notes, e.g., a $1,000 note due in 13 years at 10% interest is worth $290 now.

INTERNAL RATE OF RETURN

THREE EXAMPLES

Observe that the three properties (A, B, & C) all have the exact same investment, i.e., $3,000. Now let's see what happens when the "income stream" is different for each property.

	Property A		Property B		Property C	
Year	Investment	Cash Flow	Investment	Cash Flow	Investment	Cash Flow
Today	$ 3,000-	$ -0-	$ 1,000	$ -0-	$ 3,000	$ -0-
1	-0-	1,500	2,000	800	-0-	-0-
2	-0-	1,500	-0-	1,700	-0-	-0-
3	-0-	1,000	-0-	1,600	-0-	-0-
4	-0-	500	-0-	1,000	-0-	6,000
Totals	$ 3,000	$ 4,500	$ 3,000	$ 5,100	$ 3,000	$ 6,000

Dollar Amounts can be increased ten or a hundred times with no changes in the IRR.

Note that property C has a total cash flow of $6,000, exactly double the original investment, and that property A and B have lesser total cash flow. Since property C has the greatest cash flow, it must therefore be the best investment . . . right? Wrong! It is not only how *much* return you receive on an investment, but *when*.

TIME-VALUE

What Einstein did to show that time is important (read *vital*) to space, the Internal Rate of Return (IRR) does to show that time is important to the value of an investment.

If you knew absolutely nothing of IRR, would you notice that the investment in property B gives you a one year grace period before requiring the balance of $2,000? Would you notice that property B has a total cash flow of $600 more than property A? Would you notice that property C receives no cash flow until the end of the fourth year? Would you guess that property B, all other things being equal, was the best investment? If the answer is "yes" you would be correct.

The actual Internal Rates of Return are:

Property A   24%
Property B   35%
Property C   19%

Your accountant can verify this on his hand calculator.

It is interesting to calculate that property C has an *average* rate of return of 25%, i.e., $6,000 divided by 4 is $1,500, or 25% per year. Note that an average rate of return of 25% is a long way from an IRR of 19%.

Please note Letter to Author, On Calculators, pg. 376.

IV
CREATIVE
FINANCING

BUBBLES BURSTING

Physics teaches us that equal pressure in all directions from one center point, or one medium suspended with equal pressure in another, e.g., gas in liquid, forms a perfect sphere, or bubble.

Australian pearl divers in the 1850's literally exploded when they popped through the surface of the water. The hand-crankers on the air pump had overestimated the amount of air needed. The combination of the diver's blood nitrogen bubbles expanding, and the air (oxygen) in the suit expanding at the decreased sea level pressure . . . blew the diver apart.

The analogy is fair to apply to the housing bubble's expanding pricing. As long as the price of a house expands proportionally to the expanding inflation (or a touch more), the pressures are all equalized, and the bubble remains intact.

The National Association of Realtors records indicate the median sale price of a single-family house in 1973 was about $30,000, and for 1979 it is about $58,000. This is approximately 16% a year increase. Although this is a greater increase than, say—food inflation, with food you have nothing left (you eat the expensive steak). Your house *remains*—you don't eat your house.

REFINANCE DOWNWARD

The usual thinking is to take money *out* of a property with an 'equity loan,' or new loan (which is refinancing upward). What about paying down the loan? Refinance downward? If the interest rate on the loan is high, and you have no better investment opportunity, then consider paying down your loan (in a corporation it would be a 'sinking fund'). The interest payments on a conventional thirty year loan are amazingly two to four times the amount of the loan. It is a simple matter to multiply your own monthly payment by 360 payments (30 years) to determine the total dollar cost of your loan.

If you have borrowed money on a second loan to put in a new roof (which is usually a good move), your next best move may be to pay off this loan. If the lender is a private party the loan can probably be discounted (price reduced because of early pay off) to save even more dollars.

Many knowledgeable investors prefer to invest in second mortgages because of their excellent return and security (in most cases.)

Paying off (or down) your highest interest short term loans, e.g., second note, or credit card loans are the benchmark by which to judge all other investments. You might do better, but you could easily do worse.

MIRRORS & JELLY BEANS

Joel Elekman, investment banker, who handles multi-million dollar projects throughout the nation, stated when the author asked him about IRR and DCF, "You can crystal-ball rate of return to death. A priori math modeling is all done with mirrors and jelly beans. You must determine how it relates to your objectives." If you know the "cash on cash" return is 10%, does it help your objectives to know that the Internal Rate of Return, using five variable parameters, is 9.83%? If it does, then use it. If it doesn't, then don't bother.

BETTER NOW THAN LATER

After several all day conferences with Lars Gantzel, legal counsel to the California Association of Realtors, he replied rather clearly (for an attorney), "It is better to have money now than later. It is better to borrow money now for repayment later."

THE LEGACY OF OWNERSHIP

Ownership is the right to capitalize (the present value of all expected future benefits) the consequences of one's actions. An owner of a building exercising good taste in decorating adds to its value and utility. Consequences of all actions are, in fact, capitilized, and they fall upon the owner (government or private).

GIVE ME SHELTER

Property held free and clear (no debt) is an excellent hedge on inflation, or deflation. The huge equity is like a bank. When funds are needed for a future fortuitous purchase, they are easy to obtain with a first loan. It is future purchasing power, in a near liquid, untaxable, inflation protected, continually enjoyable form. It is *real* estate.

Poor Abe Lincoln lived in a log cabin. One might note that he had the productive use of leisure to study law, because his log cabin was free and clear.

EQUITY REVEALED

In speculation (buying and developing a property for the purpose of selling at a higher price) the money to pay seller's profit comes from the down payment, and new loan of the new buyer.

The buyer's debt becomes the seller's equity.

SYNDICATION BASICS

A *syndication* is a group of persons who combine their financial and managerial resources to carry out a real estate transaction with the stated intention of earning a profit. A syndication is the way to purchase the 'cherry' property you always wanted, but could not afford. If one person can't handle the deal, then ten can. Because syndications involve *investment contracts* (securities) your project may fall under the Securities Act of 1933, or other federal and state laws. It is imperative that legal counsel be sought. In California, for example, there is the 10/25 rule: if the syndicator sells to no more than ten persons, and contacts no more than twenty-five persons, then the requirements under the Securities Act are less stringent.

TYPES OF SYNDICATIONS

Ownership can be either by a corporation, or a more typical general partner with limited partners. The syndication can be of two main types: *specified property*, or *unspecified property* ('blind pool'). Specified property is as the name implies—a specific property has been purchased, or optioned by the syndicator (general partner). An unspecified property means that the investors are placing their money in a 'blind pool' and relying on the syndicator's good judgement to select a property after the funds are all collected.

COMPENSATION

In a typical syndication, the syndicators (managing general partners) receive a real estate sales commission and a management fee for handling all of the paperwork and day to day property management. One caution is to note the amount of 'front-end' load that the syndicator receives. Better to have all parties to receive their monies equally, so that the syndicator will be motivated to see the project to completion. Syndications last from about one to eight years. A rule of thumb is to look for a doubling of your investment in five years.

A & B SYNDICATIONS

An *A & B Syndication*, or partnership, refers to the well known Mr. Able and Mr. Baker, who both want to invest, but have very different goals. As with the *Hawaiian Technique* you can divide a property into two parts, the land and the building. By assigning all of the property cash flow to the land (say A), and all of the tax write-off to the building (say, B), you can now satisfy Mr. Able's investment goal of cash flow, and Mr. Baker's requirement for tax shelter. Mr Charlie, of course, would want a little of each, so he can have a portfolio with a half of A, and a half of B investment.

THE HAWAIIAN TECHNIQUE

William Zeckendorf thought of a new method for selling real estate while surf-casting off of Oahu, Hawaii. He named it "The Hawaiian Technique."

His concept was to sell different types of ownership to different people. For example: (1) building ownership, (2) land ownership, (3) building and land rental ownership, (4) lease ownership, and (5) the right to future ownership.

CORPORATION ANALOGY

His concept is analogous to a corporation that does *not* sell the corporation outright, but rather issues stock, which relates to a lease, and bonds, which relate to first and second loans. Ownership can be further broken down into common and preferred stock, warrants, options, or convertible debentures.

IV
CREATIVE
FINANCING

HAWAIIAN TECHNIQUE — EXAMPLE

- The usual sale of a property with a $200,000 net income, would be to sell it for . . . . **$ 2,000,000**

- Using the *Hawaiian Technique* the same building would be sold as follows:

		RECEIVE
1. Lease property ($200,000 net income) for $1,000,000 (A fair 20% return to lessee).	CASH DOWN = $ / LOAN = $	200,000 / 800,000

2. Refinance. The $1,000,000 lease puts you in a stronger credit position. The loan proceeds equal $2,000,000 cash.

First loan (75%)	= $	1,500,000
Second loan (25%)	=	500,000
TOTAL OF STEPS **1** & **2**	= $	**3,000,000**

Using the *Hawaiian Technique* the money received went from $2,000,000 to $3,000,000; an increase of $1,000,000, and *you still own the property!* The building could then be sold for an additional million.

The combinations in this technique are as varied as the needs of the potential buyers, and the skill of the seller in 'packaging the deal.'

THE BEST LOAN

PURCHASE MONEY FIRST

The best loan is almost always obtained from the *seller lending the money*. This is called a "purchase money loan," and is indicated on the purchase agreement in the "seller to carry" clause (seller "to take back paper").

Using this method of borrowing, the author has *obtained properties for nothing down, 100% financed, no points, no loan fees* and *no prepayment penalties.*

BLANKET MORTGAGE

To convince the seller that he is secure in giving a 100% (or 90% or 80%) loan, it helps to have good credit, and it may be necessary to secure the loan with not only the subject property, but with *one or more* other properties—a so called **OVERLAPPING DEED OF TRUST** *(or mortgage).*

BUILT-IN FINANCING

When creating the purchase money loan, consider writing in a "right of one transfer" clause. When the property is eventually sold, this clause assures built-in financing for the new buyer to assume the loan.

BALLN PAYMENTS

The final payment on an installment note—usually considered a balloon if it is more than twice the regular payment. Be very careful of maturity dates on loans. Be sure to mark your calendar, and allow enough time to secure funds to pay off the loan, or to re-negotiate the terms. A $10,000 balloon payment that you were not expecting can be quite a shock.

BANKER'S VIEWPOINT

If you owe a thousand dollars to a bank and can't pay it back, you have a problem.
If you owe a million dollars and can't pay it back, then the bank has a problem.

THE BANK AS A CLOCK

Bob Moriarity, vice president with Barclay's Bank, stated, "The banking system is a time mechanism, it helps to close the deal. If you have enough time to raise capital by selling other property, you probably don't need a banker." He then personalized it by adding, "Roy, your deal would never have closed if we had not given you the $400,000 loan." Be sure to allow yourself plenty of time to secure financing—at least two months. The ticking of the investment clock never ceases.

I MUST BE RICH

They tell a story of Walt Disney, when asked if he was rich. He replied, "I must be, I owe seven million dollars."

ANOTHER LOOK AT THE STOCK MARKET

Although this book concerns itself with real estate, there are interrelationships between real estate and the stock market. All of the offices and plant facilities of all corporations involve real estate. Corporations must either own real estate, or lease it. They can not exist in a vacuum.

Also, there are businesses listed on the exchange, whose business is doing business in real estate, e.g., REIT's.

Two very succinct analyses of the stock market are as follows: Will Rogers' successful formula for investing was, "Don't gamble. Take all savings and buy some good stock and hold it till it goes up, then sell it. If it don't go up, don't buy it."

J. P. Morgan's classic answer when asked what the market was going to do was, "It will fluctuate."

CREATIVE
FINANCING

IV

HOME OWNER'S POLICY (HOP)

A Home Owner's Policy covers possessions stolen or damaged even away from home. Be sure to read the fine print. It is a good idea to engrave all items (or use special ultra-violet ink) with your driver's license number. Also take photos of all items to aid the police in identification, and to establish insurance loss. The author has saved thousands of dollars by proving loss with a simple set of snapshots.

KEEP RECORDS & RECEIPTS

In 20 or 30 years when you finally pay off a loan, it will be important to have the original loan document in order to record that the loan is paid off (Deed of Reconveyance, if a deed was used).

INCOME AVERAGING

Five years of income averaging means five years of tax documents to review (for an IRS audit).

COMPUTER RECORDS

If all of the information concerning your properties is placed in a computer memory, and coded for easy retrieval, you could then sort out the exact amount spent on paint, hardware, electricity, water. etc. over a ten year period. Based on five full IRS audits, the author has found that the government tax examiners are very partial to well organized computer printouts.

FULL DISCLOSURE BY BROKER

It is in the National Association of Realtor's ethics, and also the law in most states that a real estate broker must disclose, 'all material facts' concerning a transaction—even facts that are not asked about but that are relevant, must be disclosed. If this is not done a broker could be accused of 'negative fraud.'

One investor puts a clause in all of his deals, "seller acknowledges that buyer is a real estate broker, buying for his own account, and at a *huge* potential profit, or loss."

Please note Letter to Author, Litigation Prevention, pg. 379.

INSURANCE COVERAGE

BETTER TO HAVE:

A $1,000,000 umbrella (or blanket) liability insurance policy. . .

THAN:

Three each $300,000 policies

BECAUSE:

It is much less expensive to have one policy covering all of your property. It can include buildings, cars, boats and planes.

A one million dollar policy can be obtained to cover liability *over and above* the regular policies on each property. Also, check your policies each year to be sure the amounts keep pace with inflation. This helps to illustrate the advantage of dealing with an insurance expert.

MOF, MOFING & MOFED

MOF is the author's acronym for Mount Olympus Formula, or, if you prefer, Modified Option Formula. It was first thought of while negotiating on top of Mount Olympus. No claim is made that it is a unique idea, although it may have elements of 'new truths of old creation'. Tom La Lanne, attorney, was responsible for the legal framework of the MOF. The fact of the matter is that all of the author's best ideas were already thought of by some greek over 2,000 years ago. No doubt, before that, the first caveman was saying to the second caveman, "I will give you the option on my cave during the six months that I am away hunting, if you give me three sacks of dried fish."

The basic concept is extremely simple. The subject property, usually a very desirable one, is optioned and leveraged up to the hilt—up to 100%, using your own funds, borrowed funds or joint venture capital. If possible, the building is converted to condominiums. The MOF option is held for the capital gains period, and then the option is sold or traded. As an investor (not a dealer) you are entitled to take capital gains taxation on a capital asset held for the required capital gains holding period. This is the most favored tax rate. It is also the reason the option is assigned (sold), and not the property or the individual condominiums. By trading your option upwards for a more expensive option, there is no tax when done properly.

The downside risk is clearly spelled out. The non-refundable option money is what is lost if you can not perform. The upside potential is rather startling, since the rule of thumb is a selling price on condominims of 1.5 times the original pruchase price. A $1,000,000 property is therefore worth $1,500,000 as condominiums. Since the option is sold, and not the property or the individual condos, it is sold for less than the market value of the converted property.

If you option a $1,000,000 property and sell the option for $300,000, your gross profit is $300,000 on the transaction. If you have four similar options going at once, the return is well over a million dollars profit in a single year. You have at risk only the option money, and if need be you can walk away from the deal. Stock brokers would speak of this as a 'stop loss.'

The author is not acquainted with a better system for making money in real estate.

MOF TERMS

The following ten MOF clauses are typical of the type of Option Agreement contracted by the author's attorney. The clauses can be changed at will as reason and circumstances dictate. In every case the purchase price was for all cash, and was more than the Optionor (or seller) was asking. The dollar amounts indicated are used solely as examples.

(1) Optionee (or buyer) is to deposit $5,000 into escrow upon acceptance of this option offer. Upon delivery of a current "Certificate of Occupancy" (or equivalent document) to escrow the deposits become non-refundable, and are to be delivered from escrow directly to the Optionor, and credited to the purchase price. The Certificate is to be delivered within two months.

(2) Optionee is to pay Optionor $500 per month starting the first of the fifth month, after acceptance of this offer. This payment is to be made to escrow and paid from escrow directly to the Optionor, and is to be non-refundable after delivery of certificate. A $500 payment is to be made monthly thereafter until close of escrow. All payments thereafter are non-refundable, and are to be paid from escrow directly to the Optionor, and credited to the purchase price.

(3) Optionor agrees to allow Optionee to convert building to condominiums, or a cooperative stock corporation. Optionee agrees to use due dilligence to expeditiously accomplish such conversion. In the event the Optionee does not complete the conversion, then the Optionee has the right to null and void this option agreement, and the Optionor to retain all non-refundable deposits.

(4) Optionor agrees to cooperate with Optionee in signing all documents required for a conversion. The terms of said documents are to be in accordance with this option agreement.

(5) Optionee agrees to be legally responsible for the conversion process.

(6) Optionee agrees to provide Optionor with a monthly status report of the conversion, if requested.

(7) Optionee and Optionor agree to mutually cooperate, as far as possible, on a tax-deferred exchange.

(8) Optionee shall have the right, at his expense, to improve the property, and all such improvements shall conform to the building code.

(9) During the escrow period, any new leases shall be on a month to month basis only. Optionee is to have the "right of first refusal" to rent any apartment, and the Optionee is to guarantee the present rent payment on any vacancy.

(10) If escrow has not closed within 370 days after the acceptance of this option agreement, then the Optionor has the option to null and void this contract and retain all non-refundable deposits.

IV

CREATIVE FINANCING

THE TEN PIECES OF MONEY

PARABLE OF THE TALENTS

St. Luke, Chapter 19: *And he called his ten servants and declared them ten pounds (talents), and said unto them. Occupy till I come . . .Then he commanded these servants to be called unto him, to whom he had given the money, that he might know how much every man had gained by trading.*

Then came the first, saying, Lord, the pound hath gained ten pounds. And he said unto him, Well, thou good servant. . .And the second came, saying, Lord, thy pound hath gained five pounds. And he said likewise to him.

And another came, saying, Lord, behold, here is thy pound, which I have kept laid up in a napkin: For I feared Thee, because Thou art an austere man. . .And he saith to him, Out of thine own mouth will I judge thee, thou wicked servant. Thou knewest that I was an austere man, taking up that I laid not down, and reaping that I did not sow: Wherefore then gavest not thou my money into the bank, that at my coming I might have required my own with usury?

And he saith unto them that stood by, Take from him the pound and give it to him that hath ten pounds. . .For I say unto you, That unto every one which hath shall be given; and from him that hath not, even that he hath shall be taken away from him.

DISCOUNTED CASH VALUE

A BOWL OF SOUP

Genesis, Chapter 25: *And Esau said to Jacob, Feed me, I pray thee, with that same red pottage; for I am faint. . ..And Jacob said, Sell me this day thy birthright. And Esau said, Behold, I am at the point to die: and what profit shall this birthright do to me? . . .and he sold his birthright unto Jacob.*

Esau sold his birthright (his right to inherit all of his father's goods, and the right to be leader of the clan), a future capital asset, for a bowl of soup. The discounted cash value (one bowl of soup) for a future inheritance, does not show fiscal responsibility. Esau should have first checked with an investment advisor, or at least a soothsayer. He was later to regret this dumb move.

CHAPTER
V

REAL ESTATE LAW and TAXES

REAL ESTATE LAW & TAXES OVERVIEW

Unfortunately, ours is a litigious society. 'Sue the bastards' seems to be the rallying cry for persons suffering even the slightest of indignities. The author has had calls from an irate buyer, in a lather because the pilot light went out on the hot water heater. Somehow, such calls seem way out of context when they arrive in the middle of a multi-million dollar transaction. Apparently we must become adjusted to individuals who are not prepared to direct their own destiny, or accept responsibility for their own actions.

It is an indication that our laws are complex when lawyers hire lawyers. Also, it would indicate that those who make the law are becoming entwined in their own doing, to be hoisted on their own petard. The author has 'won' a full jury trial after three weeks preparation and a one week trial involving about fifteen witnesses. The accusation was the 'violent eviction' of eight trespassers. Not only was it nonviolent, it was not even rude (as one tresspasser was to later testify). There is a certain satisfaction in 'winning' a trial, shaking the hands of the twelve jurors, and 'proving' in court that you are not of canine ancestry, but it is a hollow victory. Losing a month out of your life on a trial is a no-win situation. The conclusion is try sweet reasonableness, pay the bucks (even if you are right), clean it up in an hour, and go on to the next project.

If you must go to court, then remember the attorney's shibboleth, "If the evidence is against you, argue the law. If the law is against you, argue the evidence. If both the evidence and the law are against you, pound on the table and yell like hell."

In this chapter a few of the more common points of law are reviewed, as well as the more important tax aspects. A special emphasis is placed on the exchange of property, since this is probably the most advantageous method of legally avoiding taxes. As long as you continue to trade up, you pay no taxes. It is only when you finally sell that you get clobbered.

V
LAW &
TAXES

GENESIS OVERRULED

.

In the beginning God created the heaven and the earth. And the earth was without form, and void; and darkness was upon the face of the deep. And the Spirit of God moved upon the face of the waters. And God said, "Let there be light." And there was light. And God saw the light, that it was good.

At this point in the project, He was faced with a class action suit for failing to file an Environmenal Impact Report (EIR) with the Heavenly Environmental Protection Agency (HEPA), an agency staffed by angels dedicated to keeping the universe free of pollution. He was granted a temporary permit for the heavenly portion of the project, but was issued a "Cease and Desist" order for the earthly portion, pending further study by HEPA.

The staff also demanded to know how the light would be made, and were told that the light would come from a huge ball of fire. Nobody at the agency really understood this, but it was provisionally accepted under the following terms:

(1) No smog or smoke would result from the ball of fire,
(2) A separate burning permit would be required, and
(3) Since continuous light would be a waste of energy, darkness should prevail at least half of the time.

He agreed. Everything appeared in order until He said He wanted to complete the project in six days. He was advised that His timing was completely out of the question, and that it would take at least 180 days to review the application, check credit references and study the impact report. Then there would be public hearings, and it would be 10 to 12 months before a final construction permit could be granted.

And God said, "To hell with it."

FORECLOSURES

The author wishes to thank Theodore Bayer (Teddy Bear), attorney, for insisting on this page. He has an excellent point.

Just when you are convinced that skyrocketing interest rates, ever-expanding governmental meddling and the wild-fire spread of rent control have made residential income property about as appealing as a cocktail party at a nuclear plant, someone mentions *foreclosure sales*. Sounds like a bad actor, something to be avoided regardless of how good the property looks, right? Wrong! With the upward spiral of the cost of money at the same time that big government is attempting to relegate the expression 'private property' to an archaism, loan foreclosures *will increase* markedly. The wise investor will be well advised to become familiar with the mechanics of the foreclosure process in his or her area, in order to benefit from the often-ignored opportunity to buy property below its market value.

FORECLOSURE SALES

Foreclosure sales—which occur when a borrower is no longer able, or desirous of meeting his loan obligation—are either *judicial or private*. *Judicial sales* are conducted *by the courts* and, as expected, require an inordinate amount of time. Thus, *most foreclosure sales* are conducted by a *private trustee*, usually a *title company*, under the *power granted in the deed of trust or mortgage*.

Once a loan has gone into default, the trustee must give the borrower, and certain other parties who request it, written notice of the default. Here's an opportunity to get a jump on other prospective foreclosure sales purchasers; if there is a piece of property in which you are particularly interested, or one where you learn that the owner is having financial problems, *record* a simple 'request for notice of default' against the property—you'll have two to three additional months to attempt to get financing.

DEFAULT

If the default is not *cured*, i.e., paid off during a period of time after the notice (the period varies from state to state), a *notice of sale* will be posted in a *public place* and/or *published* in a local newspaper. It is extremely advisable to learn where the title companies in your area post these notices and in which newspapers they are published. Check these sources at least weekly. The sale will occur anywhere from twenty to forty-five days after the notice has been posted/published.

HIGHEST BIDDER

At the sale, most states require the property to be sold to the highest bidder. Period. Only the *foreclosing creditor* may credit bid, i.e., bid up to the outstanding balance of his loan without putting up any cash. All other parties are required to *have cash* with them to complete the deal at the sale. It's a good idea to have *cashier's checks* or similar instruments *in increments of $1,000.00 and $5,000.00 to cover increases* over the initial bid. Some states permit the trustee conducting the sale to accept other suitable payment, e.g., loan committment letter from a local bank. If such is the case, *contact the trustee and the foreclosing creditor, before the sale* and discuss other possible methods of payment. Note that in many states a bid is *binding* once it is accepted by the trustee; failure to complete the purchase could *subject you to a civil and/or criminal liability.*

RESEARCH

Simple research and regular checking on foreclosure sale notices can open *a whole new world of income property investment opportunities.* Foreclosure sales represent an excellent mechanism for buying property below its market value, often *well below market.*

THREE-WAY EXCHANGE
TWO BUYS + ONE SALE

CREATIVE FINANCING TO AVOID TAXES

A three-way trade is required when one of the parties in the trade wants to cash out. Mr. Able buys Mr. Baker's property. Mr. Baker buys Mr. Able's property. Mr. Baker sells to Mr. Jones. This equals two buys and one sale, and is called a *three-way exchange*.

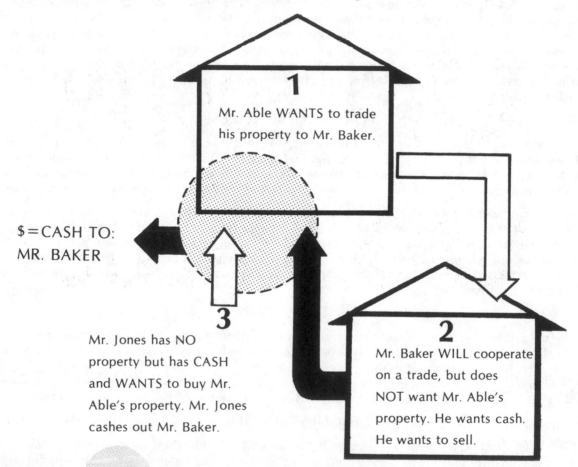

1

Mr. Able WANTS to trade his property to Mr. Baker.

$ = CASH TO:
MR. BAKER

3

Mr. Jones has NO property but has CASH and WANTS to buy Mr. Able's property. Mr. Jones cashes out Mr. Baker.

2

Mr. Baker WILL cooperate on a trade, but does NOT want Mr. Able's property. He wants cash. He wants to sell.

IN ESCROW	AT CLOSE OF ESCROW

IN ESCROW

1. A 3-way escrow.
2. SIMULTANEOUS.
3. Mr. Able and Mr. Baker have a LEGAL EXCHANGE.
4. Mr. Able gets Mr. Baker's property.
5. Mr. Baker gets Mr. Able's property in escrow only.
6. Mr. Baker sells Mr. Able's property to Mr. Jones.
7. Mr. Baker has traded with Mr. Able, and sold to Mr. Jones for cash.

AT CLOSE OF ESCROW

$ = 2   **1**

TRADING BASICS

BOOT = EQUITY

UP EQUITY

UP VALUE

You must trade "like for like" as defined by the IRS, i.e., investment property for investment property, and both held for investment.

For a *tax-deferred exchange* you must *trade up* into an equal or larger *equity, and also* an equal or *larger* property value.

The *difference between* the *equities* is called the *"boot"* and is paid in cash or other consideration.

Even if you trade up in value, if you trade down in equity you are subject to *taxation* on the difference (boot), because of *"mortgage relief"*.

The secret to trading if the equity and value of your property are *higher* than the property you desire to trade into, is to *adjust the equities and values of the properties before you trade.*

Further, you can *trade into one or more* properties to assure trading up into higher equity and value. The properties could even be in different states, but you will need escrow to close "simultaneously".

Remember that when you finally sell the traded-into property, your taxes are based on the gain going all the way back to your original cost basis. This is the reason why people with million dollar properties say, "I can't afford to sell."

TAX DEFERRED EXCHANGE

'Tax-free' = Tax-deferred
An important distinction

	Able	Baker
Fair Market Values	$100,000	$120,000
Loans	40,000	60,000
Equities	60,000	60,000
Cash Transfer	0	0
Recognized Gain	0	$ 20,000

Mr. Able exchanges his property for Mr. Baker's . . . must be 'of a like kind.'

Mr. Able pays NO tax on this exchange, but will in the future if he SELLS at a profit or trades down.

Mr. Baker has a gain of $20,000 in 'MORTGAGE RELIEF.'

TAX DEFERRED EXCHANGE

If you have unequal equities, consider
refinancing BEFORE a trade, in order to lower taxable gain.

ABLE & BAKER TRADE

	NO REFINANCING		REFINANCED*	
	Able	Baker	Able	Baker
FMV	$ 100,000	$ 120,000	$ 100,000	$ 120,000
Loans	40,000	90,000	40,000	60,000*
Equities	60,000	30,000	60,000	60,000
Cash *(Boot)*	0	30,000	0	0
Gain	30,000	20,000	0	20,000

*By having Mr. Baker refinance from $90,000 to $60,000, the equities become even.

After refinancing, Mr. Able has NO taxable gain on the trade for Baker's property.

Please note pg. 304.

CONTRACT

Contract: An agreement to do or not to do a certain thing.
A binding promise.

Basic Essentials:

1. Capacity—persons must be capable of contracting.

2. Mutual Consent—Voluntary and communicated offer by one and acceptance by other.

3. Lawful Purpose—Purpose of contract must be lawful and possible.

4. Consideration from Both Parties—May be money, property, an exchange of promises or other benefits.

CONTRACTUAL AGREEMENTS

Anything two people agree to that is both possible and legal can be put into a contract. The contract can be a deposit receipt, contract of sale, option or other.

Writing out in plain English the terms agreed on by both parties can form the basis of the contract. An attorney can then enhance the document with the exact legal language.

It is of interest to note that courts have held that on a preprinted contract, handwriting takes precedence over typewriting, and typewriting takes precedence over the printed contract.

CONTRACT STATUS

VALID   One having all essential elements required by law.

VOIDABLE   "Able" to become "VOID," by wronged party.

VOID   One that never had any legal existence.
                   Not necessarily illegal.

HOLDING AGREEMENT

When dealing with government agencies that require (by law) constant updating of documents for new ownership, e.g., condo conversion, you may wish to consider having all documents show the Title Company as the owner.

With the Title Company as owner on a holding agreement, the ownership can be changed without disturbing the major documentation. In the stock market it is called holding in the "street name."

LESSOR & LESSEE

Lessor = Landlord or Owner.

Lessee = Tenant

Lease = A contract whereby the owner transfers possession and
use of property to another person for a period of time
in consideration for money, *rent*.
A Lease MUST be in writing if for more than one year.

A month—to—month rental agreement should be in writing, but
may be verbal.

Maximum Term:

Land leased for agriculture.	51 years
Privately owned property lease.	99 years

LEASES AND RENTAL AGREEMENTS

The Law: Implied, if not in writing.

1. The owner may claim only a reasonably necessary amount of the security deposit . . . any remaining portion to be returned to the tenant. It is a good idea to take photos of the apartment, prior to occupancy.

2. The tenant has a basic right of privacy. The owner has a right to enter in emergencies, to repair and as per any agreement.

3. It is the owner's responsibility to provide a dwelling which is habitable, and the tenant's duty to keep his area clean and sanitary, and not damage or remove any part of the dwelling.

4. Tenant has the 'covenant of quiet enjoyment.'

EVICTION PROCEDURE*

THIS IS AN AREA WHERE YOU DO NOT 'DO—IT—YOURSELF.'

1. Tenant is served with 3 day "Notice to pay rent or quit."

2. "Unlawful Detainer" is filed with Municipal Clerk and Summons is issued.

3. Summons and Complaint served on tenant.

4. Tenant has the legal right to file a pleading and answer to the Complaint and in this event, a trial will be held. If not, then #5.

5. Default of tenant is taken.

6. Default Judgement is received by owner.

7. Court issues Writ of Possession.

8. Writ of Possession to sheriff.

9. Sheriff evicts tenant.**

* Exact procedure may vary in some locations, but concept of step by step holds true.

** The world's first tenants violated one of the clauses in their lease, and were promptly evicted (without a thirty day notice) by the first Landlord. Present day landlords are probably not as fair, or smart as He was, but a precedent was established. You are in good company if you must evict a tenant for just cause from your own little piece of paradise.

LAW & TAXES V

TENANT SELECTION

Tenants are the source of cash flow and net income. Without tenants you have no income, and a rather uninspiring vacant piece of sculpture.

Good tenants are a great asset, both for cash flow and a source of confidence for a new buyer. They should be chosen with the same care that you would use to select your doctor or your lawyer.

Photos of the apartment before and after occupancy will help eliminate one of the main causes of landlord and tenant problems, namely, the condition of the apartment when first occupied.

The best lease ever written is of little value when signed by a dead-beat. As a minimum, *check references*—i.e., former landlords, personal and credit references, time on job, etc.

HOMESTEAD

For many of us, *homesteading* conjures up images of covered wagons racing across the Oklahoma plains to be first to stake a claim.

The modern equivalent is *urban homesteading*, i.e., the city government has a drawing to determine the winner of abandoned houses. The winner pays only one dollar for the property, but agrees to put the building in first class condition, and up to code. It is an excellent method for restoring the rotting core of a city.

Probably the last of the raw acreage homesteading took place in Alaska. By simply filling out a form, moving onto the property, and staying there for five years . . . it was yours.

COMMON DEFINITION

The more common use of the word *homestead* applies to state homestead laws that protect or exempt a portion of your home from creditors. Homestead rights can be lost by abandonment. As is usually the case, every state has different homestead rules. In some, your right is automatic. In others, you must file a notice of homestead.

The concept of homestead rights is to protect the debtor from being thrown out into the street. Note that it does not look good on a credit statement to have filed a homestead, as lenders then think you are in trouble.

MECHANIC'S LIENS

A MONEY ENCUMBRANCE

Move one spadeful of earth, or have one stake driven and your property is subject to a mechanic's lien. *Do not do anything to the land prior to obtaining financing.*

A mechanic's lien refers to a lien by any person, furnishing labor or material for the improvement of real estate, who has not been paid and can place a demand for payment on the property. The work must be done by contract.

The owner can protect against a mechanic's lien for work ordered by a lessee by recording a 'notice of nonresponsibility.'

NEW HIGH-RISE INFERNO CODES

When purchasing a high-rise building (say, five stories or more) it is prudent to investigate the building codes (both on the books and pending). A good contractor is usually very aware of the latest regulations and trends. On one large building, the author was particularly concerned with knowing if there were any safety or fire code violations. An off-duty fire marshall was asked to inspect and report on the building. For a building that appeared in near-perfect condition, the report was startling. He mentioned that to meet the present code, and a new code (to go in effect in a few months) it would cost about five thousand dollars per floor. Sprinkler systems, 'hard wire' (wired into the building, not battery operated), smoke and fire detectors, metal fire doors, additional exits and other safety features were required to be installed. This additional work must be considered when estimating the price.

The same reasoning applies in areas with <u>seismic codes</u>.

ACCELERATION & ALIENATION CLAUSES

An *acceleration clause* gives the lender the right to 'call' (demand payment) *all* sums owing, if borrower fails to keep covenants, e.g., default or non-payment.

An *alienation clause* gives the lender the right to 'call' all sums owing, if borrower alienates (conveys) title, e.g., transfers title by sale, trade or agreement of sale.

If you don't pay on your loan, it is rather clear that the lender can enforce the acceleration clause. Recent court rulings against the lender's right to enforce the alienation clause leave it in a rather unclear position. California cases of Lassen vs Tucker, and Wallenkamp vs Bank of America, tend to favor a new buyer assuming the existing loan.

The Garn-St. Germain Act of 1982 lists about eight ways that allow transfer without alienation. If in doubt, a legal opinion is advised.

V
LAW &
TAXES

LIQUIDATED DAMAGES

MR. BUYER, SINCE YOU BROKE OUR CONTRACT, I WILL TAKE 3% OF THE PURCHASE PRICE OUT OF YOUR DEPOSIT AND WILL GIVE MY BROKER PART OF THE MONEY.

SELLER

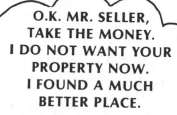

O.K. MR. SELLER, TAKE THE MONEY. I DO NOT WANT YOUR PROPERTY NOW. I FOUND A MUCH BETTER PLACE.

AND BESIDES, YOU CANNOT SUE US FOR ANY MORE MONEY, SINCE WE AGREED TO LIQUIDATED DAMAGES.

BUYER

IN ESCROW

THIS IS A HIGHLY LEGALISTIC CLAUSE AND COURTS USUALLY DO NOT LIKE LIQUIDATED DAMAGES. HOWEVER, THE DEPOSIT RECEIPT, IN THIS CASE, CLEARLY STATES I SHOULD GIVE THE MONEY TO THE SELLER.

ESCROW OFFICER

Liquidated damages is a predetermined amount of money that the parties in a contract (deposit receipt, or other) agree would be fair for the injured party to receive, in the event of a breach of contract.

EASEMENTS

Easements are land burdens restraining owners from doing certain things. A non-possessory interest in land of another giving holder right to use.

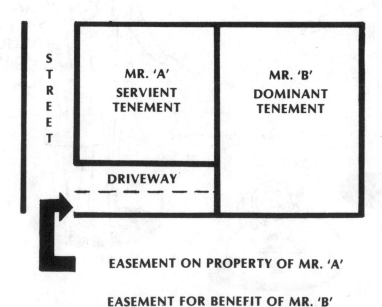

EASEMENT ON PROPERTY OF MR. 'A'

EASEMENT FOR BENEFIT OF MR. 'B'

An easement is a property interest (short of an estate) which one person has in land owned by another. It must be in writing, and is usually found in the deed.

An *easement appurtenant* would be the right to share a driveway, as illustrated above. This right, this easement, transfers with the sale of the property. It 'runs with the land.'

An *easement in gross* is more personal in nature and does not 'run with the land.' A common example is a utility or power line easement.

VIEW EASEMENT

In certain cases you can 'dedicate' to the government (city, state or federal) a portion of property you own to a view easement or green belt area in PERPETUITY. With a 'facade easement' you can dedicate just the facade to a local historical or architectural association.

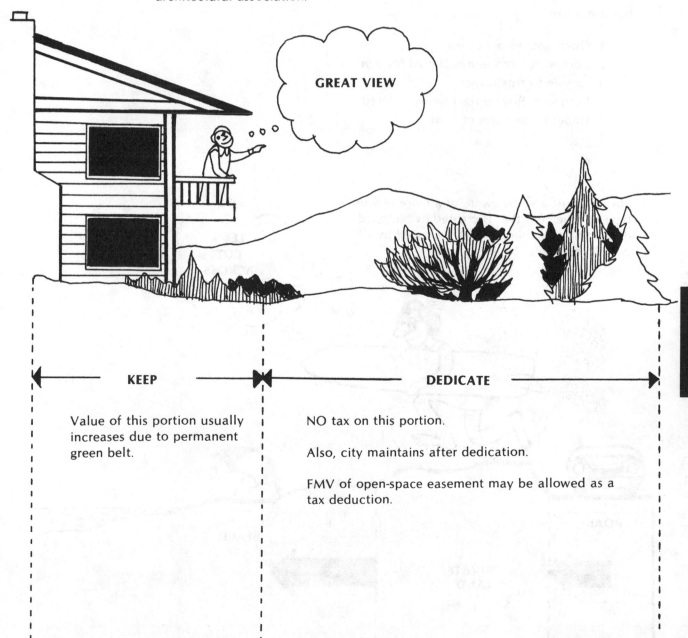

KEEP

DEDICATE

Value of this portion usually increases due to permanent green belt.

NO tax on this portion.

Also, city maintains after dedication.

FMV of open-space easement may be allowed as a tax deduction.

EASEMENT BY PRESCRIPTION

An easement can be created by prescription. . .the owner of the property would then have a burden on his land.

But it must be:

1. Open and notorious use.
2. Continuous and uninterrupted for 5 years.
3. Hostile to true owner.
4. Exclusive. Private right being asserted.
5. Under some claim of *right*.

Owners must also be aware of a more obscure type of easement that is created by "Implied dedication to public use." It is created by conditions similar to the above.

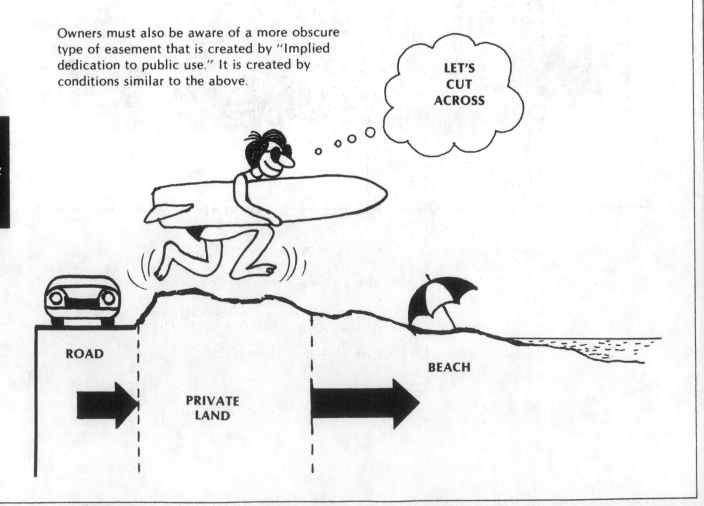

LAW &
TAXES

AVOID A PRESCRIPTIVE EASEMENT

If you allow a person(s) to use your property WITH your permission . . .
ERECT this sign:

. . . Then the person(s) can NOT claim an easement by prescription,

even if used for 5 years, because it is 'NOT hostile
to the owner.'

You should record a 'Notice of Permission.'

V
LAW &
TAXES

POWER TO THE PEOPLE

'Power to the people,' but what people? A catchy slogan and no doubt accurate for a democratic society. From the author's observations at meetings at various city halls, it sometimes appears to relate to lung power. This being the case, then opera singers should lead the pack for government reform and whoever is the loudest rules the day!

Better to qualify the statement by saying, 'Power to the elected people who have the ability to do the job.' You can always be heard loud and clear in the ballot box.

I don't believe we want unemployed beachcombers whose main qualifications are a loud voice and the ability to string puka shells deciding the complex issues of architectural covenants, traffic patterns, zoning, rent control and the like.

If "Atlas shrugged" and we had no intellect in power, but only the uneducated and uninformed, we would be in a sorry state of passionate anarchy. Let the 'cream rise,' let the able have a chance to power, let the uneducated become educated and the uninformed become informed. Let 'freedom ring'—let people who are willing to work forty, fifty or sixty hours a week on real estate or any legitimate business have the right to go as far and as fast as they can in a free enterprise system. Our founding fathers would ask no less.

EXCLUSIVE RIGHT TO SELL LISTING

Realtors are usually aware of the political climate. Documentation that requires various levels of approval, e.g., a condo conversion, new construction permits and others, are best left with someone that 'knows their way around City Hall.'

An agent dealing with a bank, or savings and loan firm which he has dealt with for ten years or more can create a more desirable milieu for obtaining a loan . . . than can an individual who walks in off the street.

With an *exclusive right to sell listing* the broker has incentive to spend his own money (up front) on advertising, and devote the required amount of time to secure a fast and efficient sale. This is usually not the case with an *open listing* (all brokers can sell, but none have an exclusive listing).

ADVERSE POSSESSION

Adverse possession is the acquiring of title to real property by possession for a period of time against the owner's will. In more common parlance it is called *squatter's rights*.

As it is with so many laws there is no universality among the states. Typical of the requirements are the five essentials for adverse possession (in California):

1.   Continuous possession for five consecutive years. The possession can be 'passed on' to a relative, e.g., a father occupies for three years and the son for two years.

2.   The possession must be 'open and notorious.' Actual occupation is not necessary, the open and notorious use could be the grazing of cattle on the property, the planting of crops, or the parking of trucks.

3.   The possession must be hostile to the will of the owner and must be by a sole user. An owner's 'no tresspassing' sign is not enough protection for the owner.

4.   The user must hold the property under a *color of title* (some defect of title), or *claim of right*.

5.   The user must pay the property taxes for the five consecutive years.

For the adverse possessor to obtain a marketable title to the property, he must obtain a *Quitclaim Deed* from the owner, or a *quiet title action* (court action).

It is interesting to note that *adverse possession* is similar to a *prescriptive easement*, but an easement is only a burden on the owner's land: it is not loss of ownership.

These statutes tend to emphasize the obligations involved with the 'right of ownership.' The law, in its wisdom, feels that property is so important that owners who do not protect and defend this right may lose it to those individuals who intend to make better use of the property.

The moral is to keep tabs on your real estate, or it may not *be* yours.

QUITCLAIM DEED

Used to remove 'cloud of title,' *doubt of clear title,* or ANY INTEREST grantor may have. If grantor has nothing, then nothing is conveyed.

EMINENT DOMAIN

YOUR LAND

The government (Federal, State or City) has the right (the right of Eminent Domain') to take your land 'for the public good.' The reason could be to convert the land into a freeway, road, public building, park or other. If you do not believe the government's appraisal is fair, you have the 'right to appeal.'

V
LAW &
TAXES

PREPAYMENT PENALTY

State laws vary throughout the United States on the use of prepayment penalties.

For example, the California Broker's Loan Law, which regulates acitivites of real estate licensees who negotiate new loans provides that:

1. Prepayment penalty is NOT allowed after seven years from date of execution.

2. 20% of the unpaid BALANCE is permitted to be prepaid in any year, *non-cumulative*, WITHOUT *penalty*.

3. Prepayment charge in any instance is limited to an amount equal to 6 months interest on the amount pre-paid in excess of 20% of the unpaid balance. Therefore, no penalty on the first 20%.

PROPERTY TAX DATES

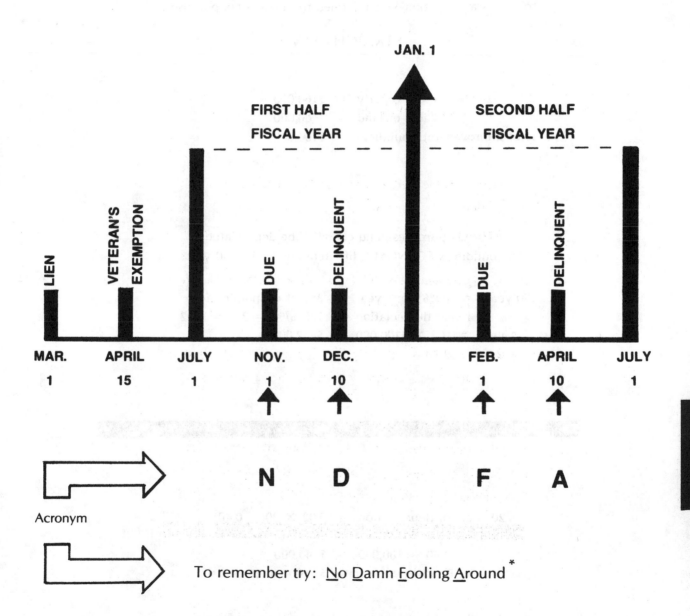

JAN. 1

FIRST HALF
FISCAL YEAR

SECOND HALF
FISCAL YEAR

LIEN	VETERAN'S EXEMPTION		DUE	DELINQUENT		DUE	DELINQUENT	
MAR.	APRIL	JULY	NOV.	DEC.		FEB.	APRIL	JULY
1	15	1	1	10		1	10	1

Acronym

N **D** **F** **A**

To remember try: <u>N</u>o <u>D</u>amn <u>F</u>ooling <u>A</u>round *

LAW &
TAXES
V

* The acronym applies to most of California. For other states you may have to make up another saying.

DEPRECIATION

Depreciation is a loss in value as an accounting procedure
to use as a deduction, when defined for income tax purposes.

STRAIGHT LINE:

$$
\begin{aligned}
\text{Value of Property} &= \$160{,}000 \\
(-)\,\text{Value of land} &= 60{,}000 \\
\text{Value of improvements (building)} &= \$100{,}000
\end{aligned}
$$

For tax purposes, land can NOT be depreciated.
The building's ECONOMIC life (rentable life) = 50 years

$$
\begin{aligned}
50 \text{ years} &= 100\%, \text{ so: } 1 \text{ year} = 2\% \text{ of economic life.} \\
1 \text{ year depreciation} &= 100\%/50 = 2\% = 0.02 \\
1 \text{ year} &= 0.02 \times \$100{,}000 = \$\;2{,}000
\end{aligned}
$$

$$
20 \text{ years of depreciation} = 0.02 \times 20 = 0.40
$$

$$
0.40 \times 100{,}000 = \$\;40{,}000
$$
So: Building depreciates $40,000 in 20 years!

NOTE: Effective Jan. 1, 1987 residential real estate will be depreciated over 27.5 years on a straight line basis. Commercial real estate will be depreciated over 31.5 years on a straight line basis. Investments made prior to that date will be grandfathered. After that date certain business property can still have accelerated depreciation. More tax information starts on page 303.

V
LAW &
TAXES

DEPRECIATION

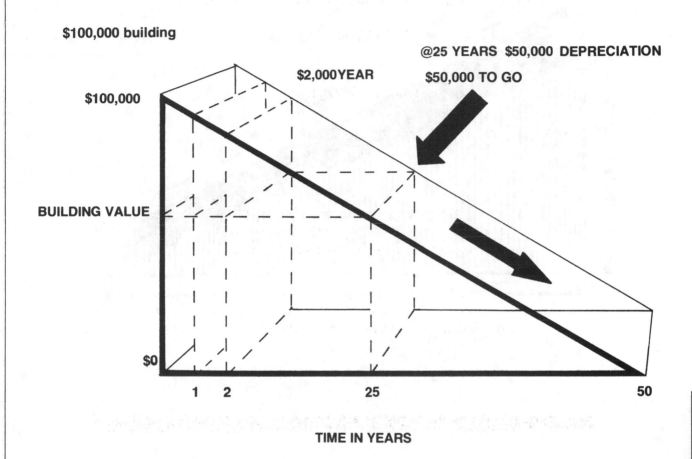

STRAIGHT LINE:

$100,000 building

$100,000

BUILDING VALUE

$0

$2,000YEAR

@25 YEARS $50,000 DEPRECIATION

$50,000 TO GO

1   2   25   50

TIME IN YEARS

FIRST YEAR OF NEW OWNER

2%/YEAR × 50 YEARS = 100%

2%/Year = $2,000 YEAR DEPRECIATION

New owner can start with a clean slate and set up a **NEW** schedule.

DEPRECIATION

STRAIGHT LINE

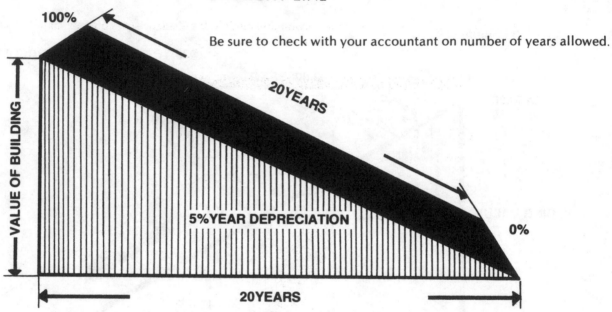

Be sure to check with your accountant on number of years allowed.

100%

20YEARS

VALUE OF BUILDING

5%YEAR DEPRECIATION

0%

20YEARS

$100,000 Building with a 5%/year depreciation.

This is considered a 'return OF investment.' Equal to $5,000 yearly

depreciation—equals a *$5,000 tax write-off.*

DEPRECIATION SUM OF DIGITS

(ACCELERATED)

Effective Jan. 1, 1987 you must use the straight line method for residential or commercial real estate. Investments made prior to that date will be grandfathered.

Add the number of years of a building's life. Say 5 years:

1
2
3
4
5
___
15 = Total

Then use a fraction of this total in REVERSE order. Depreciation:

First year	= 5/15
Second year	= 4/15
Third year	= 3/15
Fourth year	= 2/15
Fifth year	= 1/15

100% = 15/15

EXAMPLE:

First year = 5/15 = 1/3

1/3 of $300,000

$100,000 = First year depreciation

DEPRECIATION: DOUBLE DECLINING

You can take 2 times (or 200%) of the straight line method
each year of the REMAINING balance.

EXAMPLE

$$\frac{100\%}{20 \text{ years}} = 5\%/\text{year depreciation, straight line}$$

$$2 \times 5\% = 10\%/\text{year depreciation}$$

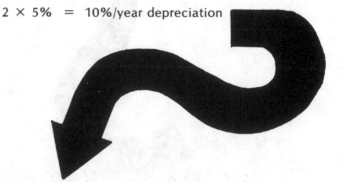

$100,000	=	Building
-10,000	=	10% = first year depreciation
$ 90,000	=	balance, end of first year
-9,000	=	second year depreciation
$ 81,000	=	balance, end of second year
$ 8,100	=	third year depreciation, etc., etc., etc.

NOTE: Effective Jan. 1, 1987 residential real estate will be depreciated over 27.5 years on a straight line basis. Commercial real estate will be depreciated over 31.5 years on a straight line basis. Investments made prior to that date will be grandfathered. After that date certain business property can still have accelerated depreciation. More tax information starts on page 303.

DEPRECIATION AS A TAX WRITE—OFF

Gross income from property (rentals) = $ 12,000 year
TOTAL EXPENSES on property
that are deductible; i.e., taxes
insurance, maintenance, etc.

= $ 7,000 Year

NET INCOME = $ 5,000 Year

$ 100,000 BUILDING with

5% per year straight line

DEPRECIATION. = $ 5,000 Year

Taxes owed based on above. = $ 0

$5,000 PER YEAR DEPRECIATION (STRAIGHT LINE)

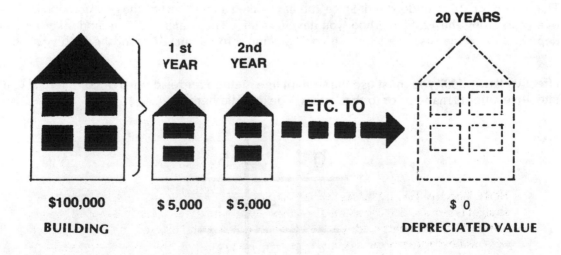

| 1st YEAR | 2nd YEAR | ETC. TO | 20 YEARS |

| $100,000 BUILDING | $ 5,000 | $ 5,000 | $ 0 DEPRECIATED VALUE |

V

LAW &
TAXES

COMPONENT DEPRECIATION

This is a sleeper. Many prominent personalities pay no, or little tax because of depreciation, using depreciation of a building, or peanut farm machinery. *Probably the most overlooked, safest, and best tax shelter that exists is depreciation.* The author has had excellent tax write-offs with oil, cattle, debts, night clubs and others (also never saw the money again).

Component depreciation is simply taking the parts of a building, other than the shell of the building, and depreciating them separately. For example, take a refrigerator that costs $1,000 and straight line depreciates for 10 years, and you have a depreciation of $100 per year, carpets at $14,000 for 7 years is $2,000 per year, plumbing that has a value of $25,000 with a "life" of 10 years is depreciated $2,500 per year, etc. The shell of the building can be depreciated either straight line or accelerated, following the usual guidelines.

All of the other parts of the building are depreciated separately and given their individual straight line life. Obviously, if you are depreciating a big chunk of the property in five or ten years, instead of 30 years, the depreciation is much greater for those 5 or 10 years (greater shelter).

Component depreciation is no longer available, but you may continue using it if you elected this method in a prior year.

DEPRECIATION SWITCH

You are allowed to switch from an accelerated method of depreciation to the straight line method (at least that is the law as the ink is drying on this page). You are *not* allowed to switch from straight line to accelerated. Why would you want to switch? If you use the 125% method, you actually receive *more* depreciation after the fifth year by using the straight line method.

The reason is easy to understand. Since you have taken a large part of the depreciation in the first five years using the 125% method (you have less left). The straight line method takes much less depreciation in the first five years, so you have more to depreciate from the sixth year on.

Effective Jan. 1, 1987 you must use the straight line method for residential or commercial real estate. Investments made prior to that date will be grandfathered.

0		$
	$	0
$		0

RECAPTURE

Government (IRS) recaptures depreciation by taxing gain. . . when property is SOLD. IRS recaptures (taxes) your 'return of investment' if any gain. It is a point of interest and law, that only the profit which is above straight line depreciation is recapture. Below straight line is capital gain (short term or long term).

Purchase BUILDING for $150,000
Land can not be depreciated, but it can increase in value and be taxable. For this example say zero gain.

If economic life (rentable life) is 50 years, then depreciation is 2% or $3,000 per year.

In 10 years, depreciation = $30,000.

$150,000 = cost basis of building
−30,000 = depreciation
$120,000 = adjusted cost basis ("book value") 10 years later.
Also add any IMPROVEMENTS to basis.

10 years later building SOLD = $160,000
Less adjusted cost basis = 120,000
_____
Taxable gain = $ 40,000

TAX-FREE VS. TAXABLE INCOME

A big advantage of real estate is that it can produce tax sheltered (tax free) income. A lower tax free investment can be equal to a higher taxable investment.

To compare tax-free and taxable returns:

1. *First determine* your *tax bracket*, e.g., say 40%.

2. Then *subtract your tax bracket from 100%*, e.g., 100% minus 40% equals 60%. This percent represents the amount of the return you can keep, the non-taxable portion.

3. *Multiply the percent amount you can keep times the taxable percent return on the investment.* This represents the equivalent tax-free percent, e.g., if 60% is the percentage you can keep and 10% is the amount of the taxable return on an investment, this is equivalent to a 6% tax-free return.

EXAMPLES

Taxable Return % On An Investment	×	Portion of Investment *Not* Taxable	=	Equivalent Tax-Free Percentage
5%		70%		3.5%
10%		50%		5%
10%		60%		6%
14%		50%		7%
20%		40%		8%

DEALER VS. INVESTOR

If you plan on doing a large amount of real estate investing, sooner or later, you will have to decide if you are a Dealer or an Investor. A friendly tax audit can do this for you.

Being an investor is better, since you can take advantage of the relatively low tax rate associated with capital gains. *A dealer's profit, on the other hand, is taxed as ordinary income.*

You can be considered a dealer on some properties, and an investor on others.

It is difficult to define precisely the differences, but out of the tax maze come the following simple guidelines:

DEALER 1. Holds property as "stock in trade" for sale to customers in the course of his trade or business.

2. Buys and sells property as his main business. You also may be considered a dealer if it is not your main business.

3. Has specific intent to resell property shortly after acquisition. One quick turnover may not classify you as a dealer, but frequent turnovers are indicative of dealer status.

4. Is identified in the field as a dealer. Has sales office, sales force, advertising, etc.

5. Dealers are subdividers of property. Although limited sales of subdivided property may be treated as capital gains.

INVESTOR 1. Few and infrequent sales of real estate.

2. Seller is relatively passive during the transaction, e.g., no sales office, no salesmen, no advertising, etc.

3. Rents property for a time prior to sale, the longer the better.

4. Investment is the main objective in purchase.

Note that the IRS wants to know what you are thinking: *your* intent of *purchase* is significant. You may want to write on all of your deals, so that you are not considered to be a dealer, "Buyer purchasing for investment."

JOINT VENTURE SYNDICATION

LIMITED PARTNERSHIP

A *joint venture* (JV) can be a huge syndication (even between countries), or it can be a few investment friends who have common goals (usually to make money). There are as many combinations of *joint ventures* as there are people. A typical JV (the type the author has been involved in) is as follows:

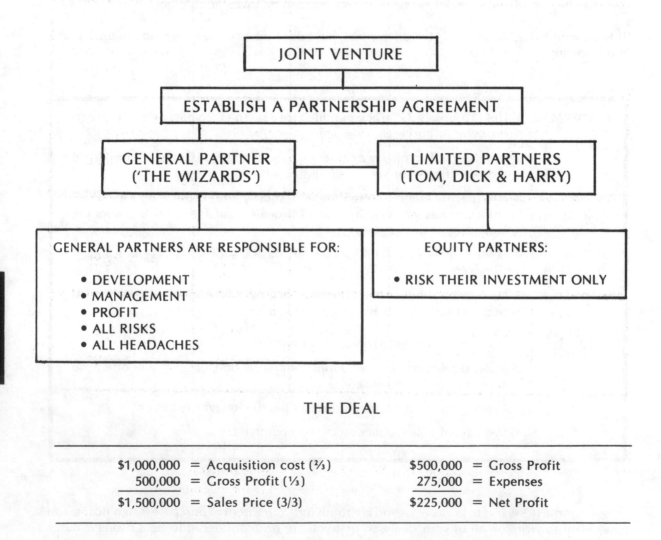

```
                    ┌─────────────────────┐
                    │    JOINT VENTURE     │
                    └─────────────────────┘
          ┌─────────────────────────────────────────┐
          │   ESTABLISH A PARTNERSHIP AGREEMENT      │
          └─────────────────────────────────────────┘
    ┌──────────────────────┐       ┌──────────────────────┐
    │  GENERAL PARTNER      │───────│  LIMITED PARTNERS     │
    │  ('THE WIZARDS')      │       │  (TOM, DICK & HARRY)  │
    └──────────────────────┘       └──────────────────────┘
```

GENERAL PARTNERS ARE RESPONSIBLE FOR:

- DEVELOPMENT
- MANAGEMENT
- PROFIT
- ALL RISKS
- ALL HEADACHES

EQUITY PARTNERS:

- RISK THEIR INVESTMENT ONLY

THE DEAL

$1,000,000	= Acquisition cost (⅔)		$500,000	= Gross Profit
500,000	= Gross Profit (⅓)		275,000	= Expenses
$1,500,000	= Sales Price (3/3)		$225,000	= Net Profit

First, limited partners receive all of their invested funds plus **10%**.
The remaining profit is split 50/50.

SYNDICATION

A syndication is:

A group of persons who come together to perform a transaction . . . it is an investment group.

INVESTMENT & TAX ANALYSIS

Name	Type Investment	Amount Invested	Cash Flow %	Write-Off On Orig. Investment
'Sea Inn'	High cash flow, tax sheltered. No write-off on original investment.	$20,000	$3,000 = **15%**	$0 = **0%**
'Able Apt's'	Cash flow, medium. Write-off on original investment.	$20,000	$2,200 = **11%**	$6,000 = **30%**
'Navel Citrus Ranch'	NO cash flow. High write-off on original investment.	$20,000	$0 = **0%**	$28,000 = **140%**

A syndication, as with any investment, should first be a
good buy . . . it should then be ANALYSED for investment
and tax advantages.

TITLE IN COMMUNITY PROPERTY
COMPARED WITH JOINT TENANCY

SURVIVOR TAX ANALYSIS

Property sold after the death of one's spouse.

	COMMUNITY PROPERTY*	JOINT TENANCY
Original Purchase Price	$ 80,000	$ 80,000
New Selling Price	$ 120,000	$ 120,000
Survivor Acquires 50%	$ 60,000 Steps up to F.M.V.	$ 60,000 Steps up to F.M.V.
New Cost Basis	$ 120,000 100% Steps up to F.M.V.	$ 60,000 (½ of original price) +40,000 Only 50% Steps up $ 100,000 to F.M.V.
Taxable GAIN	NONE!	$ 20,000

*Not in all states.

V LAW & TAXES

WILLS, TRUSTS & ESTATE PLANNING

As illustrated on the opposite page, one-half of the property *inherited* by the surviving spouse reverts back to the original value in a *joint tenancy*, and with *community property* the entire property is valued at *present fair market value.*

This is an oversimplification of an involved subject. The point of emphasis is that how you take title, i.e., joint tenancy, community property, tenants in common, separate property, etc., is of vital importance, and can have great tax consequences.

How you take title (vesting) should be established with expert help *before* you purchase a property. Vesting should relate to your will and any trusts. A *trust* being a legal arrangement by which you transfer assets such as money or real estate to another person (trustee) to manage for a beneficiary you name.

Vesting, wills, trusts, and tax planning are all included in the big picture of *estate planning.*

Vesting should conform with the intent of the will. The will should match the trust. The trust should conform with the entire estate plan.

BINDER TITLE POLICY

A *binder title policy* can save you money. The usual binder requires a payment of 10% more for the title policy, but if you have a sale within two years the new policy costs *nothing.*

BINDER INSURANCE POLICY

A *binder insurance policy* is a temporary policy issued so that you may close escrow. The conventional policy follows later. It is an excellent practice to establish a routine with your insurance broker, so that one phone call gets you a binder when you need to close escrow in a hurry.

RECORD THE OPTION

Always consider recording an option agreement. The recordation of options, or any other legal document, gives 'notice to the world.' It will help protect your option in the first position from any liens that develop after recordation.

Priority of liens (money encumbrance) are usually determined by date of recordation.

INCOME TAX & OTHER JOYS

In keeping with the philosophy of this book, the author asked many tax authorities to review and give a Quick & Easy synopsis of the Federal Tax Codes and the laws of the fifty states. Also the author read over a thousand pages of the tax codes and rulings, prior to falling asleep. When the reader has a grasp on real estate investing, try reading just a hundred pages of the tax law for a lesson in humility.

Representative of the responses to the author's questioning was the two word reply of Randy Sugarman, CPA and accountant to millionaire firms and individuals. He simply pointed to his *thirty foot long shelf of books* on tax law (updated daily) and said, "Right here."

Apparently it is an easier task to explain whether the universe is expanding, contracting, pulsating, finite, infinite, or a little of each, than it is to explain the U.S. Tax Codes. The most disturbing part of the law is when you finally do come to a logical conclusion, based on the printed word in the law books, answers evolve such as, 'That ruling has not been tested in the courts yet, so it will probably change,' or, 'Congressman Flannelmouth's amendment will change all of that section of the code if it passes next month.'

The unfortunate conclusion is that unless you are a genius, a tax attorney or an accountant, you will need expert guidance in order to work your way through the tax maze. Income tax is like interest on a loan that can never be paid off and never matures.

On the other hand, the two happiest words in the English language are, 'Tax refund.'

GOALS OF THE WIZARDS

Steve Zakula, president of The Wizards (an investment group), stated that their goal, "is to make lots of money and never pay any taxes." He admits that the latter is very difficult, unless you continue to trade up.

TAX PLANNING WITH SKIP

Skip Rupp, B.S., M.B.A., C.P.A., and a professional planner, says, "In order to prepare yourself for tax planning you must: gather all of the facts; clearly outline your objectives; prepare yourself with knowledge of the law; study your crystal ball, and then say a prayer."

TAX CREDIT vs TAX WRITE-OFF

Tax credits are the best as they come directly off of your income tax, whereas write-offs are subtracted from your adjusted income. For example, a $10,000 tax credit would be subtracted directly from a $10,000 tax liability for a net result of no taxes owed. The same $10,000 as a tax write-off (for a person in a 50% tax bracket) would result in a tax of $5,000, as opposed to zero.

Tax credits can be obtained for solar energy systems and historical buildings.

PROPERTY MANAGEMENT

Property management is a active business. It is nothing like passive investments such as bank deposits, stocks or bonds. You are dealing with people on a day-to-day basis, or at a minimum, from month to month.

If you don't like dealing with people, hire a property manager. A Realtor could refer you to a list of property managers, as could your local apartment owner's association (or related business groups).

You must have quality tenants, or you are in trouble. Ability to pay is one thing, collecting is another. Does the local motorcycle club practice hill-climbing on your stairs? The character of your tenants is reflected not only in ability to pay the rent, but also to pay it on time and to take a certain pride in living in the building (and keeping it in one piece).

If you have properties that are making you miserable, get rid of them. Select buildings and investments that you can live with. Rather to splash in the surf with a little less profit, than to have ulcers and law suits.

ACCURATE RECORDS

The name of the game in property management is accurate records. You must have an accurate 'audit trail' and be able to prove that you did, or did not receive a certain rent check, or did pay the plumber three hundred dollars. You can give receipts (date and photocopy of all checks received), or another solution for proof of receipt is to have a conveniently located bank collect all rentals. It would be rather difficult for a tenant to say they paid the bank, when the bank has no record of payment (and the tenant has no receipt). The burden of proof would fall on the tenant, and not on the landlord. This system works equally well for the tenant who has paid (and has a receipt) and the landlord says they did not.

Proof of all expenses and income is also vital when it is time to fill out the new 'simple' income tax forms.

If you find this entire subject a burdensome bore, why not hire a good property manager and accountant and let them handle the collections, maintenance and bookkeeping while you are touring Europe? The rule of thumb on costs is 5% of the gross income for a property manager, plus any repair and advertising expenses.

If you like to do your own repair and maintenance on your buildings, be sure it is worth your time. If you can hire an expert to do the job for $30 per hour, and your time is worth $100 per hour locating property to purchase . . . you have lost $70 per hour by doing the work yourself.

After the frantic comings and goings of a new purchase have settled down, and you feel confident that you could handle the entire operation, then it is time enough to consider being your own property manager.

As a minimum, have a property manager, accountant or lawyer 'set up the book's' for you, and outline a modus operandi. Visit any large stationery store to obtain a Rent Schedule Record Book, and keep in mind that if you don't select your tenants properly you may have no record problem, because you will have no income.

Making money with properties can be fun, but it is still a business.

YOUR PARTNER = UNCLE SAM

THIS WEEK'S TAX CODES

YOUR PARTNER

"THE LEGAL RIGHT OF A TAXPAYER. . .
To decrease the amount of
what otherwise would be his taxes.
or altogether AVOID them,
by means which the law permits,
CANNOT BE DOUBTED."

GREGORY vs HELVERING
293 U.S. Tax Court 465

LAW &
TAXES
V

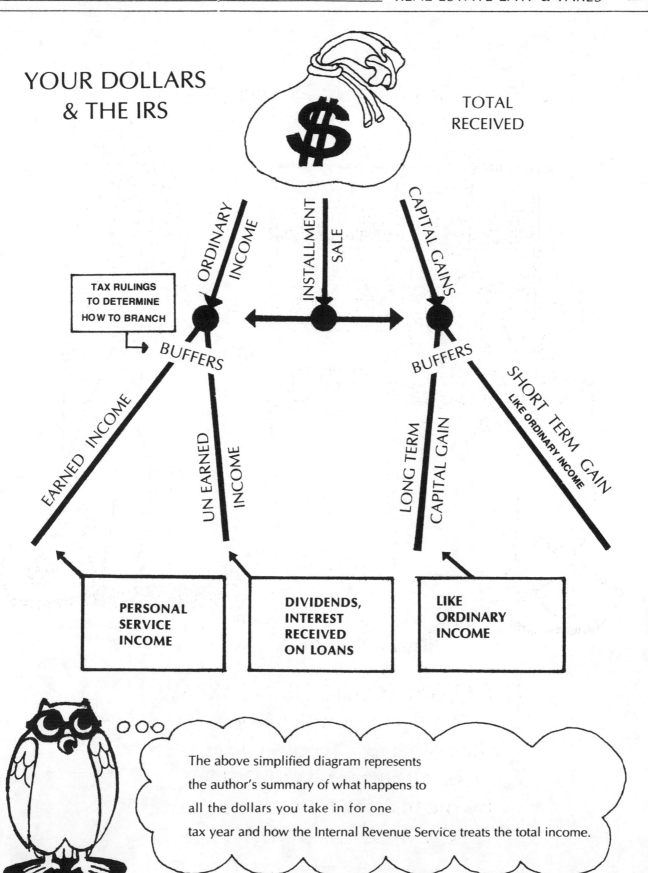

YOUR DOLLARS & THE IRS

TOTAL RECEIVED

ORDINARY INCOME

INSTALLMENT SALE

CAPITAL GAINS

TAX RULINGS TO DETERMINE HOW TO BRANCH

BUFFERS

BUFFERS

EARNED INCOME

UN EARNED INCOME

LONG TERM CAPITAL GAIN

SHORT TERM GAIN LIKE ORDINARY INCOME

PERSONAL SERVICE INCOME

DIVIDENDS, INTEREST RECEIVED ON LOANS

LIKE ORDINARY INCOME

The above simplified diagram represents the author's summary of what happens to all the dollars you take in for one tax year and how the Internal Revenue Service treats the total income.

CHAPTER VI
ARCHITECTURE
AND
APPRAISAL

ARCHITECTURE & APPRAISAL OVERVIEW

"BEAUTY IS PLEASURE REGARDED AS THE QUALITY OF A THING."
— *George Santayana*

In this chapter we look at architecture and appraisal, One discipline considers the design of the physical structure as it sits upon the land. The other places a dollar value on these elements.

To understand the development of architecture is to place a window on the history of civilization encompassing a span of time of about five thousand years, from the oldest structures that still exist—the pyramids of Cairo, to the modern world Transamerica pyramid of San Francisco. In between are all manner of sizes and shapes on all parts of our terrestrial ball.

ARCHITECTURE

One of the most beautiful architectural examples ever constructed is the Parthenon. By choice, there are no straight lines in the design. All of the columns bulge slightly outward. The facade is also slightly convex, as well as the top entrance step. The columns are not evenly spaced. The center columns are farther apart than those at the ends. The entire front facade fits perfectly into a Golden Rectangle. The number of columns on the side are exactly two-times plus one the number of columns on the front (8 columns × 17 columns) as is true of most Greek architecture.

If you consider the columns as long notes, and the three vertical grooves that repeat across the top of the columns in the entablature as short notes, a musical beat can be established of one long and three short—a rhythm that was marched to by Greek and Roman legions.

When the structure is viewed from a distance, a sinuous path invites you to rise to the top of the Acropolis. The path does not enter directly into the Parthenon, but rather delights the eye by first viewing from afar, then from below, and finally from the side before the entrance is completed.

Why would a Greek architect, over two thousand years ago, not use straight lines and even spacing of columns? The answer is found in an ancient intellect that this writer finds dumbfounding. The architect was aware of the curvature of his own eyes, in both the horizontal and vertical planes. This minute curvature of the eye is reproduced in the scale of the Parthenon. He knew, that by reproducing the curvature of the eye and the uneven spacing of the columns, it would create an optical illusion in the sight center of the brain, which would be viewed as perfectly straight lines and exactly even spacing.

GOOD DESIGN, GOOD INVESTMENT

What has this to do with real estate and making money? Plenty. All you have to do is look at the design of most government housing or the rabbit hutch tract homes of an architecturally illiterate land developer, and you know instinctively that these are disasters designed for people not fortunate enough to have a choice.

If you would believe 'that once the mind has been stretched with a new idea, it can never return to its original shape'. . .then it would follow that many modern developers have their minds in an architectural vice that is squeezed inward. If they ever had the occasion to view the Parthenon, they would observe that it is without a roof and they would no doubt suggest that this problem could be immediately remedied with 4' x 6' sheets of corrugated green plastic.

Good design, good architecture, is money in the bank—not only for the original investor but for generations of investors yet to come. It takes no architectural giant to realize that anodized aluminum is not brass, striated plastic is not marble, pine is not oak, galvanized pipe is not copper, two by fours are not carved millwork, rotating red lights are not a wood-burning fireplace and plastic swans and cement are not Monterey cypress and stream.

If you need proof that good design is not incompatible with a profitable investment, simply check the present values in your area between an architectural award-winning building, and a comparably sized and located building designed by a former army barrack's architect.

As time allows, you may want to explore the works of some of the great masters in order to determine how their designs could compliment your own investment, e.g., Mies van der Rohe and his brilliant "less is more", Richard Neutra's rectilinear understated elegance, or the soaring curves of John Lautner, to mention a few of many.

APPRAISAL

There are three basic approaches to appraisal. First, the income approach: the value of the building is determined by the amount of income it is producing, or could produce in a fair open market. No income, no value. The value by income is determined using the Gross Rent Multiplier, Cap Rate, Internal Rate of Return, etc.

The second method of determining value is by using the Cost Approach. The value of the property is determined by the cost to construct the building and other improvements, added to the cost of the land. The methods used include the cost per square foot, the Replacement Cost Technique (whereby all the component parts of a building are priced individually and then added together, less depreciation).

The third method is the Market Data Approach (comparison). Please note pages 278 and 280.

FRANK LLOYD WRIGHT* ON ARCHITECTURE

This sense of space, space alive by way of the third
dimension, isn't that sense, or feeling for architecture, an
implement to characterize the freedom of the individual?
I think so. If you refuse this liberated sense of building
haven't you thrown away that which is most precious in
our own human life and most promising as a new field for
truly creative artistic expression in architecture? Yes, is
there anything else, really? All this and more, is why I
have, lifelong, been fighting the pull of the specious old box.

* From an address to the Junior Chapter of the AIA, New York City, 1952.

THE WORLD'S TALLEST REAL ESTATE

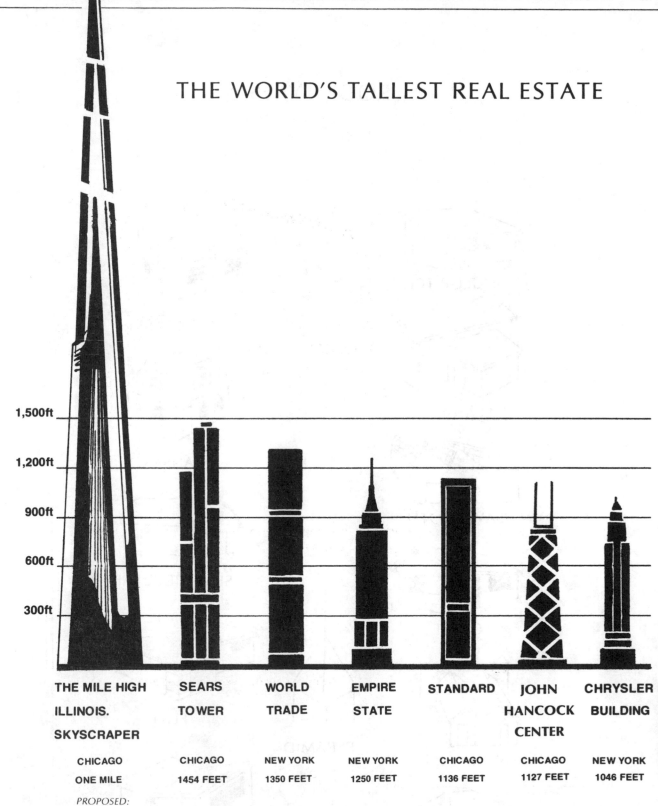

THE MILE HIGH ILLINOIS. SKYSCRAPER	SEARS TOWER	WORLD TRADE	EMPIRE STATE	STANDARD	JOHN HANCOCK CENTER	CHRYSLER BUILDING
CHICAGO	CHICAGO	NEW YORK	NEW YORK	CHICAGO	CHICAGO	NEW YORK
ONE MILE	1454 FEET	1350 FEET	1250 FEET	1136 FEET	1127 FEET	1046 FEET
PROPOSED:						
FRANK						
LLOYD						
WRIGHT						

ROOF TYPES

SINGLE-PITCH

GAMBREL

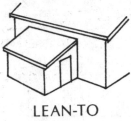

LEAN-TO

MANSARD

SAW-TOOTH

SEMI-CIRCULAR

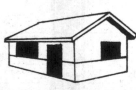

GABLE

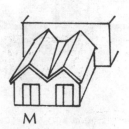

M

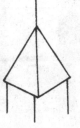

PYRAMID

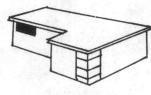

FLAT

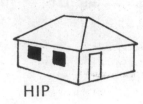

HIP

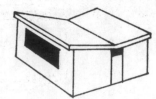

DOUBLE-PITCH OR BUTTERFLY

WINDOW TYPES

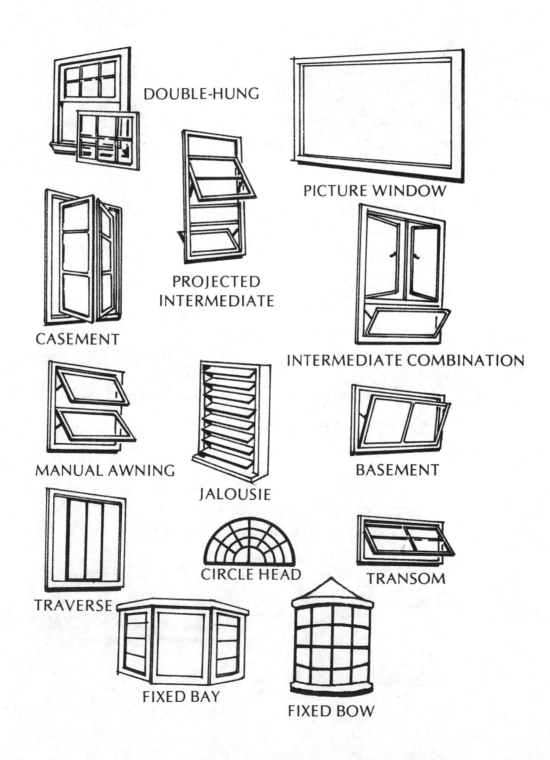

DOUBLE-HUNG

PICTURE WINDOW

PROJECTED INTERMEDIATE

CASEMENT

INTERMEDIATE COMBINATION

MANUAL AWNING

JALOUSIE

BASEMENT

TRAVERSE

CIRCLE HEAD

TRANSOM

FIXED BAY

FIXED BOW

ARCHITECTURAL STYLES

FRENCH PROVENCIAL

VICTORIAN

CAPE COD

NEW ENGLAND COLONIAL

DUTCH COLONIAL

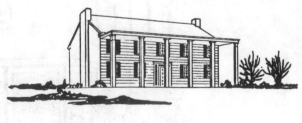

SOUTHERN COLONIAL

GEORGIAN

SPANISH

RANCH

"A" FRAME

CONTEMPORARY

FORM & FUNCTION

BEAUTIFUL ARCHITECTURE IS LIKE 'FROZEN MUSIC.'

FORM   Classic: function follows form

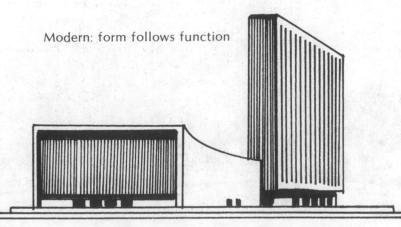

In the classic architecture of Greece and other ancient cultures, they were not concerned with cost effective, time motion studies of the inhabitants, but rather with creating a lasting beauty. They did rather well.

GREEK ARCHITECTURAL ORDERS

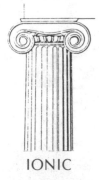

DORIC   IONIC   CORINTHIAN

FUNCTION   Modern: form follows function

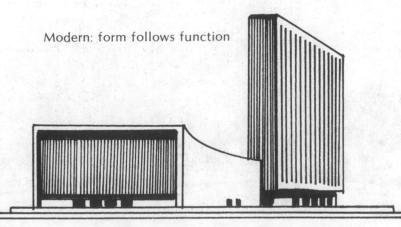

Modern architecture considers the occupant's use of the structure, and then attempts to add a 'beautiful skin.'

POINT AND COUNTER POINT
DESIGN CONCEPT

SMOOTH
CURVILINEAR (ROUNDED)
FORM, e.g., BUILDING OR SCULPTURE

ROUGH
MASSIVE
FORM

● **POINT**

● **COUNTER POINT**

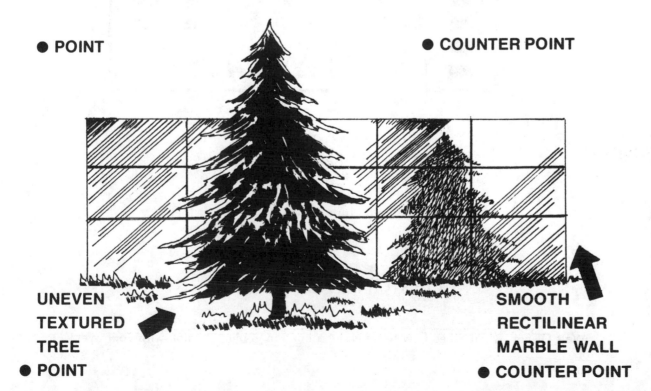

UNEVEN
TEXTURED
TREE

SMOOTH
RECTILINEAR
MARBLE WALL

● **POINT**

● **COUNTER POINT**

ASYMMETRICAL BALANCE

NO:

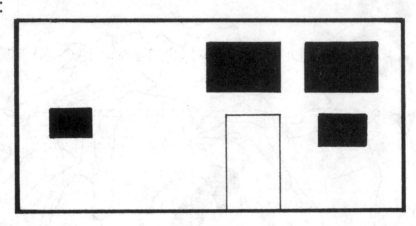

YES:

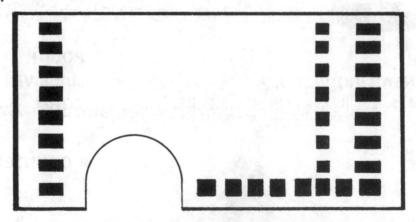

NOT NECESSARY TO BE SYMMETRICAL
(LEFT & RIGHT SIDE THE SAME), BUT
SHOULD BE BALANCED

(even if you turn upside down)

DESIGN PARAMETER

Walt Disney, when asked how to do great animation, replied, "Think with your eyes."

THE GOLDEN RECTANGLE

It pleased the eye of many to use the *Golden Rectangle*, e.g., Le Corbusier, Georges Seurat, Mondrian, Leonardo de Vinci, and the builders of the pyramids.

The front facade of the Parthenon is a golden rectangle.
A dimensional ratio of 1 to 1.6.

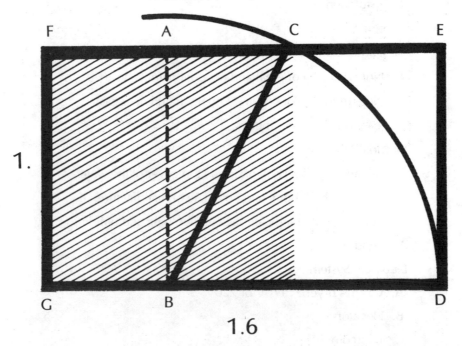

To obtain a golden rectangle, start with any square and divide it in half (A to B). Then extend a line from B to C. Using B as the center of a circle, draw an arc from C to D (length BC = BD). GDEF then outlines a golden rectangle, which can be used as a building modulus, e.g., facade, windows, rooms, walls, patios, etc. The ratio of 1:1.6 can be expanded to 2:3.2, 3:4.8, 4:6.4, 10:16, ad infinitum.

CHECKING THE BUILDING

A quick list of physical aspects:

1. Foundation and Land

    A. Type of soil

    B. Drainage, *percolation*

    C. Seismic activity

    D. Plot plan and any new zoning at city planning office

2. Framing

    A. Exterior and interior walls

    B. Floors

    C. Original plans and permits at city building inspector's office

3. Roof

    A. Drain system

    B. Vents

    C. Insulation

4. Heating System

    A. Furnace and all equipment

    B. Note dates on original and remodel permits, to determine age of system. Usually found near gas, electric and water meters.

5. Plumbing System

    Realtor's Trick: Look on inside top cover of the water closet in bathroom, and note date of manufacture. If it is original, it indicates age of plumbing and building.

6. Air Conditioning

7. Electrical System

    A. Clothes dryer ... 110V or 220V

    B. Elevators

    C. Intercom

    D. Automatic door

    IN DOUBT? ... use an appraiser.

BUILDING DETAILS

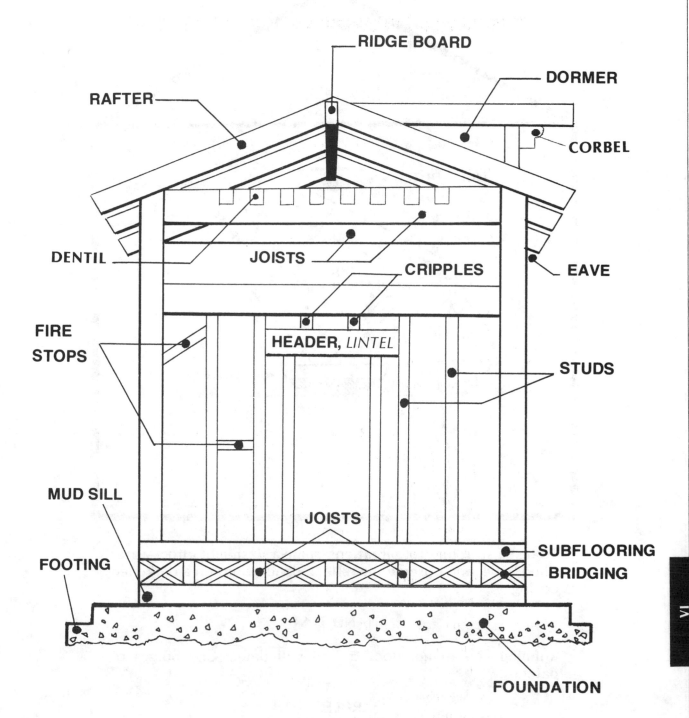

RIDGE BOARD

DORMER

RAFTER

CORBEL

DENTIL

JOISTS

CRIPPLES

EAVE

FIRE STOPS

HEADER, *LINTEL*

STUDS

MUD SILL

JOISTS

FOOTING

SUBFLOORING

BRIDGING

FOUNDATION

VIBRATION TEST

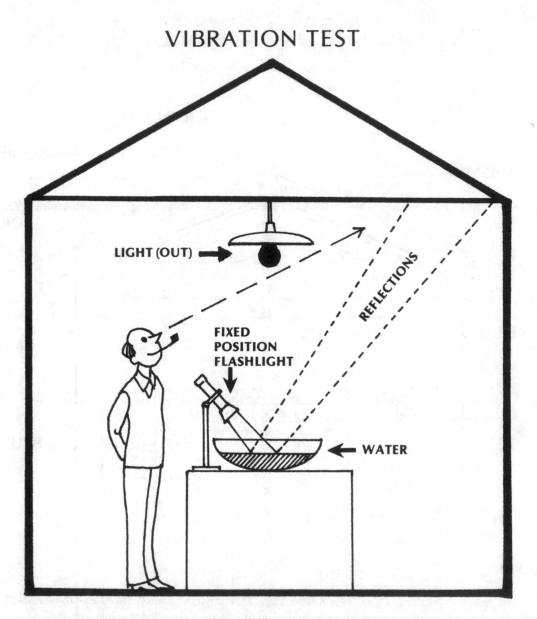

To test a structure for vibrations, shine a flashlight into a water filled bowl, and observe the reflected vibrations on a darkened ceiling.

HAND TEST

Running your hand along a wall will detect any bulges or patches.

MARBLE TEST

A marble rolled along the floor can detect the direction of any slope (so, be sure not to lose your marbles).

SOUNDPROOFING TEST

To test the soundproofing qualities of a building, place a portable radio in the room to be tested. Then turn to normal volume (gradually increase to high volume), and listen for the sound in adjoining rooms or apartments.

PASSIVE SOLAR HEATING CONCEPTS
THERMAL STORAGE SYSTEMS

Passive solar heating uses only energy of the sun for heating, as opposed to active solar heating that requires energy other than the sun, such as pumps, motors, etc.

The design for a solar storage area and the resultant design of the structure is as creative as the architect's imagination. The concept of all solar heating is as complex as knowing that the sun warms.

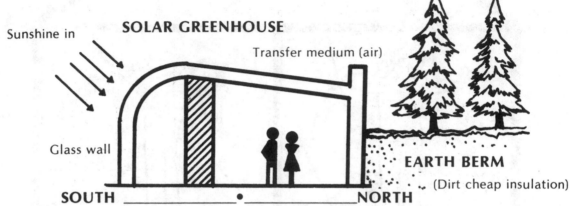

SOLAR GREENHOUSE

Sunshine in

Transfer medium (air)

Glass wall

EARTH BERM

(Dirt cheap insulation)

SOUTH _____•_____ NORTH

Greenhouse admits solar energy: Heat is stored in thermal storage wall.

By carrying a compass you can check out the building's orientation.

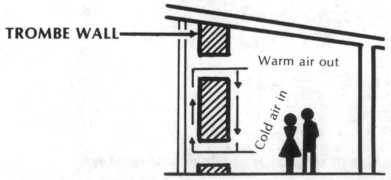

TROMBE WALL

Warm air out

Cold air in

Vents at top and bottom of the thermal storage wall permit natural circulation.

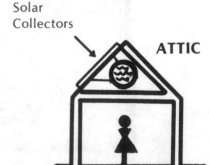

Solar Collectors

ATTIC

Solar pond

Movable insulation

INTERNAL/EXTERNAL MASS

Water bags can be flooded in hot weather.

ARCHITECTURE & APPRAISAL VI

The illustrations represent methods of passive solar storage and heating. The heat being stored in concrete, brick, rock, water, or other heat holding media.

TAX CREDIT

Be sure to consider the tax credit available for installing solar energy systems.

ACTIVE SYSTEM

A simple *active system* would employ a fan, near the solar storage area, to circulate the heat throughout the building.

CENTRAL MASS

INTERNAL MASS

A cat sunning itself on a back porch understands solar energy. Why can't humans?

Sunshine in

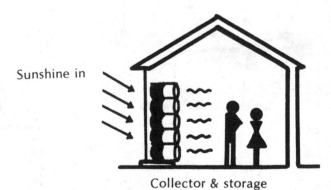

Collector & storage
(water tanks)

A PASSIVE SYSTEM

Used and cleaned 55 gallon drums filled with water offer an inexpensive way of storing heat. For more drama you can use clear plastic vertical tubes. Water weighs 62.4 pounds per cubic foot, if heated 10° F a cubic foot can hold 624 Btu's

EXTERNAL MASS

ATTACHED

TRY TO CREATE THE 'THERMAL INERTIA' OF A THERMOS BOTTLE.

INSIDE TO OUTSIDE
DESIGN CONCEPT

CLERESTORY WINDOW

ROCK WALL →

INSIDE

OUTSIDE

MITERED GLASS CORNERS →

GLASS WALL

YOUR EYE is almost forced to follow through from inside to outside with the use of glass walls and the continuity of features from inside to outside.

. . . a more spacious and dramatic feeling is created.

VOIDS AS WELL AS WALLS CREATE SPACIOUSNESS

R — VALUE

INSULATION

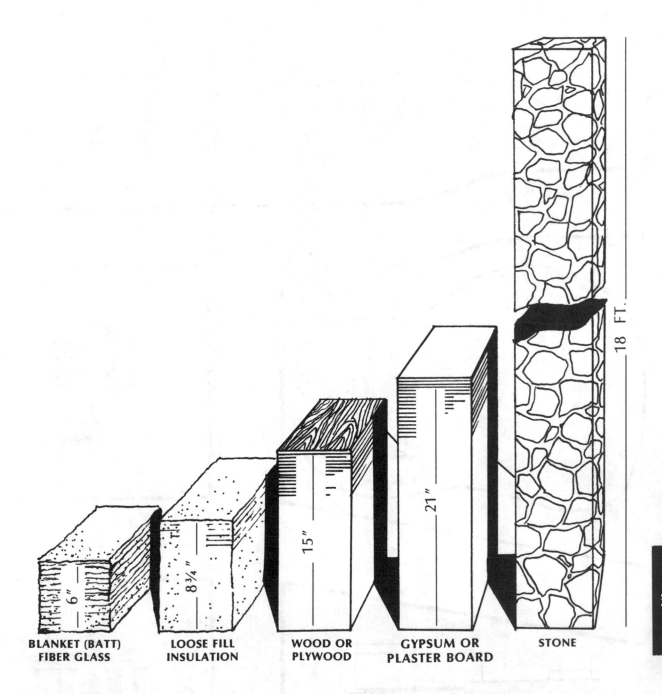

BLANKET (BATT) FIBER GLASS	LOOSE FILL INSULATION	WOOD OR PLYWOOD	GYPSUM OR PLASTER BOARD	STONE
6"	8¾"	15"	21"	18 FT.

All of the above are equal to R-19, a recommended minimum standard of insulation. R-value is any material's resistance to heat flowing through it. Six inches of fiber glass blanket or batt, has the same R-19 value rating as eighteen feet of stone. Energy experts say that using R-19 insulation on your attic floor can save up to 30% of the energy used to heat or cool your home each year.

AMENITIES INCREASE VALUE

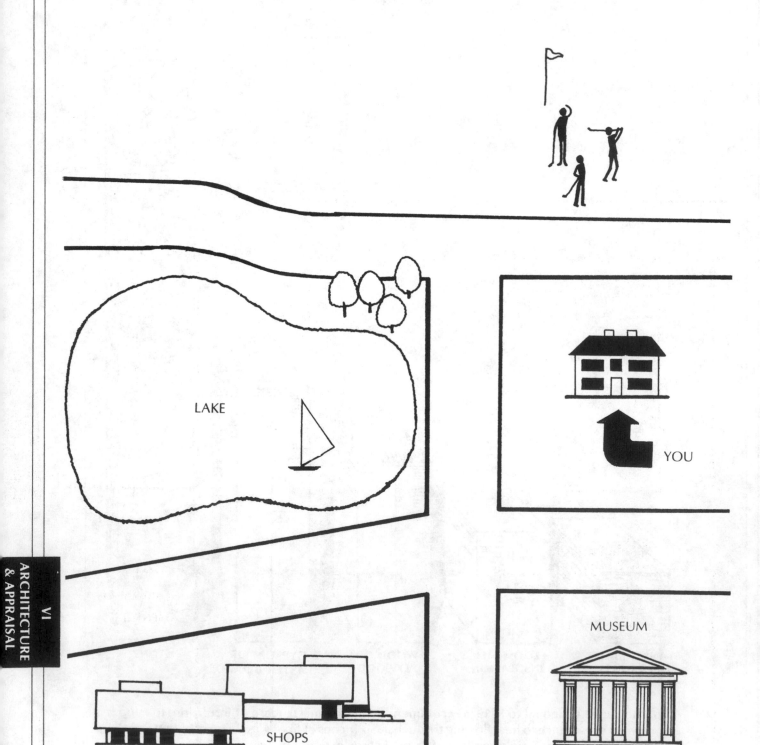

LAKE

YOU

MUSEUM

SHOPS

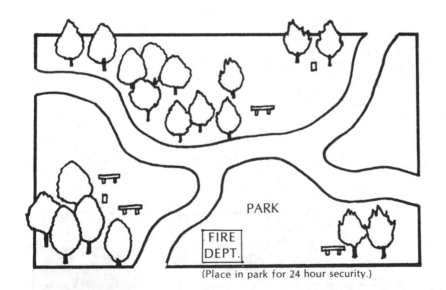

PARK

FIRE
DEPT.

(Place in park for 24 hour security.)

SCHOOL

POLICE

NEARNESS OF
AMENITIES

BUS STOP

All the above usually INCREASE VALUE.

VALUE INCREASE

The following usually increase value...the most for your $.

Landscaping and
Color coordinated Exterior
and Interior Painting

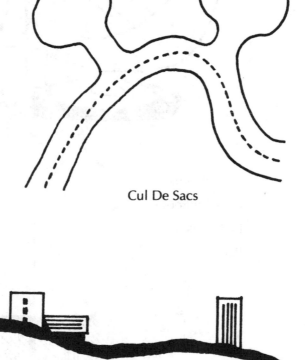

Curving Street

Cul De Sacs

Uneven Elevations of Terrain, Especially with views

Fireplaces

Extra Bathroom

Extra Bedroom

Remodeled Kitchen

Patio

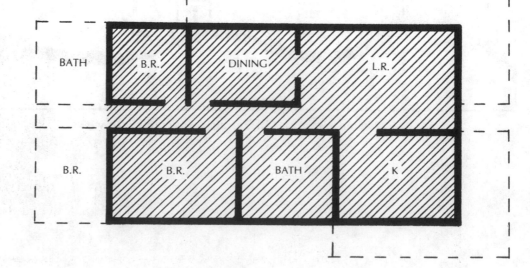

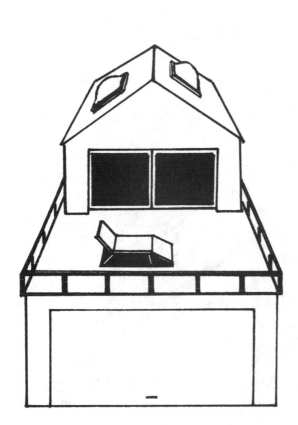

Decks

Try for Sun and View

View or Vista

Glass Doors,

Windows and

Skylights

LET THERE BE LIGHT

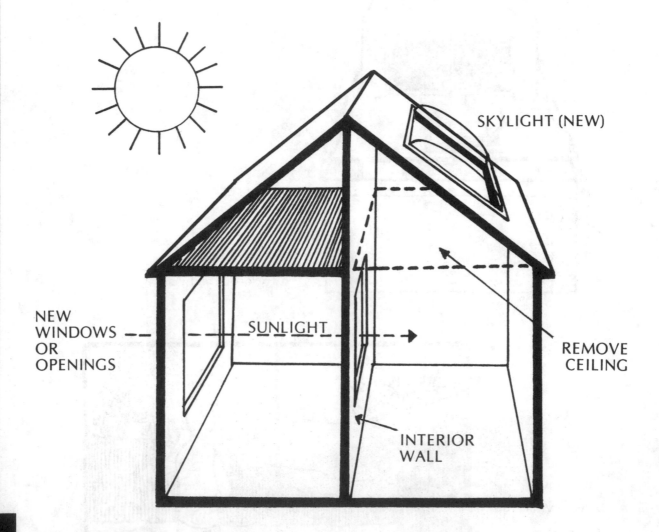

Using skylights, windows, and interior openings, a natural light environment can be created for a once dark interior room.

The author has personally knocked out the ceiling of an interior room in five minutes. This being accomplished by sitting on the joists, and pounding the top of the ceiling, and having it fall to the floor. A skylight was then added as pictured above.

THE WAY IT CAN BE . . .NOW!

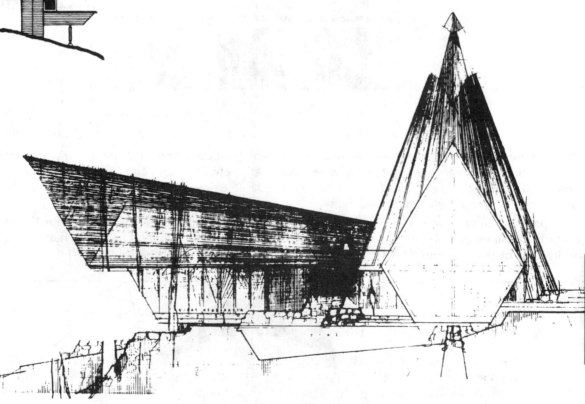

Renderings are courtesy of Lee Aaron Ward, architect, A.I.A.,
Frank Lloyd Wright apprentice,
Napa, California

VI
ARCHITECTURE
& APPRAISAL

VERTICAL ZONING & AIR SPACE

COMMERCIAL CONDOMINIUMS

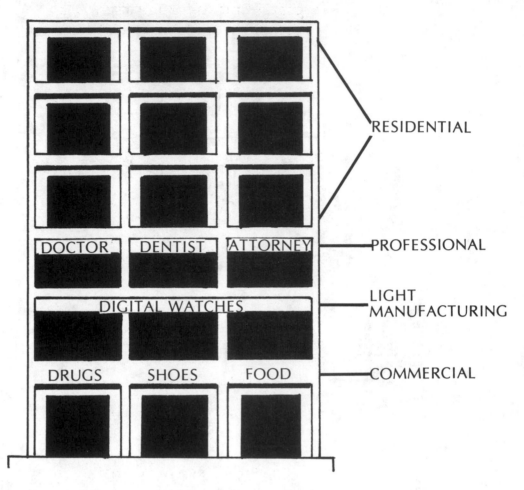

RESIDENTIAL

DOCTOR — DENTIST — ATTORNEY — PROFESSIONAL

DIGITAL WATCHES — LIGHT MANUFACTURING

DRUGS — SHOES — FOOD — COMMERCIAL

More density per acre + more home owners per usable space = CONDOMINIUMS

By combining "vertical zoning"—residential, and commercial condominiums—with the use of air space over no cost, existing government property (freeways, malls, parks, etc.) a system can be developed for a "vertical city." This would appear to be one of the few options available to create low to moderate income housing in areas where land is scarce, or even non-existant.

The combination of commercial-residential condos in one building creates a milieu whereby the residents tend to favor the businesses in the complex. One reason for this is that the commercial maintenance fees can cover the entire cost of the residential fees.

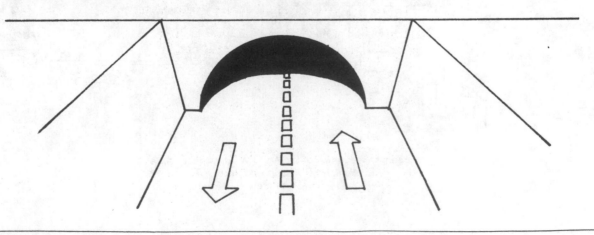

TERMITE REAL ESTATE

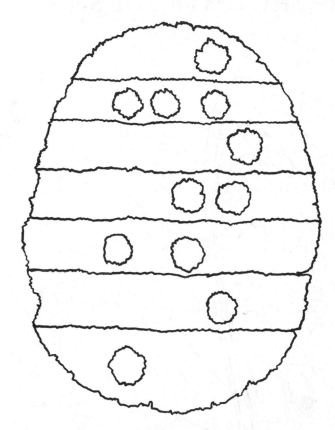

A TERMITE MOUND

Certain termites build a very mathematically precise and beautiful building. They accomplish this using their own excrement. Many modern developers would be well advised to use this medium. . . at least then their structures would be "true to the medium," i.e., wood should look like wood, glass should look like glass, steel should look like steel, etc.

One would think that man could create an environment at least as practical and efficient as a termite.

To our knowledge there are no termite architects. If there were, no doubt, their creative structures would sell faster and for a higher price, than a match box occupied by a less inspired termite.

VI
ARCHITECTURE
& APPRAISAL

THE RHYTHM OF THE SPHERES

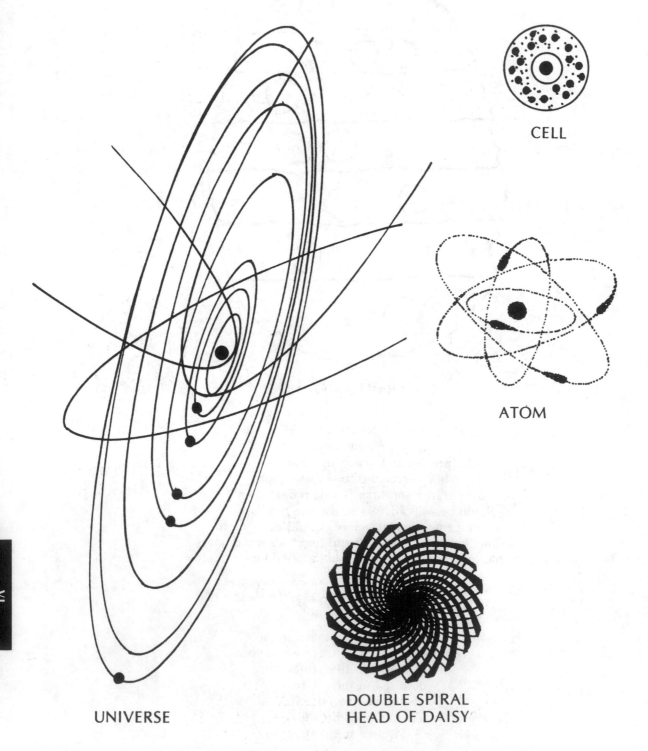

CELL

ATOM

UNIVERSE

DOUBLE SPIRAL
HEAD OF DAISY

SPIRAL GALAXY

SNOWFLAKE

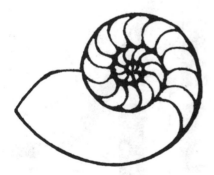

NAUTILUS SHELL

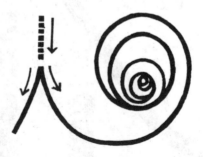

PHOTON TRACERY
IN BUBBLE CHAMBER

YOUR BUILDING

*EMBEDDED IN FOUR BILLION YEARS
OF PRIMORDIAL CREATION ARE ALL THE
DESIGNS FOR ALL THE ARCHITECTS
YET UNBORN.*

VALUE & DEMAND

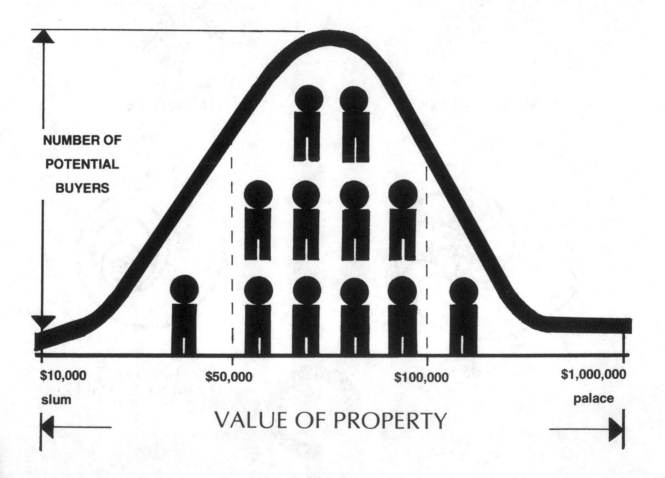

NUMBER OF POTENTIAL BUYERS

$10,000
slum

$50,000

$100,000

$1,000,000
palace

VALUE OF PROPERTY

A range in values from about $50,000 to $100,000 will interest the largest number of potential buyers. The more buyers the more liquidity, i.e., faster sale.

ELEMENTS OF VALUE

For income property and other things.

1. UTILITY: A thing must have use and ability to give satisfaction or arouse desire for possession.

LAST BEER
IN WORLD

2. SCARCITY: Limited supply of desired property INCREASES value.

3. DEMAND: Reflects desire. Created by scarcity of desired property. Implemented by purchasing power.

4. TRANSFERABILITY: Title should be easy to move.

VI
ARCHITECTURE
& APPRAISAL

AN INCOME PROPERTY'S LIFE CYCLE

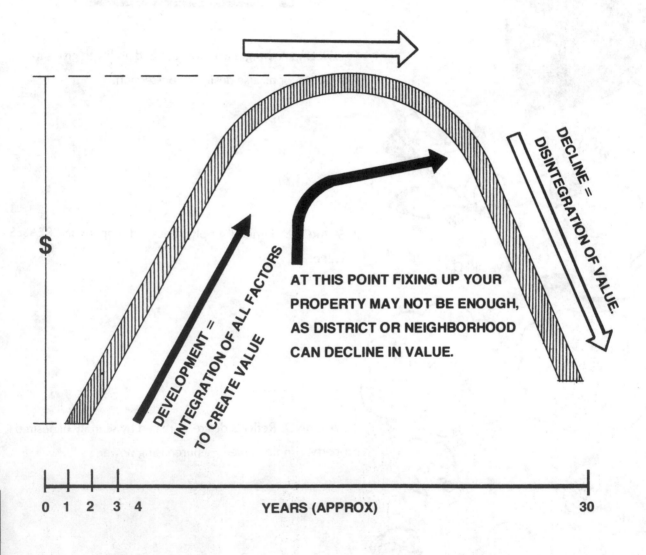

STATIC STATE = EQUILIBRIUM OF MAXIMUM VALUE.

DECLINE = DISINTEGRATION OF VALUE.

$

DEVELOPMENT = INTEGRATION OF ALL FACTORS TO CREATE VALUE

AT THIS POINT FIXING UP YOUR PROPERTY MAY NOT BE ENOUGH, AS DISTRICT OR NEIGHBORHOOD CAN DECLINE IN VALUE.

0 1 2 3 4   YEARS (APPROX)   30

Principle of change (flux): = Present and future, NOT past, is of
prime importance in appraising value.
You must recognize economic and
social forces at work...

PRINCIPLE OF CONFORMITY

NO!

YES!

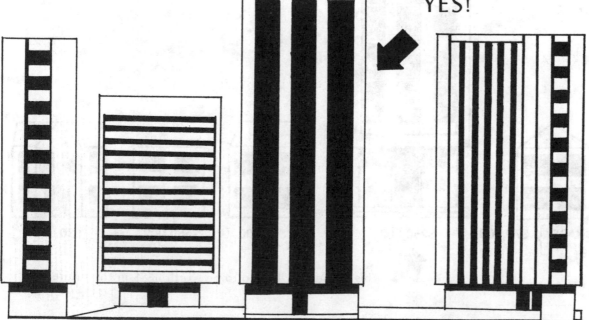

Maximum property value is realized when a reasonable degree of sociological and economic homogeneity is present. Similarity, but not monotonous uniformity; e.g., above examples relate to architectural conformity.

VI
ARCHITECTURE
& APPRAISAL

REGRESSION

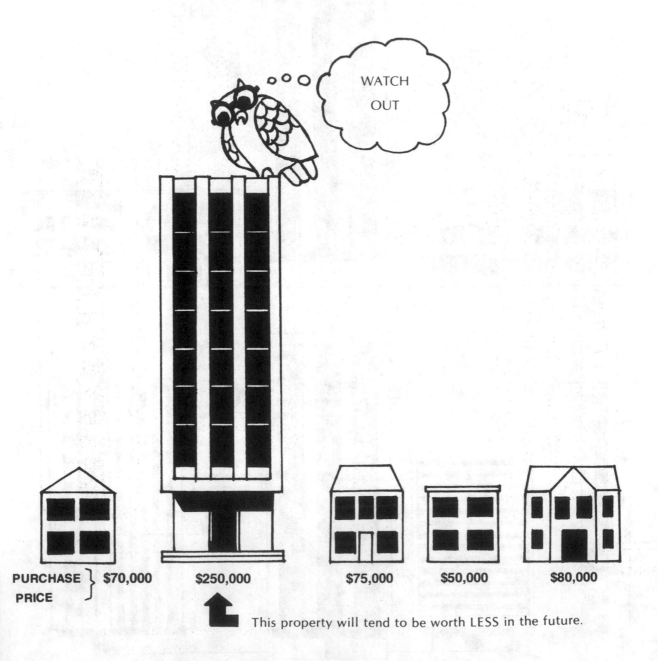

PURCHASE } PRICE $70,000 $250,000 $75,000 $50,000 $80,000

This property will tend to be worth LESS in the future.

VI
ARCHITECTURE
& APPRAISAL

'A MISPLACED IMPROVEMENT'

Regression:

An appraising principle that holds that a high valued property placed in a neighborhood of lower valued property seeks the level of the lower valued properties.

PROGRESSION

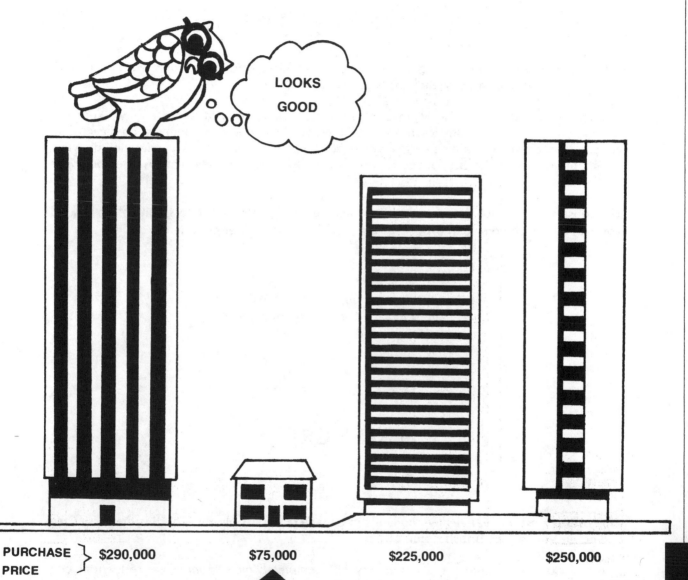

| PURCHASE PRICE | $290,000 | $75,000 | $225,000 | $250,000 |

This property will tend to be worth MORE in the future.

Progression:

An appraising principle that holds that the worth of a

lesser valued property is ENHANCED when placed in an

area with property of higher value.

REMODEL WITH ARCHITECTURAL PLANS

BRAIN EQUITY

A common mistake in remodeling is to spend a considerable amount of money with a minimum, or no increase in the value of the building.

Dollars spent and 'sweat equity' invested must be combined with 'brain equity.' You must remodel smart for maximum return on your investment. If you don't know a cornice from a cupola, then consider retaining an architect who can give you expert advice, detailed drawings, and material specifications. A budget can be established to determine exactly where you are going.

Then observe how much easier it is to obtain accurate bids from contractors. With plans and bids you can approach your loan officer for a remodel loan in greater confidence.

*Far better to erase a line on an architect's rendering
than to replace the position of a window.*

FALSE CREEK

One of the most innovative developments in Canada (and possibly the world) is the False Creek Project in Vancouver, British Columbia.

This is a 500 acre water-oriented community with *completely mixed zoning*, i.e., residential, commercial and industrial. This community has beautiful architecture, live-in boat marinas, spacious parks, and a rhythmic flow of varying heights, unobstructed views; designs for pedestrians not cars; versatile mix of shops and industries—these are the fruits of creative planning.

As Joan Byrnes, marketing consultant for Bolles Associates has said, "In Vancouver, if the rules needed changing, they changed them." At False Creek they judged the 'quality of life,' not mathematical zoning and density formulas. The poor, moderate income and rich all live together in a close knit live-work community. It appears to be a case study for the future.

A LOOK AT THE FUTURE

Encouragingly new concepts for a better way of life for all segments of our society *do* exist.

The California legislature has enacted a pilot program whereby the State *literally* goes into partnership with low-to-moderate income families. The concept is simple and creative. The State will buy 49% of a condominium (or house), the individual buys 51%. The individual has all of the usual rights of ownership, the State just goes along for the ride, and when the building is eventually sold (even far in the future), the individual owner receives 51% of the sale price.

When an investor pays part of the mortgage payment as a co-owner, it is called a Shared Appreciation Mortgage (SAM).

FACTS vs FANTASY

Concepts and abstractions are the qualitative stuff of which a property investor's dreams are made. To turn those dreams into reality, a scientific or quanitative approach is required.

Objective truth is preferable to subjective opinion.

Examples:

HOW OLD IS THE BUILDING?
Fantasy: It's quite old.
Fact: It was built in 1906 just after the earthquake.

WHAT WILL IT COST TO BRING IT UP TO CODE?
Fantasy: It won't cost much.
Fact: We have a signed and dated contractor's bid for $12,852.14.

DO YOU HAVE MANY VACANCIES?
Fantasy: We always fill it up in a few days.
Fact: Based on our records over the past three years we have a 2% of gross income vacancy factor, or $810 per year.

HOW BIG IS THE LOT?
Fantasy: It's about average.
Fact: Based on the latest city plot plan maps, the lot is 47 feet by 100 feet or a total area of 4,700 square feet.

IS IT OK TO ADD ANOTHER APARTMENT IN THE BACK?
Fantasy: It should be OK.
Fact: Yes, you can. We have a permit with approved architect's plans. However, you must add another garage and tear out the basement. One contractor estimated the cost at $25,000.

APPRAISAL PROCESS FLOW CHART

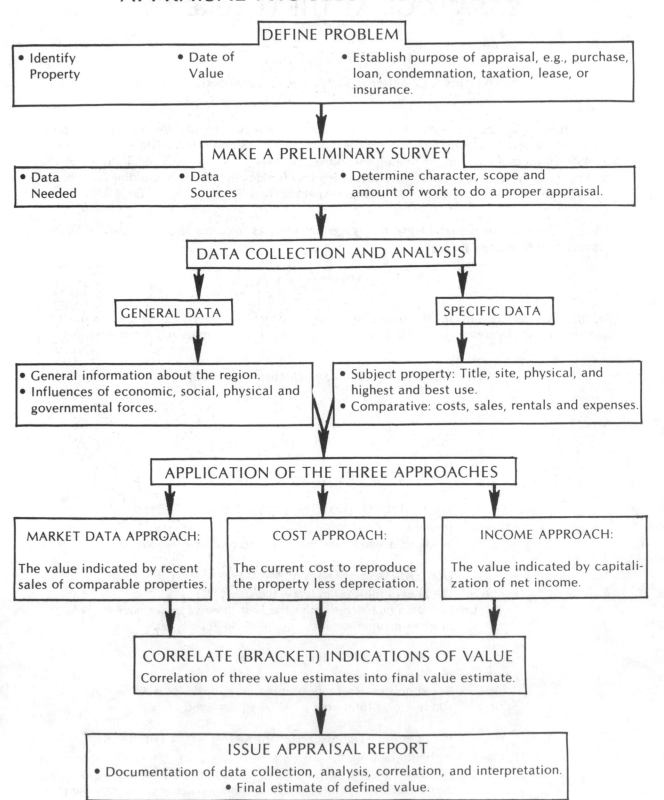

DEFINE PROBLEM

- Identify Property
- Date of Value
- Establish purpose of appraisal, e.g., purchase, loan, condemnation, taxation, lease, or insurance.

MAKE A PRELIMINARY SURVEY

- Data Needed
- Data Sources
- Determine character, scope and amount of work to do a proper appraisal.

DATA COLLECTION AND ANALYSIS

GENERAL DATA

SPECIFIC DATA

- General information about the region.
- Influences of economic, social, physical and governmental forces.

- Subject property: Title, site, physical, and highest and best use.
- Comparative: costs, sales, rentals and expenses.

APPLICATION OF THE THREE APPROACHES

MARKET DATA APPROACH:

The value indicated by recent sales of comparable properties.

COST APPROACH:

The current cost to reproduce the property less depreciation.

INCOME APPROACH:

The value indicated by capitalization of net income.

CORRELATE (BRACKET) INDICATIONS OF VALUE
Correlation of three value estimates into final value estimate.

ISSUE APPRAISAL REPORT
- Documentation of data collection, analysis, correlation, and interpretation.
- Final estimate of defined value.

APPRAISING A PROPERTY

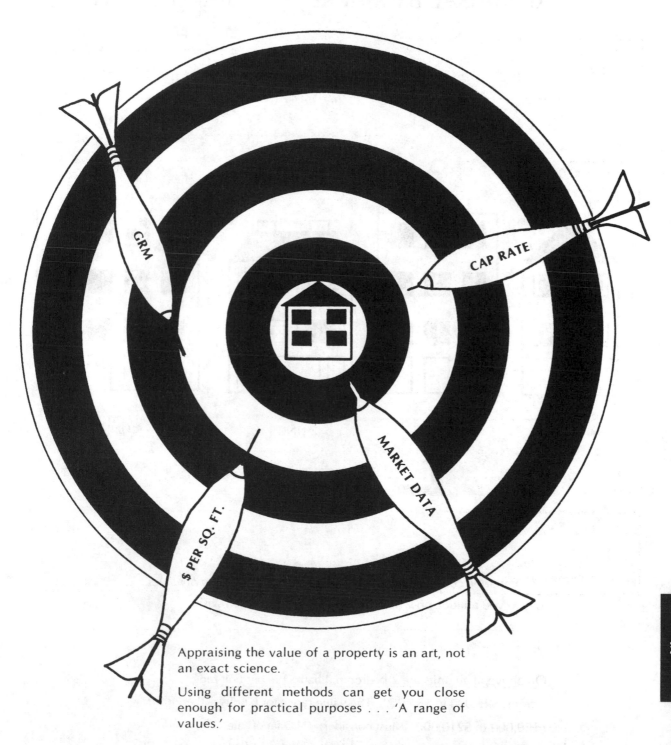

Appraising the value of a property is an art, not an exact science.

Using different methods can get you close enough for practical purposes . . . 'A range of values.'

Blayne A. Christian, S.R.A., C.R.A., says, "An appraiser who continually appraises too low for lenders who want to make loans, will receive no calls. An appraiser who continually appraises too high on FHA loans will also receive no calls. You must know the purpose of the appraisal. I try to give a range of values."

APPRAISAL BY MARKET DATA APPROACH

Obtain RECENT SELLING Prices:

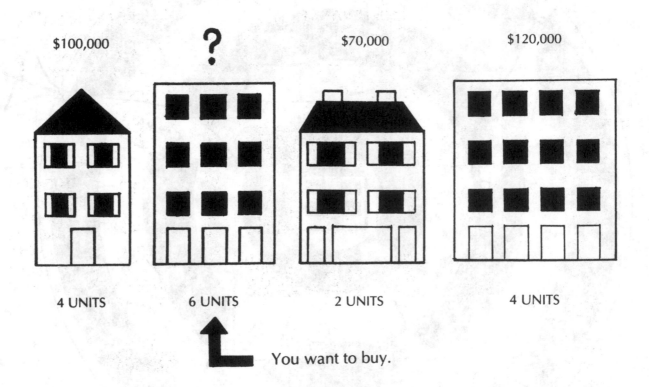

$100,000   ? $70,000 $120,000

4 UNITS   6 UNITS   2 UNITS   4 UNITS

You want to buy.

By comparing comparable properties you will have "a range of values" ...
to give you an idea on what to offer on the property you wish.

On above, if all units are 2 bedroom, I bath...the per unit range
is from: $25,000 to $35,000. The value range for 6 units is then from:
$150,000 to $210,000. Must consider: (1) Date of sale,
(2) Location, (3) Lot and building condition and size, (4) Reason for sale,
(5) Amenities; etc.

THE APPRAISAL PROCESS

BEST COMPARABLE PROPERTY

The 'best comparable property' is usually the most accurate way to appraise. All of the other methods lend evidence to support this figure.

It is *not* an average of all the methods, rather it is more like a best judgement by an experienced appraiser.

Hallmarks of a good appraiser are knowledge, experience, judgement and integrity.

3 TYPES OF DEPRECIATION

RELATED TO APPRAISING PROPERTY

Depreciation is loss in value due to any cause.

1. Physical Deterioration:

    A. Structural defects, decay, dry rot, wear and tear.

    B. "Deferred maintenance," wear due to lack of care.

2. Functional Obsolescence:

    A. Inherently poorly planned.

    B. Functionally inadequate, too big, too small, wrong style or "old fashioned."

3   Social or economic Obsolescence:

    A. Run–down neighborhood or slum, *blighted area.*

    B. Excess taxes or zoning changes, *R2 to city dump.*

CAP RATE BY BAND OF INVESTMENT

The *band of investment method* is another technique for arriving at the CAP RATE. The theory is that by analyzing the individual rates of return of the property, you can attain a more accurate Cap Rate than by other methods.

The interest return on the first mortgage, the interest return on the second, or any other mortgages, and the return the investor expects on the equity investment are totaled and then related to the entire investment.

Example:

FIRST MORTGAGE	$50,000	@	11%	=	$5,500
SECOND MORTGAGE	$20,000	@	10%	=	2,000
INVESTOR'S EQUITY	$10,000	@	15%	=	1,500
TOTAL	= $80,000				$9,000

A yield of $9,000 on a total investment of $80,000 therefore carries an overall Cap Rate of 11.25%.

CAP RATE BY THE SUMMATION METHOD

A less commonly used method of determining the Cap Rate is the summation method.

Start with a very safe rate, say the rate of return on government Savings Bonds	5%
Add the "degree of risk" inherent in the subject building, say	3%
Add an allowance for lack of liquidity	2%
Plus an amount for property management, say	1%
The total Cap Rate is, then	11%

ANOTHER SUMMATION METHOD

Another *summation method* is used by the President's Council of Economic Advisors (CEA) for determining the Cap Rate for the entire nation.

Start with a safe government Savings Bond rate, say	5%
Then add the anticipated inflation rate, say	9%
Total Cap Rate	14%

The bottom line is that *CAP RATE is based on the appraiser's analysis of estimates of real estate investor's opinion*. Just a touch of the nebulous.

VI
ARCHITECTURE
& APPRAISAL

QUICK BUILDING SITE ANALYSIS

RAW LAND COST $100,000

DIVIDED BY NUMBER OF UNITS
(Estimated for new project) . . . . .100 units

THUS, RAW LAND COST PER UNIT . . . . $ 1,000

    Number of square feet per unit 1,000

    Multiply by construction cost per square foot $40

MULTIPLY NUMBER OF SQUARE FEET (1000)
TIMES THE COST PER SQUARE FOOT ($40) . . . . $ 40,000

TOTAL ROUGH COST PER UNIT
(Before all sales, administration, loan & other costs)

TOTAL OF LAND COST ($1,000) + CONSTRUCTION COST ($40,000) . . . . $ 41,000

ADD 30% (PROFIT & OVERHEAD) = $12,300

$12,300 + $41,000 = $53,300

WILL IT SELL AT THIS COST?

COST BY SQUARE FOOT METHOD

Six unit apartment house...**NEW***.

6 units × 20 ft. wide × 50 ft. deep = 6,000 sq. ft.

6,000sq. ft.× $25 per sq. ft.= $150,000

use current price

Garage = 20 ft. wide ×50 ft. deep =1,000 sq.ft.

1,000sq.ft.× $10 per sq.ft. =$10,000

6 unit cost	=	$150,000
Garage cost	=	10,000
Land cost	=	20,000
Total property cost	=	$180,000

Remember that the VALUE of the property may be more or less than the COST depending on location and amenities.

* If NOT new, must <u>subtract depreciation</u>.

VI
ARCHITECTURE
& APPRAISAL

TWO LOTS

Given two equally priced lots, one with a destroyed structure on it, the other without. . .the lot with the structure on it is worth less (all other things being equal).

The reason is simple. The destroyed shell of a building must first be removed, and at a considerable expense. The author is familiar with small buildings that had bids of $10,000 to $15,000 to remove. One wag suggested that red ribbon should be tied around all the remaining parts, and they would then be stolen at no cost.

SALVAGE VALUE

If parts of the building can be incorporated into the new structure, e.g., a brick wall, a curving arch, a useable foundation with utilities, or other architectural elements, then possibly you can make lemonade out of the lemon.

It should also be noted that if you remove the 'scraper' (a building that should be scraped away), or keep the vacant lot, the lot will be more attractive and more likely to sell if you plant barley seed (or other appropriate ground cover) and a few well placed trees.

AVOID THE WRECKING BALL
HIGHEST AND BEST USE

HOLD IT!

AN ARCHITECTURAL
JEWEL BEING
USED AS AN
ART GALLERY.

GROSS INCOME = $10,000

A FEW OTHER ACTUAL
EXAMPLES OF
'HIGHEST AND BEST
USE' ARE: THE
CONVERSION OF A
MONEY LOSING
RIDING ACADEMY, TO
A TV STUDIO:
JOINING RAILROAD CARS
TOGETHER TO FORM
A FANCY RESTAURANT;
AND THE CONVERSION
OF AN OLD WINDOWLESS
BUILDING, TO A
MONEY-MAKING
MINI-WAREHOUSE.

JOE'S HOT DOGS

A NEW PLANNED
USE FOR THE
ABOVE SITE
. . . HOT DOGS.

GROSS INCOME = $40,000

Hot dogs may bring the 'highest and best use' (in terms of dollars), but a part
of our cultural heritage is destroyed forever.
A compromise may be in order.
Joe's could rent a space. Hot dogs with art.

VALUE INCREASE
WITH PARKS PATTERN

Long straight uninterrupted
streets are usually uninteresting . . .

PARKS
PATTERN

VS.

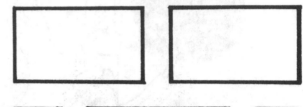

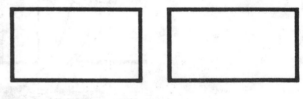

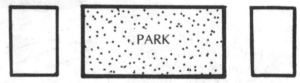

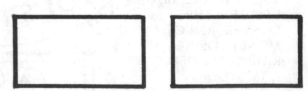

...shorter streets, vistas, green belts,

usually INCREASE VALUE!

STRAIGHT
GRID
PATTERN

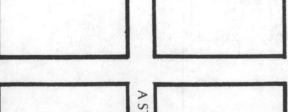

A STREET

PROGRESS IS SUBJECTIVE

THE WAY IT WAS FOR THOUSANDS OF YEARS.

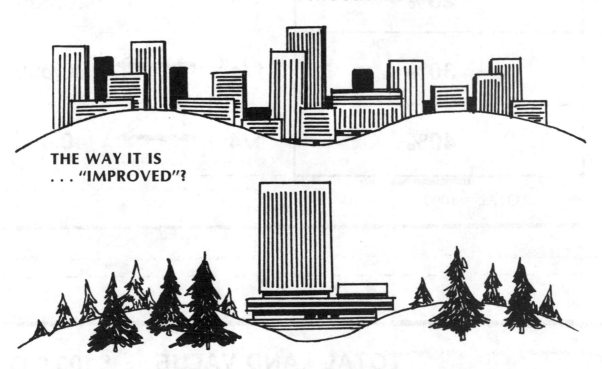

THE WAY IT IS . . . "IMPROVED"?

THE WAY IT COULD HAVE BEEN WITH PROPER "DENSITY AND ZONING" CONTROL. A BETTER ENVIRONMENT INCREASES PROPERTY VALUE.

VI
ARCHITECTURE
& APPRAISAL

4-3-2-1 RULE

TYPICAL CITY LOT

10%	**1/4** →	**$10,000**
20%	**1/4** →	**20,000**
30%	**1/4** →	**30,000**
40%	**1/4** →	**40,000**

TOTAL =100%

SIDEWALK

— STREET —

TOTAL LAND VALUE = $100,000

4-3-2-1 Rule: First 1/4 of standard lot depth = 40% of total value,

second 1/4 = 30%, third 1/4 = 20% and

fourth 1/4 = 10%

VI
ARCHITECTURE
& APPRAISAL

PRINCIPLE OF SIZE & SHAPE

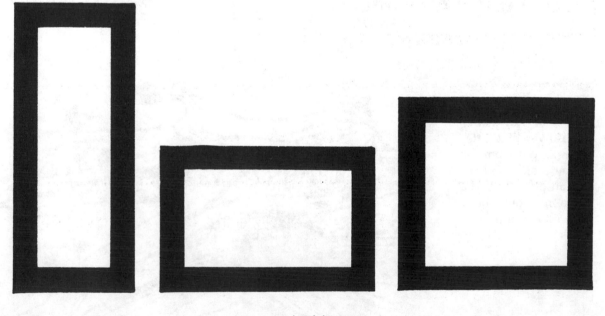

Less Valuable Lots *Odd Shapes*

More Valuable Lots

Above assumes location and all other
factors equal.

URBAN GROWTH PATTERNS

There are four main theories to explain the way cities grow. Knowing which way a city is going to go is most important for estimating future property values. The four theories are: the concentric ring theory, the star theory, the sector theory, and the special zone theory. These theories are just for openers. All, or any part of these and perhaps five others can be overlayed on top of one another to concoct the theory of your choice. They are of interest from an academic viewpoint, but it is strongly urged that you look this horse in the mouth.

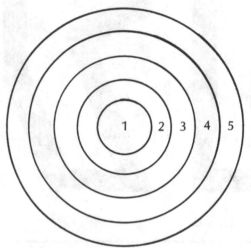

A growth theory of five concentric circles or ovals, usually named: (1) The central business district, (2) the zone in transition, (3) the zone of workingmen's homes, (4) the middle-class zone, and (5) the commuters' zone.

THE CONCENTRIC ZONE THEORY

The star theory observes that cities spread out from the center along the lines of transportation. The resultant shape resembles a star, or octopus.

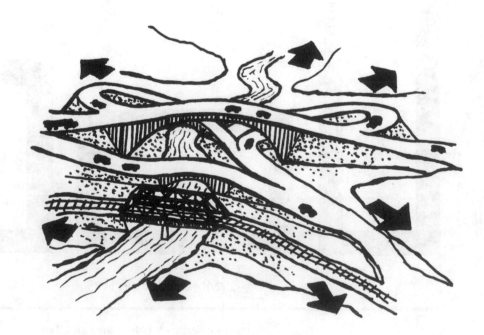

THE STAR THEORY

URBAN GROWTH PATTERNS

Reality is such that a walk around the city, a visit to City Hall with a planning officer, a review of literature from the Chamber of Commerce, and a conversation and tour with an experienced real estate broker . . . will be more rewarding than the most esoteric growth theories.

The sector theory divides the city into pie-shaped wedges or sectors, and usually explains the wedges in terms of high priced property or rent. The sectors are dynamic and represent a certain period of time, e.g., the inner portion of the sector could represent 1930, and the periphery 1980.

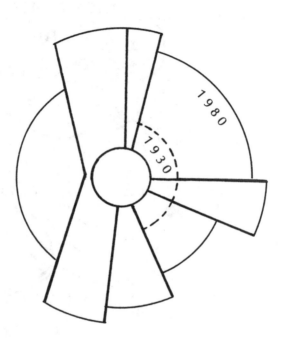

THE SECTOR THEORY

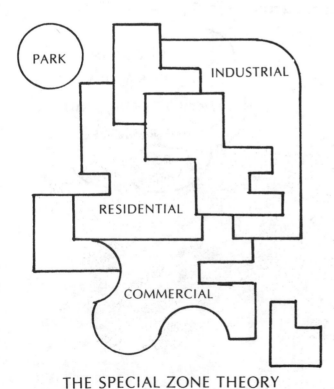

THE SPECIAL ZONE THEORY

The special zone theory simply divides the city in terms of the particular type of zoning, e.g., residential, industrial, commercial, etc.

AND THEN THERE WAS EARTH

APPENDIX

REAL ESTATE ABBREVIATIONS

AD VALOREM	In proportion to the value
AEK	All electric kitchen
AKA	Also known as
ALTA	American Land Title Association (policy)
B&P	Business and professions (code)
BONA FIDE	In good faith
BTU	British terminal unit
CAL	Cash above loan
CLEAR	Free and clear of loans
CLO	Call listing office
COE	Close of escrow
COL	Cash over loan
CPA	Certified public accountant
CPM	Certified property manager
CRV	Certificate of reasonable value
DBA	Doing business as
DOS	Due on sale (loan)
ET AL	And others
ET UX	And wife
F/A	Forced air heater
FHA	Federal Housing Administration
FMV	Fair market value
FNMA	Federal National Mortgage Association, 'Fanny Mae'
GI	Government issue, Veteran's Administration
GIM	Gross Income Multiplier
GNMA	Government National Mortgage Association, 'Ginny Mae'
GNP	Gross national product
GRM	Gross rent multiplier
KILO	Key in listing office
MAI	Member of Appraiser's Institute
MLS	Multiple listing service
M/M	Month to month (rental)
MO	Make offer
NAR	National Association of Realtors
OBO	Occupied by owner
OT	Over tub (shower)
OWC	Owner will carry (loan)
PRIMA FACIE	At first sight
SET OFF	Square away a debt by mutual deductions
SHORT RATE	Extra payment for cancelling insurance
SIR	Society of Industrial Realtors
T/G	Tongue and groove (floors)
VW	Good view
W/W	Wall to wall (carpets)

Tom Owens, a real estate lawyer, led a group of eight attorneys working with the author to arrive at what is believed to be an 'idiot proof' Deposit Receipt. It did receive a letter of commendation from the Department of Real Estate. The only limiting factor was that for simplicity we wanted the form on one 8½" × 14" legal size page, front and back. We had to condense a ten page manuscript to one page. (It is surprising that only Ten Commandments were needed by Moses.)

It should be kept in mind that different city, state and federal government rulings can change the ball game, as well as local customs, e.g., in northern California the buyer pays title fees, whereas in southern California the seller usually pays title fees.

It is believed to be written clearly, and to understand it, is to grasp the essence of an offer to purchase real property.

Real Estate Purchase Agreement and Deposit Receipt

REALTOR®

This is more than a receipt for money—It is intended to be a legally binding contract. READ IT CAREFULLY.

_____, California, _____, 19_____

RECEIVED FROM _____
(hereinafter called "Buyer") the sum of _____ DOLLARS ($_____),
evidenced by Cash ☐, Personal Check ☐, Certified Check ☐, Cashier's Check ☐, or _____ payable to
_____, as a deposit on account of the purchase price of _____
_____
DOLLARS ($_____), offered for that property in the city of _____, County of _____
State of California, consisting of land and improvements commonly known as: _____
(hereinafter called "the property") subject to the condition of title set forth on the reverse hereof.

Agent's address _____ Agent _____
Telephone _____ By (signature) _____

BUYER'S OFFER

BUYER HEREBY OFFERS TO PURCHASE THE PROPERTY FOR THE PRICE SPECIFIED ABOVE AND ACCORDING TO THE TERMS AND CONDITIONS SPECIFIED BELOW AND ON THE REVERSE SIDE. BUYER HAS READ AND UNDERSTOOD ALL OF THESE TERMS AND CONDITIONS INCLUDING THOSE APPEARING ON THE REVERSE SIDE.

I. Summary of Financing:

(A) $_____ The above deposit.

(B) $_____ Additional deposit to be placed in escrow on or before _____ (_____) days after opening thereof.

(C) $_____ Payable to escrow holder upon notification from escrow. Such notification shall also specify any additional sums necessary for closing costs and adjustments as between Seller and Buyer.

(D) $_____ First Trust Deed Note payable $_____ per month, including interest at _____% per annum (or for the first six months of loan, if variable interest rate) for a term of _____ years, plus impounds if required by lender. ☐ Buyer to take title subject to (agrees to assume if required). ☐ Buyer to obtain. ☐ Seller to carry.
Charges to secure above new loan: Buyer's _____ Seller's _____.

(E) $_____ Second Trust Deed Note payable $_____, or more per month, including interest at _____% per annum: all due and payable in _____ years. ☐ Buyer to take title subject to (agrees to assume if required). ☐ Buyer to obtain ☐ Seller to carry. ☐ Entire balance due and payable upon sale or transfer of property.

(F) $_____ Total purchase price (Sum of A through E).

(BOTTOM HALF OF FRONT PAGE)

II. Possession at close of escrow. If after close of escrow Seller for any reason should remain in possession, then Seller shall pay Buyer $_____ per day for rent until possession is given to Buyer.

III. Close of escrow shall occur on or before _____, 19____ unless extended by the terms hereof or by the mutual agreement of the parties. Escrow to be opened with and managed by _____, _____ office ("Escrow Holder").

IV. In the event Buyer is to assume or obtain financing as set forth in Paragraph I above, then this offer is subject to Buyer obtaining and qualifying for the said financing within _____ days from acceptance of this offer.

V. Unless otherwise stated herein, the purchase price includes all tacked down carpets, draperies, window coverings and all built-in and attached appliances, fixtures, keys, and if income property all personal property items used in its operation, and _____
_____

VI. Unless otherwise designated in the escrow instructions, title shall vest in Buyer as follows: _____
_____

(The manner of taking title may have significant legal and tax consequences. Therefore give this matter serious consideration).

VII. The following constitute other provisions, such as special prorations, assumption/payment of assessments, the matter of physical condition of the property, repairs, and any other terms or conditions different from this form: _____
_____
_____

VIII. If Buyer fails to complete the purchase as herein provided by reason of any default of Buyer, Seller shall be released from the obligation to sell the property to Buyer. Buyer and Seller agree that it would be impractical or extremely difficult to fix actual damages in case of Buyer's default; accordingly in lieu of any right Seller may have against Buyer at law or in equity, Seller retains the Deposit (or three [3] per cent of the purchase price, whichever is less) as Seller's sole right to damages. The amount so retained is determined by the parties to be a reasonable estimate of Seller's damages.

Seller_____ Buyer_____

IX. Buyer's signature hereon constitutes an offer to Seller to purchase the property. Unless acceptance hereof is signed by Seller and such acceptance communicated to Buyer in writing on or before _____, 19____, this offer shall be deemed revoked and the deposit shall be returned to the Buyer. THE BUYER AUTHORIZES THE ABOVE NAMED AGENT TO HOLD THE DEPOSIT IN UNCASHED FORM UNTIL THIS OFFER IS ACCEPTED BY SELLER, AT WHICH TIME THE DEPOSIT SHALL BE PLACED IN A TRUST ACCOUNT.

X. THIS AGREEMENT, when duly executed by Seller and Buyer, consists of this page and the reverse side of it and any exhibits referenced herein. There are no other terms or conditions oral or in writing except that which appear in this Agreement. It is further understood that no representative or agent has any power to change or modify any terms or conditions herein.

XI. The undersigned Buyer acknowledges a receipt of a copy hereof. The undersigned Buyer further acklowledges that Buyer has not received or relied upon any statements or representations by the above Agent or Agent's employees or representatives which are not herein expressed.

BUYER _____ Address _____
Telephone: Home _____ Office _____ _____
BUYER _____ Address _____
Telephone: Home _____ Office _____

ACCEPTANCE

The undersigned Seller accepts and acknowledges the receipt of a copy of the foregoing offer and hereby agrees to sell said property on the terms and conditions set forth herein.

A real estate commission for services rendered in the amount of _____ percent (__%) of the accepted sales price shall be paid to the above Agent. Seller agrees to pay said commission through escrow at the time of closing thereof. If completion of the sale is prevented by default of Seller such commission shall nevertheless be paid by Seller upon such default. If completion of sale is prevented by default of Buyer, then if and when Seller collects damages from Buyer pursuant to Paragraph VIII above, Seller shall pay Agent the sum of one-half (½) of the damages collected after first deducting title and escrow charges and the expenses of collection, if any.

SELLER _____ DATED _____ Time _____
Address _____
SELLER _____ Telephone: Home _____ Office _____

A Real Estate Agent is the person qualified to advise on Real Estate. No representation or recommendation is made by the above Agent, or its agents or employees as to the legal sufficiency, legal effect or tax consequences of this document or the transaction relating thereto. These are questions for your attorney.

[Office use only—do not write below this space]

Manager's Review _____ Date _____

(TOP HALF OF BACK PAGE)

Additional Terms and Conditions of Offer

1. Condition of Title. Title to the property shall be delivered to Buyer at close of escrow subject to (1) any public utility easements, zoning and set back ordinances of the City and County in which the property is located. (2) Current taxes for the fiscal year. (3) Covenants, conditions, restrictions, reservations, rights of way, easements and exceptions of minerals, oils, gas, water, carbons and hydrocarbons on or under said property now or record and in deed to file, if any, affecting the use and occupancy of said property, including liens and charges arising out or imposed by the terms of said covenants, conditions or restrictions. (4) Encumbrances to file, or of record, as disclosed by the terms of the offer shown on the front of this contract. (5) Any other encumbrance, lien, term or condition of or to the property acceptable to Buyer. If Seller fails to deliver as herein provided, Buyer at his option may terminate this Agreement and any deposit shall thereupon be returned to him.

2. Objection to Title and Posting of Balance of Purchase Price. Fifteen (15) days from the date of acceptance by Seller are allowed the Buyer to examine the title to the property and to report in writing any valid objections thereto to the agent for the Seller named on the reverse side. If no such objections to title be reported, the balance of said purchase price shall be paid by Buyer on or before the expiration of such time or the period of time stated in Paragraph III, whichever is longer, to the escrow holder for account of the Seller. Seller within fifteen (15) days of acceptance shall deliver to the escrow holder a properly executed and acknowledged grant deed to the property. If any such objections to title are reported within the fifteen day period the Seller shall use all due diligence to remove such objections at his own expense within ninety (90) days thereafter, and if so removed, the balance of said purchase price shall be paid within five (5) days after such objections have been removed and upon delivery of said deed as hereinbefore provided; but if such objections cannot be removed within the time allowed, all rights and obligations hereunder may, at the election of the Buyer, terminate and end, and said deposit shall be returned to the Buyer, unless he elects to buy said property subject to such objections. The decision of any local title insurance company shall be accepted as final by both Buyer and Seller as to all questions affecting title and Buyer agrees to accept a title insurance policy issued by any such company as conclusive evidence of the condition of the title. If said Buyer shall fail to comply with any conditions at the time or in the manner herein provided for, said Seller shall be released from all obligations hereunder. AT THE DISCRETION OF THE AGENT HEREIN, IF AN UNINTENTIONAL ERROR THAT CANNOT BE NEGOTIATED, HAS BEEN MADE BY ANY PARTY, THEN ALL DEPOSITS SHALL BE REFUNDED; AND THE AGREEMENT SHALL BE CONSIDERED NULL AND VOID. Pacific Union Co. is hereby authorized to order, for the account of the Buyer, a preliminary title report.

3. Evidence of Title. Seller shall furnish to Buyer at Buyer's expense a standard California Land Title Association (CLTA) policy insuring title in Buyer in the condition of title specified in Paragraph 1 above. If required by Buyer's lender, Buyer shall pay for an American Land Title Association (ALTA) title policy.

4. Prorations & Escrow Costs. UNLESS otherwise provided for on the reverse side, property taxes, premiums on insurance acceptable to Buyer, rents and interest shall be prorated as of the recordation of the deed and non-delinquent assessments which are a lien shall be assumed by Buyer. Buyer shall pay for title insurance and his escrow and closing costs. Seller shall pay for the cost of documentary stamps on the deed, the existing loan prepayment penalty, if any, real estate transfer taxes, and his escrow and closing costs.

5. Financial Information. Buyer hereby agrees promptly to provide such financial information to the lender as is reasonably needed to determine whether Buyer qualifies for the loan contemplated on the reverse side.

6. Present Physical Condition. UNLESS otherwise provided for on the reverse side, the property is being purchased in its present physical condition and Seller makes no warranties, guarantees, representations or promises with regard to said property. Buyer acknowledges that he is entitled to obtain copies of all reports and completion notices on the property filed with the Structural Pest Control Board within the last two years by applying for same, along with a $2.00 search fee, to the Board at 1707 11th Street, Sacramento, California 95814. Seller does agree, however, that heating, air conditioning (if any), plumbing, electrical, and other mechanical apparatus and appliances shall be operative at the close of escrow, and that Seller shall maintain landscaping and pool (if any) until close of escrow. All trash and debris shall be removed from the premises.

(BOTTOM HALF OF BACK PAGE)

7. Inspection. In amplification of the preceding paragraph, Buyer and/or his representative shall have the right to inspect the premises, during normal business hours, for a period of seven (7) days from Seller's acceptance hereof. If during said period Buyer discovers any defect in the condition of the property which is of a material nature, then Buyer may rescind this Agreement by giving written notice within said seven (7) days period. Upon such notice, all deposits shall be returned to Buyer.

8. Destruction of Premises. If the improvements on the property are destroyed or materially damaged prior to the close of escrow, then on demand by Buyer, any funds deposited into escrow shall be returned and this Agreement shall thereupon terminate.

9. Leases & Deposits. Within seven (7) days of Seller's acceptance hereof, Seller shall deposit into escrow all written leases of or concerning any part of the property. Further, prior to close of escrow, Seller shall remit into escrow all last month's rents, security deposits, cleaning fees or other monies held by Seller as security for tenant's performance under any oral or written lease or other agreement, which funds shall be remitted to Buyer upon close of escrow and shall not otherwise affect the purchase price. Buyer to take title subject to any existing leases and tenant's rights.

10. Time of the Essence. Time is of the essence of this Agreement.

11. Notice to the Public. It is the custom of the Agent, prior to the close of escrow, to give notice to the public, by publication and otherwise, of the sale in progress and to introduce therein the new owners of the property. The execution of this contract constitutes a consent on the part of the Buyer and Seller for said notice to be given.

12. Report of Residential Record. In locations where it exists, Seller shall provide to Buyer, in escrow prior to close, a "Report of Residential Record." If the report shows any existing building code violation of a material nature or other condition on or concerning the property of a material nature, then unless the violation or condition is already recognized by the terms of this agreement, Buyer may rescind this agreement within 48 hours of his receiving the report and all deposits shall be returned to him.

13. Attorney's Fees and Costs. Should Seller, Buyer or Agent commence action to enforce the respective rights of each arising out of this Agreement, the prevailing party or parties shall be entitled to reasonable attorney's fees and costs.

14. Agent not Responsible. The Agent shall not be held responsible for the failure to comply with any of the terms of this Agreement by either the Seller or the Buyer.

15. Use of Masculine, Feminine, Etc. All words used in this Agreement, including the words Buyer and Seller, shall be construed to include the plural as well as the singular number, and words used herein in the present tense shall include the future as well as the present, and words used in the masculine gender shall include the feminine and neuter.

16. Prevailing Law. This Agreement shall be subject to and interpreted by the laws of the State of California.

17. Heirs, Devisees Bound. This Agreement shall inure to the benefit of and be enforcible by or against the respective heirs, devisees, successors, executors and administrators of the Parties.

18. Escrow Instructions. Escrow instructions signed by Buyer and Seller shall be delivered to the escrow holder, which instructions shall be in conformance with this agreement.

19. Other Documents if a Condominium. If the subject property is a condominium unit, then Buyer further acknowledges he has received copies of the relevant Public Report, the Declaration of Covenants, Conditions and Restrictions, the Articles of Incorporation of the Owners' Association and the By-Laws of Owners Association. Buyer acknowledges that he understands that he will be charged a prorated assessment to cover the operational costs of the Association as provided in the covenants, conditions and restrictions which have been recorded.

Please note Letter to Author, Litigation Prevention, pg. 379.

APPENDIX

LETTER OF INTENT

A SIMPLE YET EFFECTIVE LETTER CAN HELP SECURE EVEN LARGE PROJECTS.
(An agreement to agree.)

PATHFINDER

REALTY

ROY T MALONEY

Aug. 26, 1979

TO: D. F. Keller & Co.

Dear Dave;

This letter is to outline my intention for the purchase of ten units at Kaanapali Shores.

I agree to a purchase price of one million dollars over your purchase price.

I agree to deliver option money (non-refundable) in the amount of $3,000 per month until the completion of the project and close of escrow, on or about Dec. 1981.

Upon your verbal acceptance of these terms I will have my attorney draw up a formal document for our signatures.

I look forward to hearing from you.

Sincerely,

Roy

THE INTERNAL REVENUE CODE
QUICK & EASY

The art of taxation consists of so plucking the goose as to obtain the largest amount of feathers with the least possible amount of hissing.

J.B. Colbert (1619-1683)
Financier to Louis XIV

If Patrick Henry thought that taxation without representation was bad, he should see how bad it is *with* representation.

The Old Farmer's Almanac

OVERVIEW: After culling through over 7,500 sections of the Federal Tax Code, the following represents a summary of the more important sections as they apply to real estate. They should at least help to put you in the right ballpark. Don't feel bad if these sections are not crystal clear . . . even tax attorneys and accountants argue over the fine points. To our knowledge the sections of the code have never been presented in this format. In the long run expert tax advice can be inexpensive.

These pages could not have been done without the great assistance of Frederick W. Daily, J.D., LL.M. (Tax) of San Francisco and Mr. Thomas Manolakas, MBA, CPA, J.D., LL.M., a professor of real estate tax law at McGeorge Law School in Sacramento, CA. They have done an outstanding job of making the Tax Code understandable. This writer knows of no better reference, and believes Congress should take note.

A descriptive heading is followed by the section of the Code.

RESIDENCE REPLACEMENT RULES

A. **ROLLOVER Rule** (I.R.C. 1034)

Allows you to pay no tax now on any **gain** from the sale of your residence when: (a) You purchase a new principal residence within 24 months before or after the sale of the old one, **and** (b) the new home costs as much or more than the old one, **or** (c) you start construction on a new home within 24 months before or after the sale of the old one **and occupy** within 24 months after the sale. **You** are allowed to defer gains under this rule only once every two years unless a move was work-related.

B. **OVER 55 Rule** (I.R.C. 121)

Allows individuals and married couples 55 or older to sell their principal residence without any tax liability for gains up to $125,000. The residence must have been owned and occupied by the owner for at least 3 of the 5 years before the sale. Only one spouse need be at least 55. This tax break can only be used once in a lifetime and it can be combined with the Rollover rule above, to allow a **trade down**.

REHABILITATION CREDITS (I.R.C. 42 & 48)

Up to 70% of the costs of rehabilitating certain historical or low income structures may be taken as a **credit** against federal taxes. A credit is far better than a deduction! Example: A $100,000 qualifying expenditure could cut federal taxes of $100,000 down to as little as $30,000! And, this credit taken with depreciation deductions **could reduce the building costs to zero,** after considering the reductions in federal and state income taxes!

DEPRECIATION (I.R.C. 168)

Property purchased beginning in 1987 can be depreciated over either 27.5 years (residential rental) or 31.5 years (commercial) on a straight line basis only. Land may never be depreciated, only the improvements built on land.

Any property acquired before 1987 is depreciated according to the tax code at the time of the acquisition.

HOME OFFICE DEDUCTION (I.R.C. 280A)

Allows deduction for maintenance, utilities, depreciation or rental expenses and other related expenses for the part of the home used in a business activity. The "office" doesn't need to be a separate room but must be used **exclusively** and **regularly** for business. The maximum amount of the deduction is limited to a formula based on the net income of the business less the proportion of taxes and interest (homeowners only, not renters) allocable to the office space.

TAX FREE (DEFERRED) EXCHANGES (I.R.C. 1031)

Allows you to trade property without paying any current taxes on gains unless you are a dealer in property. Taxes on your gains are postponed to the year in which the property is sold, except to the extent that you received and **boot** (cash or debt relief) in the exchange. This boot is taxable in the year received.

Exchanges may be straightforward trades, or more likely, three party trades: seller finds a buyer to buy the new property and trade it to him instead of paying him cash. Result: A 1031 exchange.

There is also another method, the delayed or "Starker" exchange. Here a tax free exchange treatment will be applied when the seller sells his property outright, designates a property to buy within 45 days and acquires title within 180 days of the original sale. Before trying this it is suggested that you talk to your lawyer.

CAPITAL GAINS (I.R.C. 1221, 1231)

Beginning in 1987 capital gains are no longer treated any differently than ordinary income by the tax code.

However, if there is a capital **loss** your deduction is limited to $3,000 per year with a carryover of any excess. If there is an overall Section 1231 (business type realty) loss, it may be fully deductible.

BEWARE THE **ALTERNATIVE MINIMUM TAX**

This is a sneaky way that the tax code can get you when it is determined that you have "excessive" income exempt from tax due to deductions as well as other items. For example, the receipt of **balloon** payments may trigger this tax. If you are concerned, check with your tax advisor.

HOME FINANCING AND RE-FINANCING (I.R.C. 163 (h))

Beginning in 1988, interest deductions for borrowings on first or second homes are limited to loans of (1) $1,000,000 to **buy** or **build** both (total), **plus** (2) $100,000 of borrowing on the equity of both (total), a total cap of $1,100,000. BEWARE: There is a **re-financing trap** here. Example: You own a home worth $250,000 with only a $50,000 first mortgage. Can you refinance for $200,000 and get a full interest deduction? NO. Because you are limited by rule (1) to $50,000, the amount of your first mortgage, **plus** $100,000 under rule (2), a total of $150,000!

PASSIVE LOSS RULES (I.R.C. 469)

Welcome to the Land of Confusion. Effective in 1987, rental income losses are designated as "passive losses". This type of loss cannot be deducted from your "active" income (wages) or "portfolio" income (interest, dividends). Excepted from operation of the rule here are taxpayers with Adjusted Gross Incomes of less than $100,000, who are allowed to use "passive losses" of up to $25,000 of realty losses to offset other income, either active or passive. As if this weren't bad enough, there is a phase-in period for these rules, which don't become fully effective until 1991.

INSTALLMENT SALES (I.R.C. 453)

Beginning in 1988 most taxpayers may once again use this provision to defer taxes through installment sales.

A qualifying installment sale is one in which all or part of the sales price is received in a year or years after the sale. Gain on the sale is taxed in the year it is received and in proportion to the total amount received. Example: Property sold for $250,000, which had an adjusted basis of $150,000; gain of $100,000. Nothing paid down with two installments of $125,000 each, plus interest, due in the next two years. Of each payment 40% the Gross Profit Ratio, e.g., $100,000 gain, divided by $250,000 sales price equals 40%, or $50,000 will be **taxable** along with the interest, and $75,000 will be **nontaxable return of capital**.

BEWARE: There is a **trap** in the example above. Any prior years of depreciation taken by the owner above must be "recaptured" (taxed) in the year of the sale; the owner may have a tax liability **even though** he did not get any cash at closing!

ESTATE & GIFT TAX (I.R.C. 2010 & 2505)

Starting in 1987 in computing **estate tax** due on the death of a taxpayer, or due on a gift by him, there is a credit against the tax due in an amount of $192,800, which in effect results in the first $600,000 of the estate, or gifts, passing tax free.

NEW IN 1988: I.R.S. FORM 1099-S required to be filed by brokers and others, such as closers of real estate transactions for **all** real estate sales by individuals.

Please note Letter to Author pg. 384.

ON BOOKS

To learn how to hang on to your property try:

> *Landlording,*
> by Leigh Robinson
> Published by Express.

One of the best books on real estate in a very easy to read narrative style is:

> *How I Turned $1,000 into Five Million in Real Estate,*
> by William Nickerson
> Published by Simon and Schuster.

Another inspirational book by a man who has been there, and knows his stuff is:

> *A Fortune at Your Feet,*
> by A.D. Kessler
> Published Harcourt Brace Jovanovich.

If you need expert advice on inspecting a building try:

> *The Complete House Inspection Book*
> by Don Fredriksson
>
> Published by Ballantine Books
> Author's Phone: (415) 459-3796

A company dedicated to books on real estate, as well as tapes, seminars, and current reports is:

> Impact Publishing Co.
> 2110 Omega Road
> San Ramon, California 94583
> Phone: (415) 831-1655, Dave Glubetich

For clues on how to succeed in life and business try:

> *How I Raised Myself from a Failure to Success in Selling*
> by Frank Bettger
> Published by Prentice Hall
>
> *Think and Grow Rich*
> by Napoleon Hill
> Published by Fawcett Press
>
> *A Whack on the Side of the Head*
> *How to Unlock Your Mind for Innovation*
> by Roger Von Oech, Ph.D.
> Published by Creative Think

AMORTIZATION TABLE
Simplified

Table of MONTHLY payments to AMORTIZE A $1,000 LOAN.

ANNUAL INTEREST

TERM OF YEARS

	5%	7%	9%
5	18.88	19.81	20.76
10	10.61	11.62	12.67
20	6.60	7.76	9.00

So:

A $50,000 loan to be amortized,
paid off, in 20 years @ 9%
interest would cost...

$ 9 per 1,000 x 50 = $ 450 per month

Please note Letter to Author bottom of pg. 364 and On Calculators, pg. 376.

APPENDIX

MONTHLY PAYMENT NEEDED TO
AMORTIZE A $1000 LOAN

YEARS	RATE 9.00%	9.25%	9.50%	9.75%	10.00%	10.25%	10.50%	10.75%
1	87.46	87.57	87.69	87.80	87.92	88.04	88.15	88.27
2	45.69	45.80	45.92	46.03	46.15	46.27	46.38	46.50
3	31.80	31.92	32.04	32.15	32.27	32.39	32.51	32.63
4	24.89	25.01	25.13	25.25	25.37	25.49	25.61	25.73
5	20.76	20.88	21.01	21.13	21.25	21.38	21.50	21.62
6	18.03	18.15	18.28	18.41	18.53	18.66	18.78	18.91
7	16.09	16.22	16.35	16.48	16.61	16.74	16.87	17.00
8	14.66	14.79	14.92	15.05	15.18	15.31	15.45	15.58
9	13.55	13.68	13.81	13.95	14.08	14.22	14.36	14.49
10	12.67	12.81	12.94	13.08	13.22	13.36	13.50	13.64
11	11.97	12.10	12.24	12.38	12.52	12.67	12.81	12.95
12	11.39	11.53	11.67	11.81	11.96	12.10	12.25	12.39
13	10.90	11.05	11.19	11.34	11.48	11.63	11.78	11.93
14	10.49	10.64	10.79	10.94	11.09	11.24	11.39	11.54
15	10.15	10.30	10.45	10.60	10.75	10.90	11.06	11.21
16	9.85	10.00	10.15	10.31	10.46	10.62	10.78	10.94
17	9.59	9.75	9.90	10.06	10.22	10.38	10.54	10.70
18	9.37	9.53	9.68	9.84	10.00	10.16	10.33	10.49
19	9.17	9.33	9.49	9.65	9.82	9.98	10.15	10.31
20	9.00	9.16	9.33	9.49	9.66	9.82	9.99	10.16
21	8.85	9.01	9.18	9.35	9.51	9.68	9.85	10.02
22	8.72	8.88	9.05	9.22	9.39	9.56	9.73	9.90
23	8.60	8.77	8.93	9.11	9.28	9.45	9.62	9.80
24	8.49	8.66	8.83	9.01	9.18	9.35	9.53	9.71
25	8.40	8.57	8.74	8.92	9.09	9.27	9.45	9.63
26	8.31	8.49	8.66	8.84	9.01	9.19	9.37	9.55
28	8.17	8.35	8.52	8.70	8.88	9.07	9.25	9.43
30	8.05	8.23	8.41	8.60	8.78	8.97	9.15	9.34
35	7.84	8.03	8.22	8.41	8.60	8.79	8.99	9.18
40	7.72	7.91	8.11	8.30	8.50	8.69	8.89	9.09

YEARS	RATE 11.00%	11.25%	11.50%	11.75%	12.00%	12.25%	12.50%	12.75%
1	88.39	88.50	88.62	88.74	88.85	88.97	89.09	89.21
2	46.61	46.73	46.85	46.96	47.08	47.20	47.31	47.43
3	32.74	32.86	32.98	33.10	33.22	33.34	33.46	33.58
4	25.85	25.97	26.09	26.22	26.34	26.46	26.58	26.71
5	21.75	21.87	22.00	22.12	22.25	22.38	22.50	22.63
6	19.04	19.17	19.30	19.43	19.56	19.69	19.82	19.95
7	17.13	17.26	17.39	17.52	17.66	17.79	17.93	18.06
8	15.71	15.85	15.98	16.12	16.26	16.40	16.53	16.67
9	14.63	14.77	14.91	15.05	15.19	15.33	15.47	15.62
10	13.78	13.92	14.06	14.21	14.35	14.50	14.64	14.79
11	13.10	13.24	13.39	13.54	13.68	13.83	13.98	14.13
12	12.54	12.69	12.84	12.99	13.14	13.29	13.44	13.60
13	12.08	12.23	12.38	12.54	12.69	12.85	13.00	13.16
14	11.70	11.85	12.01	12.16	12.32	12.48	12.64	12.80
15	11.37	11.53	11.69	11.85	12.01	12.17	12.33	12.49
16	11.10	11.26	11.42	11.58	11.74	11.91	12.07	12.24
17	10.86	11.02	11.19	11.35	11.52	11.68	11.85	12.02
18	10.66	10.82	10.99	11.16	11.32	11.49	11.67	11.84
19	10.48	10.65	10.82	10.99	11.16	11.33	11.50	11.68
20	10.33	10.50	10.67	10.84	11.02	11.19	11.37	11.54
21	10.19	10.37	10.54	10.72	10.89	11.07	11.25	11.43
22	10.08	10.25	10.43	10.61	10.78	10.96	11.14	11.33
23	9.98	10.15	10.33	10.51	10.69	10.87	11.05	11.24
24	9.89	10.06	10.25	10.43	10.61	10.79	10.98	11.16
25	9.81	9.99	10.17	10.35	10.54	10.72	10.91	11.10
26	9.74	9.92	10.10	10.29	10.47	10.66	10.85	11.04
28	9.62	9.81	9.99	10.18	10.37	10.56	10.75	10.94
30	9.52	9.72	9.91	10.10	10.29	10.48	10.68	10.87
35	9.37	9.57	9.77	9.96	10.16	10.36	10.56	10.76
40	9.29	9.49	9.69	9.89	10.09	10.29	10.49	10.70

MONTHLY PAYMENT NEEDED TO AMORTIZE A $1000 LOAN

YEARS	RATE							
	13.00%	13.25%	13.50%	13.75%	14.00%	14.25%	14.50%	14.75%
1	89.32	89.44	89.56	89.67	89.79	89.91	90.03	90.15
2	47.55	47.66	47.78	47.90	48.02	48.14	48.25	48.37
3	33.70	33.82	33.94	34.06	34.18	34.30	34.43	34.55
4	26.83	26.96	27.08	27.21	27.33	27.46	27.58	27.71
5	22.76	22.89	23.01	23.14	23.27	23.40	23.53	23.66
6	20.08	20.21	20.34	20.48	20.61	20.74	20.88	21.01
7	18.20	18.33	18.47	18.61	18.75	18.88	19.02	19.16
8	16.81	16.95	17.09	17.23	17.38	17.52	17.66	17.81
9	15.76	15.90	16.05	16.19	16.34	16.49	16.63	16.78
10	14.94	15.08	15.23	15.38	15.53	15.68	15.83	15.99
11	14.28	14.43	14.58	14.74	14.89	15.05	15.20	15.36
12	13.75	13.91	14.06	14.22	14.38	14.53	14.69	14.85
13	13.32	13.48	13.63	13.80	13.96	14.12	14.28	14.44
14	12.96	13.12	13.28	13.45	13.61	13.78	13.94	14.11
15	12.66	12.82	12.99	13.15	13.32	13.49	13.66	13.83
16	12.40	12.57	12.74	12.91	13.08	13.25	13.43	13.60
17	12.19	12.36	12.53	12.71	12.88	13.05	13.23	13.41
18	12.01	12.18	12.36	12.53	12.71	12.89	13.06	13.24
19	11.85	12.03	12.21	12.39	12.56	12.74	12.92	13.10
20	11.72	11.90	12.08	12.26	12.44	12.62	12.80	12.99
21	11.61	11.79	11.97	12.15	12.33	12.52	12.70	12.89
22	11.51	11.69	11.87	12.06	12.24	12.43	12.62	12.81
23	11.42	11.61	11.79	11.98	12.17	12.35	12.54	12.73
24	11.35	11.53	11.72	11.91	12.10	12.29	12.48	12.67
25	11.28	11.47	11.66	11.85	12.04	12.23	12.43	12.62
26	11.23	11.42	11.61	11.80	11.99	12.19	12.38	12.57
28	11.14	11.33	11.52	11.72	11.91	12.11	12.31	12.50
30	11.07	11.26	11.46	11.66	11.85	12.05	12.25	12.45
35	10.96	11.16	11.36	11.56	11.76	11.96	12.17	12.37
40	10.90	11.10	11.31	11.51	11.72	11.92	12.13	12.33

YEARS	RATE							
	15.00%	15.25%	15.50%	15.75%	16.00%	16.25%	16.50%	16.75%
1	90.26	90.38	90.50	90.62	90.74	90.85	90.97	91.09
2	48.49	48.61	48.73	48.85	48.97	49.09	49.21	49.33
3	34.67	34.79	34.92	35.04	35.16	35.29	35.41	35.53
4	27.84	27.96	28.09	28.22	28.35	28.47	28.60	28.73
5	23.79	23.93	24.06	24.19	24.32	24.46	24.59	24.72
6	21.15	21.29	21.42	21.56	21.70	21.83	21.97	22.11
7	19.30	19.44	19.58	19.72	19.87	20.01	20.15	20.30
8	17.95	18.10	18.24	18.39	18.53	18.68	18.83	18.98
9	16.93	17.08	17.23	17.38	17.53	17.68	17.83	17.99
10	16.14	16.29	16.45	16.60	16.76	16.91	17.07	17.23
11	15.51	15.67	15.83	15.99	16.15	16.31	16.47	16.63
12	15.01	15.18	15.34	15.50	15.66	15.83	15.99	16.16
13	14.61	14.77	14.94	15.10	15.27	15.44	15.61	15.78
14	14.28	14.44	14.61	14.78	14.95	15.12	15.30	15.47
15	14.00	14.17	14.34	14.52	14.69	14.87	15.04	15.22
16	13.77	13.95	14.12	14.30	14.48	14.65	14.83	15.01
17	13.58	13.76	13.94	14.12	14.30	14.48	14.66	14.84
18	13.42	13.60	13.78	13.96	14.15	14.33	14.51	14.70
19	13.29	13.47	13.65	13.84	14.02	14.21	14.39	14.58
20	13.17	13.36	13.54	13.73	13.92	14.11	14.29	14.48
21	13.08	13.26	13.45	13.64	13.83	14.02	14.21	14.40
22	12.99	13.18	13.37	13.56	13.75	13.95	14.14	14.33
23	12.92	13.12	13.31	13.50	13.69	13.89	14.08	14.27
24	12.86	13.06	13.25	13.44	13.64	13.83	14.03	14.23
25	12.81	13.01	13.20	13.40	13.59	13.79	13.99	14.18
26	12.77	12.97	13.16	13.36	13.56	13.75	13.95	14.15
28	12.70	12.90	13.10	13.30	13.50	13.70	13.90	14.10
30	12.65	12.85	13.05	13.25	13.45	13.65	13.86	14.06
35	12.57	12.78	12.98	13.19	13.39	13.59	13.80	14.00
40	12.54	12.74	12.95	13.16	13.36	13.57	13.77	13.98

MONTHLY PAYMENT NEEDED TO AMORTIZE A $1000 LOAN

YEARS	RATE							
	17.00%	17.25%	17.50%	17.75%	18.00%	18.25%	18.50%	18.75%
1	91.21	91.33	91.45	91.57	91.68	91.80	91.92	92.04
2	49.45	49.57	49.69	49.81	49.93	50.05	50.17	50.29
3	35.66	35.78	35.91	36.03	36.16	36.28	36.41	36.53
4	28.86	28.99	29.12	29.25	29.38	29.51	29.64	29.77
5	24.86	24.99	25.13	25.26	25.40	25.53	25.67	25.81
6	22.25	22.39	22.53	22.67	22.81	22.95	23.10	23.24
7	20.44	20.59	20.73	20.88	21.02	21.17	21.32	21.46
8	19.13	19.28	19.43	19.58	19.73	19.88	20.03	20.19
9	18.14	18.30	18.45	18.61	18.76	18.92	19.08	19.23
10	17.38	17.54	17.70	17.86	18.02	18.18	18.35	18.51
11	16.79	16.96	17.12	17.28	17.45	17.61	17.78	17.95
12	16.32	16.49	16.66	16.83	17.00	17.17	17.34	17.51
13	15.95	16.12	16.29	16.46	16.64	16.81	16.98	17.16
14	15.64	15.82	15.99	16.17	16.34	16.52	16.70	16.88
15	15.40	15.57	15.75	15.93	16.11	16.29	16.47	16.65
16	15.19	15.37	15.55	15.74	15.92	16.10	16.28	16.47
17	15.02	15.21	15.39	15.58	15.76	15.95	16.13	16.32
18	14.88	15.07	15.26	15.44	15.63	15.82	16.01	16.20
19	14.77	14.96	15.15	15.34	15.53	15.72	15.91	16.10
20	14.67	14.86	15.05	15.25	15.44	15.63	15.82	16.02
21	14.59	14.79	14.98	15.17	15.37	15.56	15.76	15.95
22	14.53	14.72	14.91	15.11	15.31	15.50	15.70	15.90
23	14.47	14.67	14.86	15.06	15.26	15.45	15.65	15.85
24	14.42	14.62	14.82	15.02	15.21	15.41	15.61	15.81
25	14.38	14.58	14.78	14.98	15.18	15.38	15.58	15.78
26	14.35	14.55	14.75	14.95	15.15	15.35	15.55	15.75
28	14.30	14.50	14.70	14.90	15.11	15.31	15.51	15.72
30	14.26	14.46	14.67	14.87	15.08	15.28	15.48	15.69
35	14.21	14.42	14.62	14.83	15.03	15.24	15.45	15.65
40	14.19	14.40	14.60	14.81	15.02	15.22	15.43	15.64

YEARS	RATE							
	19.00%	19.25%	19.50%	19.75%	20.00%	20.25%	20.50%	20.75%
1	92.16	92.28	92.40	92.52	92.64	92.76	92.88	93.00
2	50.41	50.54	50.66	50.78	50.90	51.02	51.15	51.27
3	36.66	36.79	36.91	37.04	37.17	37.30	37.42	37.55
4	29.91	30.04	30.17	30.30	30.44	30.57	30.70	30.84
5	25.95	26.08	26.22	26.36	26.50	26.64	26.78	26.92
6	23.38	23.53	23.67	23.81	23.96	24.10	24.25	24.39
7	21.61	21.76	21.91	22.06	22.21	22.36	22.51	22.66
8	20.34	20.49	20.65	20.80	20.96	21.11	21.27	21.43
9	19.39	19.55	19.71	19.87	20.03	20.19	20.35	20.52
10	18.67	18.84	19.00	19.17	19.33	19.50	19.66	19.83
11	18.12	18.28	18.45	18.62	18.79	18.96	19.13	19.30
12	17.68	17.85	18.02	18.20	18.37	18.55	18.72	18.90
13	17.33	17.51	17.69	17.86	18.04	18.22	18.40	18.58
14	17.06	17.24	17.42	17.60	17.78	17.96	18.14	18.32
15	16.83	17.02	17.20	17.38	17.57	17.75	17.94	18.12
16	16.65	16.84	17.03	17.21	17.40	17.59	17.78	17.96
17	16.51	16.70	16.88	17.07	17.26	17.45	17.65	17.84
18	16.39	16.58	16.77	16.96	17.15	17.35	17.54	17.73
19	16.29	16.48	16.68	16.87	17.07	17.26	17.46	17.65
20	16.21	16.41	16.60	16.80	16.99	17.19	17.39	17.58
21	16.15	16.34	16.54	16.74	16.93	17.13	17.33	17.53
22	16.09	16.29	16.49	16.69	16.89	17.09	17.29	17.49
23	16.05	16.25	16.45	16.65	16.85	17.05	17.25	17.45
24	16.01	16.21	16.41	16.61	16.82	17.02	17.22	17.42
25	15.98	16.18	16.39	16.59	16.79	16.99	17.20	17.40
26	15.96	16.16	16.36	16.56	16.77	16.97	17.18	17.38
28	15.92	16.12	16.33	16.53	16.74	16.94	17.15	17.35
30	15.89	16.10	16.30	16.51	16.72	16.92	17.13	17.33
35	15.86	16.07	16.27	16.48	16.69	16.89	17.10	17.31
40	15.85	16.05	16.26	16.47	16.68	16.89	17.09	17.30

MONTHLY PAYMENT NEEDED TO AMORTIZE A $1000 LOAN

YEARS	21.00%	21.25%	21.50%	21.75%	22.00%	22.25%	22.50%	22.75%
1	93.12	93.24	93.36	93.48	93.60	93.72	93.84	93.96
2	51.39	51.51	51.64	51.76	51.88	52.01	52.13	52.25
3	37.68	37.81	37.94	38.07	38.20	38.32	38.45	38.58
4	30.97	31.11	31.24	31.38	31.51	31.65	31.78	31.92
5	27.06	27.20	27.34	27.48	27.62	27.77	27.91	28.05
6	24.54	24.69	24.84	24.98	25.13	25.28	25.43	25.58
7	22.82	22.97	23.12	23.28	23.43	23.59	23.74	23.90
8	21.59	21.74	21.90	22.06	22.22	22.38	22.54	22.70
9	20.68	20.84	21.01	21.17	21.34	21.50	21.67	21.84
10	20.00	20.17	20.34	20.50	20.67	20.85	21.02	21.19
11	19.48	19.65	19.82	20.00	20.17	20.35	20.52	20.70
12	19.07	19.25	19.43	19.61	19.78	19.96	20.14	20.32
13	18.76	18.94	19.12	19.30	19.48	19.67	19.85	20.03
14	18.51	18.69	18.88	19.06	19.25	19.43	19.62	19.81
15	18.31	18.50	18.69	18.87	19.06	19.25	19.44	19.63
16	18.15	18.34	18.53	18.72	18.92	19.11	19.30	19.49
17	18.03	18.22	18.41	18.61	18.80	18.99	19.19	19.38
18	17.93	18.12	18.32	18.51	18.71	18.90	19.10	19.30
19	17.85	18.04	18.24	18.44	18.63	18.83	19.03	19.23
20	17.78	17.98	18.18	18.38	18.58	18.77	18.97	19.17
21	17.73	17.93	18.13	18.33	18.53	18.73	18.93	19.13
22	17.69	17.89	18.09	18.29	18.49	18.69	18.90	19.10
23	17.65	17.85	18.06	18.26	18.46	18.66	18.87	19.07
24	17.62	17.83	18.03	18.23	18.44	18.64	18.84	19.05
25	17.60	17.81	18.01	18.21	18.42	18.62	18.83	19.03
26	17.58	17.79	17.99	18.20	18.40	18.61	18.81	19.02
28	17.56	17.76	17.97	18.17	18.38	18.59	18.79	19.00
30	17.54	17.75	17.95	18.16	18.36	18.57	18.78	18.99
35	17.52	17.72	17.93	18.14	18.35	18.55	18.76	18.97
40	17.51	17.72	17.93	18.13	18.34	18.55	18.76	18.97

YEARS	23.00%	23.25%	23.50%	23.75%	24.00%	24.25%	24.50%	25.00%
1	94.08	94.20	94.32	94.44	94.56	94.69	94.81	95.05
2	52.38	52.50	52.63	52.75	52.88	53.00	53.13	53.38
3	38.71	38.85	38.98	39.11	39.24	39.37	39.50	39.76
4	32.06	32.19	32.33	32.47	32.61	32.75	32.88	33.16
5	28.20	28.34	28.48	28.63	28.77	28.92	29.06	29.36
6	25.73	25.88	26.03	26.18	26.33	26.48	26.64	26.94
7	24.05	24.21	24.37	24.52	24.68	24.84	25.00	25.32
8	22.87	23.03	23.19	23.35	23.52	23.68	23.85	24.18
9	22.00	22.17	22.34	22.51	22.68	22.85	23.02	23.36
10	21.36	21.53	21.71	21.88	22.05	22.23	22.40	22.75
11	20.87	21.05	21.23	21.41	21.59	21.76	21.94	22.30
12	20.50	20.68	20.87	21.05	21.23	21.41	21.60	21.97
13	20.22	20.40	20.59	20.77	20.96	21.15	21.33	21.71
14	20.00	20.18	20.37	20.56	20.75	20.94	21.13	21.51
15	19.82	20.01	20.20	20.40	20.59	20.78	20.97	21.36
16	19.69	19.88	20.07	20.27	20.46	20.66	20.85	21.24
17	19.58	19.77	19.97	20.17	20.36	20.56	20.76	21.15
18	19.49	19.69	19.89	20.09	20.29	20.49	20.68	21.08
19	19.43	19.63	19.83	20.03	20.23	20.43	20.63	21.03
20	19.38	19.58	19.78	19.98	20.18	20.38	20.58	20.99
21	19.33	19.54	19.74	19.94	20.14	20.34	20.55	20.95
22	19.30	19.50	19.71	19.91	20.11	20.32	20.52	20.93
23	19.27	19.48	19.68	19.89	20.09	20.29	20.50	20.91
24	19.25	19.46	19.66	19.87	20.07	20.28	20.48	20.89
25	19.24	19.44	19.65	19.85	20.06	20.26	20.47	20.88
26	19.22	19.43	19.63	19.84	20.05	20.25	20.46	20.87
28	19.20	19.41	19.62	19.82	20.03	20.24	20.44	20.86
30	19.19	19.40	19.61	19.81	20.02	20.23	20.44	20.85
35	19.18	19.39	19.59	19.80	20.01	20.22	20.43	20.84
40	19.17	19.38	19.59	19.80	20.01	20.21	20.42	20.84

HOW TO DETERMINE MONTHLY LOAN PAYMENTS IN TEN SECONDS

CONDITIONS

1. USE A CALCULATOR. PUT FACTORS IN MEMORY, OR TAPE ON BACK OF CALCULATOR.

2. IT IS AN AMORTIZED LOAN.

3. TERM IS FOR 30 YEARS, VARIABLE OR FIXED.

Percent per Annum	Factors: Multiply Factors by Number of Thousands	Percent per Annum	Factors: Multiply Factors by Number of Thousands
7.00	6.6534	12.00	10.2862
7.25	6.8219	12.25	10.4790
7.50	6.9925	12.50	10.6726
8.00	7.3379	12.75	10.8670
8.50	7.6894	13.00	11.0620
8.75	7.8671	13.50	11.4542
9.00	8.0463	14.00	11.8488
9.25	8.2268	14.50	12.2456
9.50	8.4086	15.00	12.6445
9.75	8.5916	15.50	13.0452
10.00	8.7758	16.00	13.4476
10.50	9.1474	16.50	13.8515
11.00	9.5233	17.00	14.2568
11.25	9.7127	17.50	14.6633
11.50	9.9030	18.00	15.0709
11.75	10.0941		

EXAMPLE:

An $83,212 loan @ 9.5%, 30 years, is 83.212 × 8.4086 = $ 699.70 per month.

Note that the factor for 11.75% is ten dollars per thousand or equal to one percent. Given the loan amount, simply move the decimal two places to the left for the monthly payment. A handy reference point. Therefore a $100,000 loan is $1,000 per month; $150,000 loan is $1,500 per month; $200,000 loan is $2,000 per month. By keeping this in your memory bank, you can do a rough estimate of loan payments in your head.

THE PAGE YOU MUST UNDERSTAND

OR CONSIDER BANKRUPTCY

A SIMPLE PROPERTY ANALYSIS

PURCHASE PRICE	**$100,000**
LOAN . . . . (—)	**80,000**
DOWN PAYMENT (EQUITY)	**20,000**

- -

SCHEDULED ANNUAL INCOME (GROSS INCOME)	$ 19,000
VACANCY FACTOR & BAD DEBTS . . . . (—)	1,000
EFFECTIVE GROSS INCOME	18,000
EXPENSES (FIXED & OPERATING) . . . . (—)	8,000
NET INCOME	10,000
DEBT SERVICE (LOAN PAYMENTS) . . . . (—)	9,000
CASH FLOW (GROSS SPENDABLE INCOME, BEFORE TAXES)	1,000

- -

INCOME TAX (ALLOWING FOR *DEPRECIATION, LOAN INTEREST EXPENSES,* ETC.)	NONE
NET SPENDABLE INCOME (AFTER-TAX CASH FLOW)	1,000
EQUITY BUILD-UP (APPRECIATION OF FAIR MARKET VALUE & LOAN PAY DOWN)	$ 12,000

- -

DON'T FORGET

LOAN AMOUNT = PURCHASE PRICE (—) DOWN PAYMENT

EFFECTIVE GROSS INCOME = GROSS INCOME (—) VACANCY FACTOR & BAD DEBTS

NET INCOME = EFFECTIVE GROSS INCOME (—) EXPENSES

CASH FLOW = NET INCOME (—) DEBT SERVICE

NET SPENDABLE INCOME = CASH FLOW (—) INCOME TAX

INSERT YOUR OWN NUMBERS & THAT'S IT!

QUOTATIONS FROM GREAT LEADERS
ALPHABETICAL BY AUTHOR

Real estate men sell civilization as much as land.
R. B. Armstrong [economist and author]

Buy on the fringe and wait. *Buy land near a growing city!* Buy real estate when other people want to sell. Hold what you buy!
John Jacob Astor [1763-1848]

I have always felt that the best security of civilization is the dwelling, and upon properly appointed and becoming dwellings depends more than anything else the improvement of mankind. Such dwellings are the nursery of all domestic virtues.
Benjamin Disraeli, Earl of Beaconsfield [1804-1881]

Land is part of God's estate in the globe: and when a parcel of ground is deeded to you, and you walk over it, and call it your own, it seems as if you had come into partnership with the original proprietor of the earth.
Henry Ward Beecher [1813-1887]

To see the world in a grain of sand,
Infinity in a wild flower,
To hold the earth in the palm of your hand,
And eternity in an hour.
William Blake [1757-1827]

When you own a piece of the earth, you own something *Permanent, Real* — something that cannot be taken away from you, something that, if intelligently chosen, will provide for your old age.
Arthur Brisbane [1864-1936]

Statisticians advise us to buy stock, but I advise you to buy real estate. When you buy real estate you can go to bed at night perfectly comfortable, for you know it will be there tomorrow. Investments in stocks and bonds, depending as they do largely on management, may be good today and lost tomorrow. A minority stock holder has very little say so as to how his dollar is used. In buying real estate, however, you are the sole owner and manager. You have a freedom of possession which other instruments do not give. No one can freeze you out. No one can run you off. It is yours. I made a real estate deal sixteen years ago against a banker's advise, and sold the property in five years for over $100,000 profit, plus 6 per cent income. If I had put this profit back in stock, I would have lost practically all of it when the crash came.
Senator W. E. Brock

A fool and his money are soon parted.
George Buchanan [1506-1582]

We recognize the risks of unconventional investing, but the true test of performance in the handling of money is the record of achievement, not the opinion of the respectable. We have the preliminary impression that over the long run caution has cost our colleges and universities much more than imprudence or excessive risk-taking.
McGeorge Bundy, Ford Foundation

All that is necessary for the forces of evil to win the world is for enough good men to do nothing.
Edmund Burke [1729-1797]

Ninety per cent of all millionaires become so through owning real estate. More money has been made in real estate than in all industrial investments combined. The wise young man or wage earner of today invests his money in real estate.
Andrew Carnegie [1837-1919]

Home is the summary of all other institutions.
Chopin [1810-1849]

Land monopoly is not the only monopoly, but it is by far the greatest of monopolies — it is a perpetual monopoly, and it is the mother of all other forms of monopoly.
Winston Churchill [1874-1965]

A man's dignity may be enhanced by the house he lives in.
Cicero [106-43 B.C.]

No investment on earth is so safe, so sure, so certain to enrich its owner as undeveloped realty. I always advise my friends to place their savings in realty near some growing city. There is no such savings bank anywhere.
Grover Cleveland [1837-1908]

The ownership of a home, the feeling of independence that comes with the possession of a bit of the earth are among the most powerful incentives to high civic interest and usefulness.
Calvin Coolidge [1872-1933]

If I could live my life again I would marry early—before twenty years . . . I would have an individual home, no matter where I had to move to get it. I would sacrifice everything . . . to give my bride a spot all her own. As for happiness, I would look for it not in any lasting physical allurement but in our partnership in helping our home and our children grow. For a home must grow, too, with the care and love of years until it becomes a part of life—an old friend to whom we willingly return!
Will Durant [in an editorial entitled "Modern Marriage]

Imagination is more important than knowledge.
Albert Einstein [1879-1955]

The first farmer was the first man, and all historic nobility rests on possession and use of land.
Ralph Waldo Emerson [1803-1882]

Fortune favors the audacious.
Erasmus [1466-1536]

Buying real estate is not only the best way, the quickest way, the safest way, but the *only* way to become wealthy.
Marshall Field [1835-1906]

Our stock of everything useful, which cannot be increased, becomes more and more valuable because there are more and more people to bid for it. The best example is real estate.
B. C. Forbes [business analyst]

The ownership of an urban home, or a farm, unharrassed by fear of loss either through economic pressure or political philosophy, is one of the most stabilizing factors we can have in American civilization.
Glen Frank [noted educator]

If you would know the value of money, go and try to borrow some.
Benjamin Franklin [1706-1790]
Poor Richard's Almanac

No form of property gives as much consequence to its owners as land. This is true of the past, the present and the future.
James Anthony Froude [1818-1894; historian, in his great work on Caesar]

So far as we can see with any certainty, the quality of value has longer and more constantly attached to the ownership of land than to any other valuable thing. Everywhere, in all time, among all peoples, the possession of land is the base of aristocracy, the foundation of great fortunes, the source of power. Those who own the land must be the masters of the rest. Land can exist without labor but labor cannot exist without the land.
Henry George [1839-1897]

Three things are to be looked to in a building: that it stands on the right spot; that it be securely founded; that it be successfully executed.
Goethe [1749-1822]

Wisdom is only found in truth.
[ibid]

Real estate is an imperishable asset, ever increasing in value. It is the most solid security that human ingenuity has devised. It is the collateral to be preferred above all others, and the safest means of investing money.
Hetty Green [One of the world's richest women, 1835-1916]

Believing that nothing can do more toward the development of the highest attributes of good citizenship than the ownership by every family of its own home, I am always glad to endorse effective efforts to encourage home ownership. Nothing better could happen to the United States than a very notable increase in the ownership of homes.
Warren G. Harding [1865-1923]

Land increases more rapidly in value at the centers and about the circumference of cities.
William E. Harmon [noted realty operator]

The present large proportion of families that own their homes is both the foundation of a sound economic and social system and a guarantee that our society will continue to develop rationally as changing conditions demand. A family that owns its own home takes a pride in it, maintains it better, gets more pleasure out of it, and has a more wholesome, healthful and happy atmosphere in which to bring up children. The home owner has a constructive aim in life. He works harder outside his home; he spends his leisure more profitably, and he and his family live a finer life and enjoy more of the comforts and cultivating influences of our modern civilization. A husband and wife who own their own home are more apt to save. They have an interest in the advancement of a social system that permits the individual to store up the fruits of his labor. As direct taxpayers they take a more active part in local government. Above all, the love of a home is one of the finest instincts and the greatest of inspirations to our people.
Herbert Hoover [1874-1964]

The instinct of ownership is fundamental in man's nature.
William James [1842-1910]

The small landholders are the most precious part of a state.
Thomas Jefferson [1743-1826]
Letter [1785]

To be happy at home is the ultimate result of all ambition, the end to which every enterprise and labor tends and of which every desire prompts the prosecution.
Dr. Samuel Johnson [1700-1784]

I have always liked real estate—farm land, pasture land, timber land and city property. I have had experience with all of them. I guess I just naturally like "the good earth," the foundation of all our wealth.

Jesse H. Jones [former federal government financier]

Every man has by nature the right to possess property as his own.

Pope Leo XIII [1810-1903]
Encyclical Letter [1891]

Property is the fruit of labor; property is desirable; it is a positive good in the world. That some should be rich shows that the others may become rich, and hence is just encouragement to industry and enterprise.

Let not him who is houseless pull down the house of another, but let him work diligently and build one for himself, thus by example assuring that his own shall be safe from violence when built.

Abraham Lincoln [1809-1865]

Delay is ever fatal to those who are prepared.

Lucan [A.D. 39-65]

Landlords grow rich in their sleep.

John Stuart Mill [1806-1873]

A man's true wealth is the good he does in the world.

Mohammed [circa 570-632]

There are so many elements of respectability that come to him who finds permanent shelter for his loved ones. It is a force for law, since a home owner desires protection by law. He acquires respect for the property of others. He wants good, sound government and desires to become an advocate of law and order. Ownership makes him vigilant. I think it was Gladstone who said: "Property always sleeps with one eye open."

John H. Puelicher [president of the American Bankers' Association]

Real estate cannot be lost or stolen, nor can it be carried away. Purchased with common sense, paid for in full, and managed with reasonable care, it is about the safest investment in the world.

Franklin D. Roosevelt [1882-1945]

Every person who invests in well-selected real estate in a growing section of a prosperous community adopts the surest and safest method of becoming independent, for real estate is the basis of wealth.

Theodore Roosevelt [1858-1919]

The substantial wealth of man consists in the earth he cultivates, with its pleasant or serviceable animals and plants and in the rightly produced work of his own hands.

John Ruskin [1819-1900]

Real estate is an imperishable asset, ever increasing in value. It is the most solid security that human ingenuity has devised. It is the basis of all security, and about the only indestructable security.

Russell Sage

Land is a fund of a more stable and permanent nature; and the rent of public lands, accordingly, has been the principal source of the public revenue of many a great nation that was much advanced beyond the shepherd state.

The purchase and improvement of uncultivated land is the most profitable employment of the smallest as well as the greatest capitals, and the road to all the fortune which can be acquired in that country "America."

Adam Smith [1723-1790; economist]

The renter who sings "Home Sweet Home" is kidding himself and serenading the landlord. Rent money once handed over is gone forever but the money you put into a house is still yours. It changes its form—it becomes property instead of gold and simply passes from your right pocket to your left.

Billy Sunday [1863-1935; Evangelist]

It is a comfortable feeling to know that you stand on your own ground. Land is about the only thing that can't fly away.

Anthony Trollope [1815-1882]

No matter where you live—in city, village or farm—hang on to your real estate. It's a good investment and worth all that was paid. Real estate at today's prices is the best investment of which I know. Good real estate at the right prices—is sure to be a thrifty investment. People who own real estate should make every effort to keep it. It's worth every dollar it cost.

Thomas Robinson Ward [banker]

Strongly I am impressed with the beneficial effects which our country would receive if every good citizen of the United States owned his own home!

Geroge Washington [1732-1799]

No house should ever be *on* any hill or on anything. It should be *of* the hill, belonging to it, so hill and house could live together each the happier for the other.

Frank Lloyd Wright [1869-1959; "An Autobiography," 1932]

ROY'S ROT

SUMMARY OF AUTHOR'S RULES OF THUMB
(& WORDS OF ART—WOA)

Overview: These *bons mots* come from widely divergent sources. They are presented as much for enjoyment value as content, but as the old Armenian saying goes, "Many a truth was spoken in jest."

1 You can have appreciation of equity without inflation.

2 A poor reason to buy real estate is only for inflation.

3 Inflation should be an added benefit of ownership, not the main reason to purchase.

4 The cost of money, with high interest, can be too high in relation to the benefits.

5 Don't force it, use a bigger hammer.

6 When the cost of money is too high, it can discourage initiative, and in effect act as a hidden tax on the populace.

7 How do you develop a Rodeo Drive (Beverly Hills) with two-year leases? You don't, but rather pipe rack merchandising with handwritten paper signs.

8 The landlord who does not develop longer leases to encourage the development of successful business operations is damaging his own self-interest.

9 A ten-year lease has a "value add" that is more than nine years over a one-year lease.

10 A capitalization rate using a fixed expense factor or percentage, say 40%, that does not account for the exact actual expenses... amounts to the same as an inflexible gross rent multiplier.

11 Good news, bad news. The good news is that our five million dollar offer was accepted. The bad news is that they want five hundred dollars down.

12 Main concerns of rental property owners are: rent, vacancies, negative cash flow, maintenance and management.

13 About 80% of the population cannot afford to purchase a home. Equity participation is one answer.

14 I can show you how to build a clock, but you will have to wind it.

15 Fake it 'til you make it.

16 I've been down so long it feels like up.

17 What goes around, comes around.

18 The feeling that you understand real estate is similar to being able to hit a speed punching bag at five beats per second while blindfolded.

19 On any particular job it takes about two weeks to learn the rules, and a lifetime to learn the exceptions.

20 There are as many definititions of net, or profit, as there are people.

21 Why do you spend so much time arguing over a contract when you have no intention of living up to it? To provide a basis for renegotiation.

22 It is difficult, if not impossible, to prepare an economic model when this model can be influenced by political decisions.

23 The greatest potentiating effect in real estate is to buy property with nothing or low down payment. Then sell at a profit. Or to create an increase in rental income with a disproportionate increase in fair market value, which represents an increase in equity.

24 After you have established a solid base of income property with a positive cash flow... and then lose it on a misadventure, you won't miss it anymore than you would your eyes.

25 Nothing is more dangerous than an idea when it is the only one you have.

—*Emile Chartier*

26 A simple handwritten statement of facts on an agreement that is witnessed and notarized is a very powerful tool in a court of law. Remember that with a contract, handwritten text takes precedence over typewritten, and typewritten takes precedence over the pre-printed form.

27 The way to succeed is to double your failure rate.
—*Thomas J. Watson*, founder of IBM

28 A rich man with a problem is mother's milk for an attorney.

29 A friend in Alaska states that turnkey (completed) construction by a contractor costs about $80 per square foot, including land. The same quality of manufactured housing made in the "lower 48" and shipped to Alaska runs turnkey about $50 a square foot. The difference being in the increased cost of labor and material in Alaska.

30 A capitalization rate fanatic using a percentage rate of expense that he found in an erudite statistical manual that will not vary based on the actual expenses... is like a statistician who averages the temperature of your body, even though one foot is on ice and the other on fire.

31 I have two buildings for you both priced the same... one has a cap rate of 10%, the other 11%... which one do you want? Only a fool would purchase on these facts alone.

32 The problem with a real IRR (Internal Rate of Return), or FMRR, is that there is none until after the fact.

33 On a foreclosure sale, and others, it is a good idea to come prepared for an overbid with ten or more $5,000 cashier's checks. You will be way ahead of the person who has not thought it through.

34 If you plug in too many variables into a projection, e.g. IRR (Internal Rate of Return)... the computer printout is not worth the paper it is printed on.

35 An interesting viewpoint: On a 100% financed purchase money mortgage, all of the seller's equity is the buyer's debt.

36 Time is money... don't waste it.

37 One difference between an amateur and a professional is the assumption by the professional of a positive outcome.

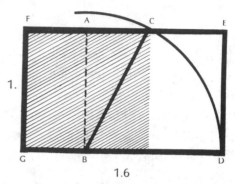

38 Both Michaelangelo and Le Corbusier observed that the height reached by their upstretched arm was two times the height from the ground to their navel. They also observed that their navel height compared to their full height was in the ratio of 1 to 1.6. The proportions of the golden section. It is interesting to note that two belly buttons were the inspiration for so much beauty.

39 This book has taken me from local obscurity to national oblivion.

40 The three circles in Chinese architecture and design represent: science, beauty and religion.

41 Beauty, charm, intelligence, health and wealth... help, but aren't everything. There is a strong relationship between knowledge, power, ability, excellence, happiness and the creation of wealth.

The ability to use knowledge is power. The ability to use this power, within the limits of your own capability in the pursuit of excellence, creates happiness and wealth.

There are many men with the knowledge of football equal to Vince Lombardi, but few apply this knowledge in the pursuit of excellence as he did. This outlook is the thread through the lives of men like Lincoln, Patton, Frank Lloyd Wright and Zeckendorf.

42 Better to have a real estate loan with limited liability than a personal loan with unlimited liability.

43 Worst case with a real estate loan, lender takes property... with a personal loan, lender takes you.

44 There has been more money lost in real estate through over optimism than through over pessimism.

45 If you can't do the time, don't do the crime.

46 Lack of opportunity is usually nothing more than lack of purpose and direction.

47 Bankruptcy is the financial equivalent of making a man a eunuch.

48 On the front door of your property place a sign that reads: In emergency phone... Number of children... Number of pets... Type of pets... Special medical information... For...

49 Tough times don't last, tough people do.

50 If, as the ads claim, all you need is knowledge of real estate to make your fortune... why aren't all the real estate agents and brokers who have this information millionaires?

51 Nothing down, wonderful. Negative cash flow, not good. Fast fuse balloon payment, bad. No financing to be had, very bad. Foreclosure imminent, disaster.

52 Go for Cash. When you must take paper... increase the note by an amount indicated on the "present value of the dollar" table. If this is not clear then review pages on "Internal Rate of Return" and "Discounted Cash Values."

53 The one who loves the least has the power.

54 I thought I was wrong, but I was mistaken.

55 Before granting a loan, a banker likes to know: Will you pay? Can you pay, and did you pay?

56 Babe Ruth led the league in strike outs the year he led in home runs.

57 Jealous people revel in drawing attention to other people's failures.

58 Living well is the best revenge.

59 Fool me once, shame on you. Fool me twice, shame on me.

60 A bird in the hand... means it's difficult to blow your nose.

61 Fixed and non-fixed loans... quick and easy: With a fixed loan the interest and loan payments do not change for the life of the loan. With a non-fixed loan (or mortgage) the interest rate can change with the CPI, treasury bill rate or other interest rate indicator. When the interest rate changes, so therefore does the loan payment and/or the length of the loan.

62 It is rare, if ever, when *all* aspects of real estate are down. If housing sales are down... rental sales increase. If residential income is down... commercial sales can be doing well. Know your market.

63 When you are reclined on your cantilevered sundeck overlooking the crashing surf and sipping your pina colada... it is hard to feel like a loser. You can create your own ambience for success.

64 When you are considering the purchase of two similar properties, one of which is in poor repair, but much less expensive... obtain firm quotes to have this property equal or exceed the quality of the other property. If the total cost of the property including remodeling is less than the cost of the improved property... then your choice becomes obvious. Fortunes are made creating beauty out of nothingness.

65 When you are calculating your potential profits on a transaction... remember to include the cost of carrying a loan. A million dollar loan at 20% is $200,000 for the year. This can eat you alive.

66 People can be divided into three groups: those who *make* things happen, those who *watch* things happen, and those who *wonder* what happened.

67 The road to success is always under construction.

68 If your goal is to have one hundred million dollars... invest one million today at ten per cent interest and wait 48 years.

69 Greed for land is unknown to the Australian aborigines. When they grasp a handful of earth and let it sift through their fingers, it is not to covet the earth, but to enhance their feeling of being as one with the universe.

70 It seems logical that the cost of a lease should be at least as much as the interest the owner could receive at the bank on the fair market value of the property.

71 If you buy property to own and not to sell... then you won't be sorry if you must hold for a distant sale.

72 The wine is more important than the bottle. The use of real estate can be more important than the property.

73 If you are the owner of two buildings consider connecting them with an arched skylight. This "streetscape," an open-ended pedestrian thoroughfare, would do well to emulate the Gallerias of Milan and San Francisco.

74 Too many people are busy being busy.

YOU PUT DOWN
$10,000

$10,000

$100,000
PURCHASE PRICE

YOU HAVE 90% LEVERAGE

75 Leveree, the one who is being leveraged.

76 The investor in an equity participation deal wants to leverage his investment about 2½ times. For example, 20% down payment to return 50% on the profit.

77 You have two diverse philosophies at work with rental property. The landlord is trying to make a living on his investment. The tenant is not concerned if the property makes money, he wants a nice place to live. These different objectives are the basis of most tenant problems. Common objectives will help solve the problem.

78 A broker on the rocks has his license on ice.

79 One point on a million dollars is $10,000 or 1%.

80 A seller who does not want to have the problems of management, but does want the benefit of appreciation on the property, should consider an equity participation plan. The seller can leave cash (equity) in for the down payment portion of his participation, say 20% for 50% of the profit (over the new purchase price) in five years. The buyer has the advantage of buying for little or nothing down. The seller can have his cake and eat it too.

81 When you have a split of spouses from a home... you have an in-house spouse and an out-house spouse.

82 Advertising costs, publicity is free.

83 Two rules of success: First, innoculate yourself with the worst possible scenario... you will then develop antibodies against failure. Second, visualize the goals you wish to obtain. When you are there it will be *deja vu*.

84 Using the "rule of 72," a property worth $200,000 and increasing in value, based on an inflation rate of 8% per year, will be worth $400,000 in 9 years. Wait another 9 years and it will be worth $800,000. Patience is definitely a virtue.

84 If your tenant is late with the rent, any late fees can be subtracted from the security deposit.

85 One standard with equity sharing is that the tenant in common who is the investor and puts up 20% of the purchase price as down payment, will receive 50% of the tax write-offs and 50% of the profit on sale of the property in five years.

86 Negative leverage, or reverse leverage, occurs when debt service is larger than the net income. There is a negative cash flow.

87 Negative amortization occurs when the loan payments are not high enough to pay all of the interest. The loan principal is therefore becoming larger, rather than smaller. Our federal government has this problem.

88 Beware of reckless eyeballing of hysterical monuments.

89 Take an expert to lunch and you pay. It is the most cost-effective way to obtain information without any phone interruptions.

90 What is scarce today will be scarcer tomorow.

91 80% of all sales are made after the 5th call.
48% of salespeople quit after 1 call.
25% of salespeople quit after 2 calls.
12% quit after 3 calls.
5% quit after 4 calls.
10% keep on calling and then make 80% of all sales.

92 People do what you _in_spect, not what you _ex_pect.

93 In lieu of cash you could put in new carpets and drapes as a security deposit.

94 Name a tax write-off received without spending any dollars? _Depreciation._

95 ABC... Always Be Closing (the deal).

96 KYMS... Keep Your Mouth Shut.

97 You have two ears and one mouth... and they should be used in about that proportion.

98 KISS... Keep It Simple, Stupid.

99 We have two choices... to be an axe or a chopping block. The neck on the block belongs to the one who does not choose.

100 One day you are drinking wine, the next day picking the grapes.

101 Better to have a 50% tax on $20,000 and keep $10,000 tax-free, than a $10,000 loss (write-off) and keep nothing. Note that the difference between the two examples is $20,000. Don't outsmart yourself with tax losses.

102 So you do not want the extra $100,000 in cash now on the sale of your property because it will put you in a higher tax bracket. Wait a minute and analyze. You will pay tax on the $100,000 when you finally do receive it. Could you not pay the tax, invest the $100,000 and make enough on the investment to pay any additional tax?

103 It's hard by the yard, but a cinch by the inch.

104 As the urban cowboy was "looking for love in all the wrong places," so the investor can with real estate.

105 Out of the mud grows the lotus.

106 Jesus saves, but Moses invests.

107 On foreclosure property, or REO (Real Estate Owned property), it is prudent to be on good terms with the bank or savings and loan manager who lists these properties as he can give you special insight.

108 Edifice complex: a mania to build.

109 If you have one million dollars going into escrow, then wire funds bank to bank (electronic transfer) without a check, in order for interest to start at the exact close of escrow.

110 When you work on solutions try not to become part of the problem.

111 Make lemonade out of the lemon.

112 Forewarned is forearmed.

113 Albert Einstein used his Princeton University paychecks as bookmarks.

114 If you are so smart, why aren't you rich?

115 Pitching always comes before hitting.

116 Publish or perish.

117 If it is too good to be true, it probably is.

118 It's not how much smoke you blow, it's how hard you blow it.

119 The most creative financing of the future could well be the limited partnership syndication, including equity participation.

120 Avulsion is fast, erosion is slow.

121 If you are going to play the market, be a bull or a bear... not a pig.

122 We will sell no house before its time.

123 Nothing down... balloons up... get a longer string.

124 The easiest person to deceive is oneself.

125 What "rosebud" was to Citizen Kane, the tattooed words above the wings on the arm of a fellow paratrooper are to me: "Death before Dishonor."

126 You can't tell... but you can *sell* a book by its cover.

127 Cash is king... but a well "seasoned" (good record of payment), high interest, and secured note is a prince.

128 You are what you think.

129 Keep your eye on the doughnut, not the hole.

130 Your goals and purpose on this planet should be crystal clear.

131 Technical information doubles every five years. Are you keeping up?

132 Try to find a job you like; don't just look for wealth.

133 Inundata... too much data.

134 Work *smart* and hard, not just hard.

135 The ring of depressed property around the center of a vibrant growing city is one area of investment opportunity.

136 Make stepping stones out of stumbling blocks.

137 Make it snappy and be unhappy.

138 A penny held over your eye can blot out your vision.

139 Move one grain of sand and you change the structure of the entire universe.

140 All the darkness in the world cannot put out the light of one candle.

141 There is more objection to the tax complications than there is to the amount of the tax. —*President Ronald Reagan*

142 If the owner of a commercial property has a problem he usually thinks in terms of selling. A possible better solution is to have a professional management firm take over and create a Master Ground Lease (MGL) with triple net to the owner.

143 Make your move. It is usually easier to apologize than to get permission.

144 A ship in port is safe, but that is not what ships were built for.

145 If you are not familiar with corbellated dentillated soffits, rococo entablatures, and italianate curvilinear broken pediments. . . you are probably not familiar with good architecture. But you can still appreciate it.

146 The harder you work, the luckier you get.

147 You can judge a country by the way it treats its least favored citizen. —*John F. Kennedy*

148 Truth hurts less than a discovered lie.

149 Color code a floor plan of all exits and place in halls.

150 SET... Spendable, Equity and Taxable.

151 I know you think you know what I mean, but I am not sure you realize that what you thought I mean was not what I said.

152 It only takes twenty years for a liberal to become a conservative without changing a single idea.

153 Stalin's paranoia was a self-fulfilling prophecy; so is Bucky Fuller's optimism.

154 In monopoly capitalism, price usually equals at least cost plus taxation plus rent plus interest.

155 Poverty doth make cowards of us all. —*Joseph Labadie*

156 Every law creates a whole new criminal class overnight.

157 If this is an out-of-the-body experience, I may never have to go out of my mind again.

158 It is not possible to step into the same river twice. —*Heraclitus*

159 Don't be a captain steering by the wake.

160 There is nothing so unthinkable as thought, unless it be the entire absence of thought. —*Samuel Butler*

161 WHO DARES WINS.
Motto of the British SAS.

162 When a project is in trouble, the investor from Jackass Flats says, "How many days have I left?" The investor from Beverly Hills says, "How much money will it take to cure the problem?"

163 If an investment property breaks even, it is making money because of the tax factors and equity build-up.

164 If you purchase a $60,000 condo for investment and it breaks even... then, worst case, with no inflation for 30 years... you should have a $60,000 nest egg. If you had five you could probably retire in style.

165 Wealth is something other than money... as wisdom is something other than knowledge.

166 There is no five-year lease on life renewable at your option.

167 Avoid the "big pot" concept of throwing everything into one project... have individual profit centers so that you can track performance.

168 If people say "yes" to me fifteen days out of the year, I am a success.

169 Rewards are not automatic.

170 Property management developed as a profession during the great depression... when banks took over property and were forced to manage them.

171 When done right, both making money and spending it can be enjoyable.

172 To sleep nights and not be concerned with a bank or savings and loan "demand for full payment of loan," notify the lender of assumption of any loan, and obtain the lender's approval in writing, before you assume the loan. Or see a real estate attorney to arrange a "special handling."

173 It takes all of our knowledge to make things simple.

174 Same bed, different dream.

175 The only shelter in real estate is depreciation...taxes, interest and expenses are write-offs. There is a difference between shelter and write-offs. With a shelter, there is no cash out-of-pocket, but with a write-off there *is* cash out-of-pocket.

176 Concerned about losing half or all of a property to a wife or live-in? Then consider having them sign and record a "quit claim deed."

177 On a normal foreclosure sale there is a "trustee's deed." On a probate sale there is an "executor's deed," and on a court decree there is a "decree of distribution," which is like a deed.

178 The quintessential communication for clarity was by a Navy pilot flying over the Atlantic during WWII. He stated, "Sighted sub, sank same."

179 He is only rich who owns the day.
—*Ralph Waldo Emerson*

180 Pay long term capital gains, but shelter ordinary income.

181 To be successful and happy, you should be the same person at work that you are at home.

182 The investor has a cash register, the occupant has a home.

183 In real estate you get into trouble not for what you know but for what you *don't* know.

184 Soar like an eagle — go for it.

185 To fully experience the beauty and safety of a sailing ship in a harbor, you must first experience the danger of a turbulent sea.

186 Peel the onion a bit.

187 Considering the alternatives, democracy is the best form of government.
—*Winston Churchill*

188 Knowing math does not make an engineer, any more than knowing real estate law makes an investor.

189 To eliminate "cash flow deficiency," raise rentals and lower expenses.

190 Have you noticed that highly mortgaged (leveraged) properties catch fire, and burn, more readily than free and clear property?

191 POEM... Plan, Organize, Execute, and Manage.

192 Once you have it made (or come close) you will want to consider a "diversified portfolio" for "capital preservation," and to be prepared for the unknown. Such a portfolio would include: cash to cover six months' expenses, stocks, municipal and corporate bonds, money market funds, precious metals, gold and silver coins, gemstones, etc.

193 Remember when an ice cream cone cost only 50¢? Remember when the average house cost only $50,000? Each generation has a different perspective on standard values.

194 Need a million dollar loan? It may well be worth hiring a mortgage banker to help you. It would cost about 2 points (per cent), or $20,000, for their services.

195 An insurance *replacement* policy is better than a *depreciated* value policy.

196 The right time to duplicate your keys is before they are lost.

197 When a master lease is cancelled the sub-leases are usually automatically also cancelled. Watch your sub-lease.

198 You found the perfect property, but can't swing it. Option the property. Write up a complete prospectus, with profit and loss projections, and include inside and outside photos. Obtain a top syndicator to help you form a partnership. Then purchase with up to five other people as limited partners.

199 Never step back when you can step forward... to the side if you must.

200 As per military operations: "Be prepared to hit targets of opportunity."

201 If you can't handle all of the wine, women and song... stop singing.

202 I can sometimes do the work of two men... Laurel and Hardy.

203 The poor save and the rich spend. (As told to the author by a loan officer)

204 In almost all cities the Recorder's Office posts Notices of Default on a bulletin board. Looking at these on a regular basis (or by subscribing to a local private service) you might find an excellent property to bid on.

205 Non-veterans can obtain veteran's property and loans by bidding on them in foreclosure.

206 The tax laws written for the Rockefellers and the Vanderbilts also apply to the self-employed.

207 The key to taxes on the self-employed is the net income, not the gross.

208 You *pay* taxes all year long, so *think* taxes all year long. Keep a log of expenses.

209 In the past two years at least eight non-descript buildings have been converted to bed and breakfast inns in the San Francisco area. The rentals increasing from about $300 per month, or $10 per day, to $100 per day, a tenfold increase in rental income.

210 For an instant MBA remember three things:
  1) Sign all checks yourself until gross sales exceed one hundred million dollars.
  2) Never spend money in anticipation of closing a deal.
  3) Starting small borrow increasingly large amounts from your banker, but pay it all back punctually.   *—Victor Palmieri*

211 The lintel low enough to keep out pomp and pride.
The threshold high enough to turn deceit aside;
The doorband strong enough from robbers to defend.

This door will open at a touch to welcome any friend.

—*Henry Van Dyke*

212 Bottom line on loans: Don't assume you can assume.

213 The grapevine is a goldmine.

214 So the seller wants $200,000 and not a penny less. Fine... I will buy it. Here are my terms: Buyer closing costs and real estate agents commission to be used as the total down payment. Real estate agents commission to be in the form of a straight note, due in full in one year, at an interest rate of 12% per annum. Remaining balance to be in the form of a first loan, payable on a monthly basis, based on an amortization rate of 30 years, with no payment for 90 days from close of escrow, and due in full in 15 years. Buyer to have the right of one transfer of the loan with the same terms and conditions, to a person of worthy credit.

215 Upon the sale of your property the chances are excellent that you have pre-paid your insurance for one year, and have a rebate or credit available to you in escrow. Remember the insurance company will not be looking for you with money in hand.

216 Most title and escrow companies extend a considerable discount on their fees if you buy and sell the same property within two years. Just ask.

217 Success is never certain, failure is never final.

218 If you have a property in foreclosure, consider having the holder of the first loan sell it back to you at the foreclosure sale. The price you pay being the balance of the first loan plus all foreclosure costs, and this total amount being in the form of a new first loan. You are gambling that the holders of the secondary financing will not outbid you. If they don't, you have wiped out all secondary financing with the foreclosure sale.

219 If it looks like a duck, quacks like a duck, and walks like a duck... it's probably a duck.

220 To cover both a high and a low price for tax purposes you may want to have a clause on your deposit receipt that reads: Price is estimated to have a fair market value of $80,000, but is being sold for $70,000 to help cover any repair expenses.

221 Taking a secret profit and then trying to give it back, is like trying to un-rob a bank. Kickbacks are a form of secret profit. The statute of limitations for secret profit is usually ten years.

222 Dead bodies surface.

223 On a deposit receipt the phrase "Property to be purchased in 'as is' condition" is an illusory phrase and cannot apply to hidden or latent defects that are known by either the seller or the agent and not disclosed to the buyer. The seller can write on a deposit receipt, "to the best of his knowledge" there are no latent or hidden defects, and that it is recommended that the buyer hire a licensed contractor to prepare a full report.

224 Weak case, ask for jury; strong case, ask for judge.

225 In a jury trial, the tenant screens jurors for tenants, the landlord screens jurors for landlords.

226 It's not the principle of the thing, it's the money.

227 Knowledge of agent is knowledge of fiduciary of that agent.

228 An agent must present all offers to the seller, even after another offer is accepted. In that case the agent should tell the seller it can be used as a "back up" offer, and should be careful of "breach of contract" if seller breaches the accepted offer.

229 The agent of the seller has the duty to be "fair and honest" to the buyer, even though there is no fiduciary relationship.

230 Use different colored checks for each property account.

231 Landlord can state on lease, "To be occupied only by humans."

232 When a contractor wants to lower the interest rate on houses that he is selling, he can "buy-down" the interest rate. To lower the interest rate 1% for two years would cost about 2 points (2%). For example: If the actual rate of a loan is 13% and the lender wants to have an interest rate of 10%, the rate can be bought-down for 2 points times 3%, or 6%. The buy-down on a $100,000 loan would therefore be $6,000. After two years the interest would revert back to 13%.

233 A future trend in building is to have two or more identical master bedrooms, with a shared living area and kitchen. The house then lends itself to an easy division for two or more persons.

234 The number of shell houses, that is, houses that you finish yourself, is on the increase.

235 TIP... Tailored Installment Program, a variable loan usually with lower initial payments and then payment increases.

236 To calculate 6 months' interest, take ½ of the yearly interest. So 16% per annum is equal to 8% for 6 months.

237 To help sell income property guarantee the rents for one year. Also, you can pre-pay the real estate taxes (tax write-off), so that you can advertise no real estate taxes for one or more years.

238 Having trouble selling a property? Consider selling only the building, and leasing the land to the buyer. You can then sell the land lease to someone else, or keep it for the cash flow.

239 Blended rate... your old loan is at 10% interest, and you want to increase the principal amount, but you don't want to pay the new higher interest, say 14%. Then negotiate with the lender for a blended rate on the new loan of 12%.

240 Great spirits have always encountered violent opposition from mediocre minds.
—Albert Einstein

241 Leasing the land under improved property is a form of financing.

242 Watch out for reverse leverage... where the leveragor becomes the leveragee.

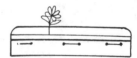

243 Sometimes the means to an end becomes the end.

244 The disruption in your life of five moves is about equal to one fire.

245 What you think of me is none of my business.

246 The map never equals the territory.

247 Of two explanations, the simpler one is more likely to be correct.

248 Knowing when not to make, is as important as knowing when to make a deal.

249 Be sure to determine who are the buyers and who are the sellers.

250 Be careful of what you dream about. You may get it.

251 A high interest note that is unsaleable can be wrapped (AIDT) with a lower interest note with a higher principal.

Example: An $80,000 note at 16% interest can be wrapped with a $100,000 loan at 12%.

Conclusion: Wrap a bad loan with a good loan, and work on the lower interest (a negative wrap), and the increased principal amount.

252   Greater uncertainty, then you need greater liquidity.

253   Vigorish... Mafia interest on a loan has been reported at 5% per week.

254   When the interest rate goes up, the equity goes down.

255   It's difficult to soar with eagles when you work with turkeys.

256   Go duck hunting where the ducks are.

257   What isn't what it is, until it isn't what it is? Answer: Equity.

258   Only a mediocre person is always at his best.

—Somerset Maugham

259   Equal dignities rule... have authority in writing even if you have a telegram.

260   Certain government agencies... Never have so few spent so much for so little.

261   If it was easy, everybody would be doing it.

262   A $100,000 loan with an interest of 11.75% per annum, and fully amortized in 30 years, will have a monthly payment of $1,010 (round number) per month. In 30 years when paid off, you will have paid $363,600!... Will they take $90,000 cash?

BUT I CAN
LIVE IN IT

263   Look for opportunity, not guarantees.

264   A billion here, a billion there, and pretty soon you have spent some real money.

265   In earthquake country, consider seismic anchor bolts. A steel bracket is placed on the stud, a bolt is then placed through the bracket, mud sill, and foundation. By securing the mud sill to the foundation, it helps to prevent the house from slipping off its foundation.

SpaDome.

266   Need an extra room and can spare about $2,000? Consider the SPADOME of Redondo Beach, CA, a most interesting geodesic dome. It is made of clear Lexan, and one model is 12 feet in diameter by 9 feet high. The design is based on futurist Buckminster Fuller's 1951 patent.

267   My price, your terms; your price, *my* terms.

268   ABC — Abundance of Caution.

269   AITD — All inclusive trust deed (wraparound).

270   A first or second loan could be paid in ounces of gold (as law allows) to protect the lender from inflation. For example, you could have a contract to accept two ounces of gold per month for ten years.

271   An individual who joint ventures with a 'dealer,' may then become a 'co-dealer.'

272   As the twig is bent, so the tree grows.

273   A ten — A scale from one to ten used for buildings and women (or men). There are no tens, but you can have two fives.

274   A visit to or by the IRS is now a part of every businessman's life. If you keep good records you will look forward to an IRS audit the way St. Augustine looked forward to confession.

275 Avoid the financial PIT (Probate, Inflation & Taxes).

276 BAR SALE — The seven services of the real estate industry: Buy, Appraise, Rent, Sell, Auction, Lease & Exchange.

277 Battles are won in the tents of generals before the battle begins.

278 Better a $200 attorney's fee than a $20,000 legal error.

279 Better to make a fortune slowly than a bundle quickly.

280 Be your own banker; lend money.

281 A Financial Market Rate of Return (FMRR) is an Internal Rate of Return (IRR), but with more sophistication. It means simply that the interest return on the IRR is invested, as it comes in, in the financial market place. For example, the interest could be invested in a money market fund, or in stocks, bonds, real estate partnerships, et al. The added interest that is received on the interest from the IRR (which is really interest on interest) is then calculated as part of the overall return on the principal.

282 Bigger fool theory — It doesn't matter what you pay for a building, there is always a bigger fool to pay more.

283 Bluebird — A semi-professional with the MOFIA.

284 Buy vacation property during the worst weather, and sell during the best.

285 Capital punishment — is when the government taxes you to get capital in order to go into business in competition with you, and then taxes the profits in your business in order to pay for its losses.

286 CCCL — Elements of a contract: Consent, Capacity, Consideration & Lawfulness.

287 Checking credibility — If the borrower doesn't ask about the interest rate, then the lender better.

288 CIGAR — Major sub-markets of real estate: Commercial, Industrial, Governmental, Agricultural & Residential.

289 COC — Cash On Cash.

290 COLIC — Essentials of a contract: Competent parties, Offer & acceptance, Legality of object, In writing & signed, & Consideration.

291 Concretion as opposed to abstraction.

292 COW — Code Of West (gentlemen's agreement).

293 CRAM — Condominium Reverse Annuity Mortgage.

294 Curtilage — The enclosed ground space around a building, such as lawn or patio.

295 DIC — Doric, Ionic & Corinthian in order of architectural antiquity.

296 Do it once, do it right, and do it now.

297 Don't use a meat cleaver for eye surgery.

298 Don't use your money, use other people's money (OPM).

299 DUE — Disposition, Use, Exclusions, as they relate to ownership.

300 DUST — Essentials of value: Demand, Utility, Scarcity, & Transferability.

301 Economic history teaches us that adversity breeds opportunity.

302 Economies of scale — The more units, the greater the volume discount.

303 Figures don't lie, but liars can figure.

304 GAM — Gross Annual Multiplier (same as GRM — Gross Rent Multiplier).

305 Gather ye rosebuds while ye may.

306 Gift your house to a charitable organization, then take a tax write-off for the value of the house, and live in your gift for the rest of your life.

307 GIGO — Garbage In, Garbage Out.

308 GNOME—ENCLATURE.

309 Golden Rule — Whoever has the gold makes the rules.

310 Go to a stationery store (or title company) and buy a pre-printed *note*. Then type in an amount equal to the equity in your house, and with payment terms that are comfortable. You have now created an instrument that can be used as down payment on any property you desire. Note that no cash has been used, only a piece of paper that represents value.

311 Hemingway buyer — A rich person. When Hemingway was aked how the rich are different, he said, "They have more money."

312 If interest rates rise — all other things being equal — the price of property should fall.

313 If it is not money, it is not a lien. An *encumbrance* is not always a *lien*, but a lien is always an encumbrance.

314 If there are no 'right to light' laws in your city, be sure before you install a solar energy system that you won't be 'overshadowed.'

315 If there is a chance you will not qualify for a loan on a property, have the seller refinance and take out a large portion of his cash in this manner. As a buyer you can then assume the new loan from the seller. It is easier to assume an existing loan than to create a new one.

316 If the seller wants your cash and not paper, use your property as down payment, but 'guarantee the sale of property within 18 months.'

317 If you do not know a city, try a sightseeing bus tour (both the pleasure tour and the business tour). At a minimum you will then know the key areas and not appear to be a real estate dummy.

318 If you work 40 weeks a year (excluding all vacations and holidays), five days a week, or 200 days per year, and make $200,000, you are averaging $1,000 per day. If you make $100,000, it is $500 per day. $50,000 per year is $250 per day, and $25,000 per year is $125 per day. Equity build up could be included as part of the income as it is adding to your net worth. Did you make your quota today?

319 In certain sections of government, they keep the monkeys and cut down the tallest trees.

320 In contracts, the big print giveth and the small print taketh away.

321 In direct relation to the costs of transportation, energy, fuel, land, etc., the move back to the city becomes more practical, and the need to improve the rotting core increases.

322 In the land of the blind, the one-eyed man is king.

323 Invest in inflation. It's the only thing going up.

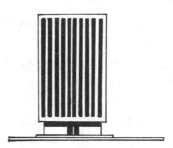

324 Investors should have the ability to visualize property *after* improvements.

325 It is easier to get in a project than to get out.

326 It is possible and practical under certain circumstances to make a *'two-tier price offer.'* One price under one condition, and an increased price under another condition.

327 It only makes sense to borrow money when the cost of borrowing is less than the return on the invested money.

328 KELVIN MOF — A MOF with no money down. Kelvin refers to the term in physics of "absolute zero."

329 Land has an infinite useful life.

330 Land salesmen have a lot on their minds.

331   Land should double in value every five years. This will help cover inflation, taxes and payments.

332   Leverage is the use of borrowed money to magnify gains and losses.

333   Lost opportunity cost. Take the money and run. The dollars you must discount to receive the money now, subtracted from the dollars to be made by having the money now, is the *lost opportunity cost.* So why lose?

334   Margin of Appreciation (MOA) — The difference in interest between the inflation rate and your loan rate, e.g., if inflation is 14% and your loan is 12%, you have a 2% MOA. It can be positive or negative.

335   MOF — Mount Olympus Formula, or modified option formula.

336   MOFIA — Mount Olympus Formula Investment Advisor.

337   Mondo Com Condo — All (100%) commercial condominiums.

338   Much easier to squeeze the toothpaste out of a tube than to put it back.

339   New things succeed, as former things grow old.

340   Next to a bad tenant, a vacancy is a delight.

341   Number of square feet times the cost per square foot (average for area), equals the estimated price of the building or unit.

342   On a lease, set the rent at, say, $500 per month, but if paid on the *first* of the month it is $475.

343   On a tax deferred exchange — Too much equity, then refinance. Too little equity, then pay down the loan.

344   One hand washes the other.

345   One story of a building is about 10 feet high. A ten story building is about 100 feet high.

346   Pay all cash to lower the purchase price, on the order of a 20% discount, then immediately obtain an 80% loan.

347   People who know how, work for people who know *why.*

348   Prepayment penalties for paying off a loan early run about the cost of six month's interest.

349   PSZTUL — (PISTOL): Physical Structure, Zoning, Transportation, Utilities & Land are points to check in the purchase of an industrial site.

350   RAW — Ready, Able & Willing. Referring to buyers in an open market to establish a fair market value.

351   Record options and other contracts to help protect your position against future liens.

352   REDI — Rapport, Empathy, Demeanor & Integrity. The author's guidelines.

353   Regarding tax shelters — Consider paying taxes and keeping a smaller profit. Taxes as yet do not exceed 100%.

354   Return on capital is less in a richer country and more in a poorer country.

355   Reverend Ike might be right, "Money is beautiful," (at least what can be done with it).

356   REX — Real Estate Exchange, a tax-deferred exchange (Section 1031, Federal Tax Code).

357   RIC — Reverse Income Condominium (a turkey).

358   RIP — Reverse Income Property (another loser).

359   RURBAN — Transition area from rural to urban.

360   Since cold water is used the most, check the cold water flow on the top floor when inspecting a building.

361 SIP — Sensible Income Project (a winner).

362 Six 'P' Formula — Poor prior preparation = pretty poor performance.

363 Tenants who lose keys and then break windows and doors to gain entry . . . and then ask why the landlord doesn't take care of the place, are a little like the man who killed his mother and father, and then asked for mercy because he was an orphan.

364 The best advice you will ever pay for is professional real estate counseling.

365 The best investment on earth . . . is earth.

366 The building is not overpriced, you are under-paid.

367 The buyer who has himself as a real estate agent may have a fool as a client.

368 The cost approach for appraising buildings usually results in the *highest* appraisal. It is practical to use on new buildings, and *one of a kind* buildings, *e.g.*, post office, church, or city hall.

369 The cost of having nothing is going up. Being broke isn't the luxury it used to be. High inflation irrevocably separates the rich from the poor.

370 The essence of good architecture is not only superb design, but also superior economics.

371 The four C's of credit are Capacity, Collateral, Character & Cash.

372 The goal of government should be to provide the opportunity for all citizens to own a home.

373 Throughout recorded history a fine suit cost about one ounce of gold; a superior dwelling, a thousand ounces.

374 'Time spent on reconnaissance is never wasted.' —*A military dictum*

375 The Robie house in Chicago, and "Falling Waters" in Bear Run, Pennsylvania, are probably two of the most architecturally important houses in America.

376 To establish a good credit rating, deposit $1,000 (or more) in three (or more) banks. One week later borrow $1,000 from the same banks. Make three payments on each loan and then pay off the loan. You have now established a good credit rating and three references.

377 To invest in real estate is to play "Monopoly" with real money.

378 To obtain a building with no cash down, consider giving the seller a loan the *principal* of which *increases* with the CPI (Consumer Price Index). The seller is covered for inflation, and is more inclined to accept nothing down (or low down).

379 Uncle Sam Demands Taxes — This helps to remember the elements of value: Utility, Scarcity, Demand & Transferability.

380 Use about ¼% to ½% of the purchase price per month on an option payment.

381 Use accoustical glass (like shatter-proof glass) or double-pane to eliminate traffic noise.

382 Use equity in one project to leverage into another.

383 Use lead-lined sheetrock (used in recording studios) to stop outside noise.

384 WADED — Five methods of acquiring title to property: Will, Adverse possession, Deed, Estoppel & Descent.

385 We have so much democracy we can't get anything done.

386 We usually undervalue *cash flow* and overvalue *capital gain*.

387 When Joe Smith is buying for another party, it is usually best to write on the *Deposit Receipt,* "Joe Smith and/or assignee," rather than "nominee."

388 When renting two or more units the tenants tend to balance out each other's behavior. If only one tenant, they would not call the landlord to mention their misdeeds.

389 When selling a property, consider *carrying the first loan* (a purchase money first). The value of the building and equity of the buyer are known facts. It could represent your best investment choice, with positive cash flow, management free, and from a well known security.

390 When you are at the top of your profession you can achieve in an hour what previously took up to a year.

391 WIZARD — A professional with the MOFIA, who helps you along the yellow brick road.

392 Yellow Brick Road — the road that leads to the Bluebird, the Wizard, and the pot of gold (POG).

393 You can depreciate property, not people. If you owned people (slavery) you could depreciate them. This is not moral or legal, so you cannot take a depreciated value of your own life.

394 You make your money when you 'package' and buy right.

395 You should make at least 3.5 times in salary the amount you spend on your loan payments plus expenses.

396 Fifteen billion years ago (round number) all of the real estate in the universe could fit on the head of a pin.

397 God needed but ten commandments to direct our lives, our federal government needs 7,500 codes just for taxes.

398 Any man can make paper, only God can make dirt.

399 Don't sell when the price goes down, "I'm locked in;" dont sell if it goes up, "I can't afford the taxes."

400 Obstacles are opportunities to develop one's sense of humor.

401 Beware of self-fulfilling prophesies.

402 One man's ceiling is another man's floor.

403 Under all is the land.

eugene legend

HOW DO I START?

You start in real estate they way you start in any new venture. Read all you can on the subject (the library has free books), and talk to the most knowledgeable people you can find, e.g., Realtors, bankers and investors. Free literature and information is available at the nearest real estate association. Colleges, high schools and private schools either have courses on investing or can direct you to such a course.

BASICS

After you understand some of the basics, select an area that appeals to you and your pocket book, say an area one mile in diameter. Know the area you select as well or better than the police and firemen responsible for its safety (and contact these people for inside information). Buy a three-ring binder and fill one or more with all the data you can find on your specific area, with emphasis on current property values. In effect *everyone* in your area is a source of information. The more people you know the more information you have. Sources of information are endless but you could start with the postman, salesmen working in the area, Chamber of Commerce, real estate offices, architects, contractors, real estate attorneys, accountants, local merchants, and be sure to visit city hall and obtain maps, zoning regulations, building codes, property tax information, and any future plans or policies.

START LOOKING

Once you have gathered all the necessary facts it is time to look at a minimum of fifty properties, and compare gross rent multipliers, costs per square foot, and amenities. When you are able to look at a property and determine within three percent what it sold for, you then know the territory.

THE FIRST PURCHASE

The first real estate purchase is usually your own home. This is a logical choice and when purchased properly (fair market value with leverage) a very wise one.

From this first stepping-stone you can trade up into a finer home or income property. Or you can retain your home and purchase another house or units.

From this small seed corn can evolve your eventual fortune.

WHERE DOES ALL OF THIS LEAD?

Do you want to continue to trade and buy up and up, until finally you can say, "today Czechoslovakia, tomorrow the world"? Everyone must establish their own goals, and at least have some idea when a level of success and peace of mind has been attained. For one, it could be owning free and clear a few self-sustaining acres with a log cabin in the woods; for another, it could be owning a triple net leased multi-million dollar shopping center.

A good friend practically single-handedly changed the face of a mountain in southern California, and for the better with beautiful architecture and construction. Spending a day with him was intellectually stimulating and physically exhausting. Typically, he would show me three or four homes he was working on, all perfectly integrated to the site and completely unique. He was not adverse to travelling four hundred miles to hand select a particular load of agate, and then build a massive wall fireplace. In between doing this he negotiated ten new building sites and the construction loans. A month after my last fascinating visit with him, he died of a heart attack. I wish he would have stopped for awhile to smell the flowers.

IN CONCLUSION

The author admits to having an enjoyable five years writing this book. The many brilliant investors, accountants and attorneys who added their comments and ideas have provided numerous stimulating days of entertainment and education.

It is not intended that these ideas are set in concrete never to change, or even that they are correct for all time. Rather that these ideas, in total, offer a 'feel' for investing that comes intuitively to the long-standing professional. After a time you 'can smell a good deal,' or a bad one.

At the onset it was determined that no punches would be pulled. . .that we would only play 'hard ball.' No self-serving concepts would be included that were of benefit only to the buyer, seller, agent, owner or renter. The criteria was to serve the truth, and the ideas presented are limited only by the scope and bias of the writer.

The concepts presented herein are the 'best of the best' that the author is aware of in over twenty years of investing. I hope the reader feels it has been a worthwhile journey.

After a few investment battle scars, it becomes as Quick & Easy as rolling off a mortgage.

REAL ESTATE INVESTING
IS A GAME
AND YOU KEEP SCORE
WITH MONEY

IF THE PAGES BETWEEN THESE COVERS
HAVE BEEN READ AND UNDERSTOOD, THEN
IT IS BELIEVED THAT YOU SHOULD GO TO
THE HEAD OF YOUR INVESTMENT CLASS. . .
AT <u>LEAST</u> TO THE HEAD OF THE
SLOW GROUP.

THE END OF THE BEGINNING

INDEX
(CONCORDANCE)

INDEX

INDEX

INDEX

INDEX

INDEX

INDEX

INDEX

Q

INDEX

INDEX

INDEX

ORDER FORM

QUANTITY	ITEM	EACH PRICE	TOTAL
	DROPZONE PRESS · BOOKS		
	REAL ESTATE QUICK & EASY · *FULLY ILLUSTRATED* · *400 PAGES* · *10TH EDITION*	$16.95	$
	WIT & WISDOM OF THE WORLD · *215 PAGES, (ILLUSTRATED)* OVER 2,000 OF THE BEST ONE-LINERS · **RETAIL $12.95**	$4.95	$
	DROPZONE VIDEOS · VHS		
	KENYA · *60 MIN.* · *ON SAFARI* · *THE LAND,* · *THE PEOPLE,* · *THE ANIMALS* · **RETAIL $23.95**	$13.95	$
	EGYPT · *1 HR. 47 MIN.* · *NILE CRUISE FROM CAIRO TO ABU SIMBLE* · *TEMPLE TOURS* **RETAIL $23.95**	$13.95	$
	A MAGNET CALLED EARTH · *THE UNIVERSE QUICK & EASY* INTRODUCTION BY ASTRONAUT RICHARD F. GORDON, JR. (IN PRODUCTION)		
	DROPZONE POSTERS (TUBE OF 10 POSTERS = $19.00)		
	THE AMAZING ANALEMMA · *22"x 27"* · *4 COLOR* · *UNIVERSE* · *ECLIPTIC* · *ZODIAC*	$3.95	$
	THE UNITED STATES OF AMERICA · *22"x 27"* · *4 COLOR* · *FULLY ILLUSTRATED* · *HISTORICAL CHRONOLOGY* · *SUITABLE FOR CLASSROOM OR CITIZENSHIP TEST*		
	THE POINT-SPHERE RADIAL VECTOR, CELESTIAL NAVIGATION SYSTEM *4 COLOR* · *ILLUSTRATES A NEW CONCEPT OF "DEAD RECKONING" SPACE TRAVEL* · *22"x 27"*		
	OTHER DROPZONE PRODUCTS		
	ANALEMMA CARD · *4"x6"* · *2 COLOR* · *PLASTIC* · *THE VIKING'S SECRET* · *A CELESTIAL NAVIGATION ANALOG (CARTON OF 50 =$25.00)*	$2.00	$
	T-SHIRTS · *100% COTTON, BLACK WITH 14" WHITE ANALEMMA* · *S, M, L, & XL* (CIRCLE ONE)	$11.95	$
	CERAMIC TILE · *8"x8"* · *WHITE* · *WITH COMPASS ROSE* · *GLAZED AT 2,000°F* · *TEXT : "ON THIS SPOT YOU ARE OVER THE EXACT CENTER OF EARTH".*	$11.95	$
		TOTAL ORDER	$

I have enclosed my check of money order. I understand each price includes shipping and handling charges.
Please, make checks payable to : R. Maloney, **DZ PRESS** · **FAX : (415) 921– 6776**

<u>SEND ORDER TO: (Please print)</u>

NAME_____ ADDRESS_____

_____ CITY _____

_____ STATE _____ ZIP_____

PHONE (AREA CODE) _____

ORDER FORM

QUANTITY	ITEM	EACH PRICE	TOTAL
	DROPZONE PRESS · BOOKS		
	REAL ESTATE QUICK & EASY · *FULLY ILLUSTRATED* · *400 PAGES* · *10 TH EDITION*	$16.95	$
	WIT & WISDOM OF THE WORLD · *215 PAGES,* (*ILLUSTRATED*) *OVER 2,000 OF THE BEST ONE-LINERS* · **RETAIL $12.95**	$4.95	$
	DROPZONE VIDEOS · VHS		
	KENYA · *60 MIN.* · *ON SAFARI* · *THE LAND,* · *THE PEOPLE,* · *THE ANIMALS* · **RETAIL $23.95**	$13.95	$
	EGYPT · *1 HR. 47 MIN.* · *NILE CRUISE FROM CAIRO TO ABU SIMBLE* · *TEMPLE TOURS* **RETAIL $23.95**	$13.95	$
	A MAGNET CALLED EARTH · *THE UNIVERSE QUICK & EASY INTRODUCTION BY ASTRONAUT RICHARD F. GORDON, JR.* (*IN PRODUCTION*)		
	DROPZONE POSTERS (*TUBE OF 10 POSTERS = $19.00*)		
	THE AMAZING ANALEMMA · *22"x 27"* · *4 COLOR* · *UNIVERSE* · *ECLIPTIC* · *ZODIAC*	$3.95	$
	THE UNITED STATES OF AMERICA · *22"x 27"* · *4 COLOR* · *FULLY ILLUSTRATED* · *HISTORICAL CHRONOLOGY* · *SUITABLE FOR CLASSROOM OR CITIZENSHIP TEST*		
	THE POINT-SPHERE RADIAL VECTOR, CELESTIAL NAVIGATION SYSTEM *4 COLOR* · *ILLUSTRATES A NEW CONCEPT OF "DEAD RECKONING" SPACE TRAVEL* · *22"x 27"*		
	OTHER DROPZONE PRODUCTS		
	ANALEMMA CARD · *4"x6"* · *2 COLOR* · *PLASTIC* · *THE VIKING'S SECRET* · *A CELESTIAL NAVIGATION ANALOG* (*CARTON OF 50 = $25.00*)	$2.00	$
	T-SHIRTS · *100% COTTON, BLACK WITH 14" WHITE ANALEMMA* · *S, M, L, & XL* (CIRCLE ONE)	$11.95	$
	CERAMIC TILE · *8"x8"* · *WHITE* · *WITH COMPASS ROSE* · *GLAZED AT 2,000° F* · *TEXT : "ON THIS SPOT YOU ARE OVER THE EXACT CENTER OF EARTH".*	$11.95	$
		TOTAL ORDER	$

I have enclosed my check of money order. I understand each price includes shipping and handling charges. Please, make checks payable to : R. Maloney, **DZ PRESS** · **FAX : (415) 921– 6776**

<u>SEND ORDER TO: (Please print)</u>

NAME_____ ADDRESS _____

_____ CITY _____

_____ STATE _____ ZIP_____

PHONE (AREA CODE) _____

DROPZONE PRESS UNCONDITIONAL GUARANTEE : *YOU MUST BE SATISFIED, IF YOU FEEL ANY PRODUCT IS NOT SATISFACTORY, YOU CAN RETURN IT WITHIN 30 DAYS FOR A FULL AND IMMEDIATE REFUND.*

Please, fold this envelope as indicated on other side and staple or seal.

PHOTOCOPY ACCEPTABLE

FOLD

FOLD

FROM: _____

_____

_____

_____

DROPZONE PRESS
P. O. Box 882222
San Francisco CA 94188

FOLD

FOLD

MAILING LIST

HI, DROPZONE PRESS
PLEASE ADD MY NAME
TO YOUR FLOPPY DISK
FOR FUTURE MAILINGS!

Please print using one square for each letter.

NAME

ADDRESS

CITY

STATE   **ZIP**

Please fold this envelope as indicated on other side and staple or seal.

354

FROM: _____

_____

_____

_____

 DROPZONE PRESS
P. O. Box 882222
San Francisco CA 94188

A LETTER TO THE AUTHOR

Dear Roy:

The following comments and ideas are for the next edition of your book. I hereby give you permission to publish. I understand that my name will be mentioned and that I will receive a free copy of your book if this letter is used.

Signature ....

Please Print: Name ....

Address ....

....

Phone ....

356

✂

FOLD --- FOLD

FROM: _____

_____

_____

_____

 DROPZONE PRESS
P. O. Box 882222
San Francisco CA 94188

FOLD --- FOLD

LETTERS TO THE AUTHOR

Since the first edition, I have received many letters and book reviews. Readers were kind enough to contribute their ideas, and the following is a selection of excerpts.

...concepts are interesting and fascinating.

California Association of Realtors

Roy, I found your book *very interesting and your illustrations were some of the best I've seen... the concepts are so well explained and illustrated,* I commend you on the enormous amount of work and time it must have taken to gather and organize so much information into one book.

There is one quote... I would like to adopt in my forthcoming book. It is, "Wealth is large results from small efforts. Poverty is small results from large efforts." I think that is a profound thought.

Robert G. Allen
Author of the national bestseller
NOTHING DOWN

A tool that can quickly and effectively bridge the gap between the lay person and the real estate professional.

E. A. Miller, President
Land Use Company

A unique way of presenting a complex subject. Each page says more than mere descriptive words.

Col. Katsuyuki Yokoyama, Ph.D.
President, Dymeo National Investments Corp.

...The most illustrated and well-written book on real estate I have ever seen or heard of.
Waldren Vorhes
Property Manager, Topanga Canyon, CA

358

Whether you are a professional realty investor, a real estate agent, or a novice home buyer who wants to understand basic real estate concepts, this new oversized book is for you. Roy is a writer of few words, but he's big on using simple methods to explain essential real estate concepts. His unique book uses diagrams, drawings, examples, acronyms, and anything else which works to simplify realty ideas. It would be an ideal textbook for a basic course in real estate.

...Explanations of internal rate of return, discounted cash flow, and capitalization rates make hazy concepts clear.

Reading this book can save dozens of hours of taking real estate courses or learning by making mistakes. Maloney has written a book which lives up to the promise of its title.

Robert Bruss,
Author and
Nationally Syndicated Columnist

Your book leverages real estate.

Kenichi Takeda
Nishiku, Osaka, Japan

I distributed a dozen copies of *Quick and Easy* to our office. The response has been one of uniform enjoyment mixed with a little healthy envy.

You've done a truly remarkable job and I keep my copy near at hand.

Larrie Furst,
Urban Partners Corp.,
Real estate investment and development

The book is clear, humorous, and fully illustrated with particularly good explanations of investment property concepts such as tax-free exchanges, internal rate of return, cap rates and gross rent multipliers. The guidance it provides on negotiating and creative financing is worth the price alone.

The Real Estate Market
NEWSLETTER

I have OD'd on seminars by bestselling authors. Your seminal diagrams on cash flow, break-even points and the largest collection of real estate quotes I have seen was worth the price of the book.... You may become the
Barry Manilow of real estate.

Ted Mareno
Real estate and painting contractor,
Pompano Beach, FL

With your book **REQE** I have the confidence to explain any concept in the field of real estate... to the expert or neophyte. When is your next book coming out?

Tom Pattinson, *President*
Sausalito Bay Company

Unique methods simplify concepts in new book.

BUFFALO COURIER EXPRESS

Real estate book of the month... by one of the outstanding authors in our midst... interesting... should serve as an extremely useful guide.

San Francisco Board of Realtors

I consider it necessary reading for novices to enable them to understand all the other real estate books. For the more sophisticated real estate operators, and in particular many of my lawyer associates, I recommend it for simplifying concepts many of us used to think were complicated.

Thomas J. LaLanne
Attorney, San Francisco, CA

...How much I enjoy looking over your book... having been a teacher of real estate for years... City College... Anthony Schools... how useful are all the charts and illustrations to display a given subject or concept.... I have never seen anything from training programs which illustrates the basics of real estate as well as your book.

Donald D. Dong
Managing Partner, City Properties
Century 21
Director, Continental Savings of America

True genius... the most entertaining and informative sales tool to cross our path in years.

Many think that we here at the CIA know it all, and we must admit that you have brought to light many of the "secrets" of the industry... finally getting real estate out of the closet and into the homes and minds of all Americans.

Your book has been put on our required reading list for all agents, as the manual of success it surely is! Thank you for this marvelous effort that will make our company more interesting, better informed and rich.

Christy Wright
Director,
California Independent Agents, Inc.

REQE is my source reference ... great ideas for finding real money for real property.

Charles Cubellis, investment broker
A. G. Edwards & Sons, Inc.
Member New York Stock Exchange, Inc.

360

...Well presented... not necessarily directed toward a real estate licensee but more toward the general public.

Department of Real Estate
State of California
Sacramento, CA

A wonderful book... it is truly the real estate book for all seasons. In addition to explaining the arcane mysteries of infinite leverage, there is also sound advice about paying off one's debt as soon as possible. "You might do better but you could certainly do worse." ...It is a serious book in a light manner and it is a pleasure to read.

G. David, M.D.,
Psychiatrist, San Francisco, CA

It seems to uniquely fit what perhaps is the largest real estate education market... the beginners.... I believe it serves that market in a very competent fashion. The concepts are presented in a very succinct and memorable manner.... I commend your excellence.

John Bakas
Broker, Hanford-Freund Co.
Director, California Association of Realtors

...Your idea to explain internal rate of return and discounted cash flow in terms of "one cent" is a winner!

DWIGHT CASIMERE
Field Producer & T.V. Reporter
Independent Network News

How did you ever come up with the idea for this book before I did? It's a natural. When I first picked it up, I said, "What a great book for beginners." Then I started reading it and realized how much *I* was learning. The thing I like best is your quote on page 172: "You can't use a mathematical model for something that is politically controlled. Capital gains, laws and taxes are regulated by acts of man and are unpredictable."

To me that sums it all up right there. Real estate is a people business. You can work out all the numbers and have everything come out perfect on paper and it doesn't mean it will work in the real world. If people don't get another thing out of the book, they will be getting more than their money's worth right there. In fact, I'd like to steal the quote and use it for my new book.

DAVID A. CHODACK
Author of Fortune Builders *and* Magic Contracts

Your book... unlocks, clarifies and explains real estate problems in a fashion easily assimilated by the layman. You reinforce your points with quotes and advice of important people who have made it using perseverance, wisdom and common sense. The sun can be enjoyed by all who choose to partake of it, and do not elect to live in the shadow of ignorance. Thanks for sharing your knowledge.

Nivaldo Saraiva, *Vice-Consul of Brazil*
Beverly Hills, CA

If some inventor could fashion a still, to distill the essence of real estate principles and techniques, then the product of that still would be **REQE**. It's 100 proof!

Leigh Robinson, author of the national bestselling, *Landlording*

I wonder if you have any more miracles left. The first is a real estate book that is easily understood, despite its technical completeness. The second will be turning a chronic renter into a property owner.

John C. Yannucci, *Tenant*
Babylon, L.I., NY

The illustrations are helpful, and the information clearly responds to the author's intention: "Inclusion in this book is based on two criteria: (1) the idea must be of general interest and (2) have usefulness in the real world," The book should be useful to both brokers and investors who are intrigued by the opportunities offered by investment real estate. *The appendices alone, containing explanations of common abbreviations, a simple property analysis (headed "The Page You Must Understand"), and the author's rules of thumb (Roy's **ROT**). . . are worth the price of the book.*

REAL ESTATE TODAY
Official Publication of the
NATIONAL ASSOCIATION OF REALTORS

It is simply astonishing to me how you have managed to reduce to such succinct terms concepts like internal rate of return and discounted cash flows. As far as I am concerned, anyone who has anything to do with the concept of money should read your book.

Mark Lester, Inc.
Real estate
San Francisco, CA

After . . . *REQE*, I realize I can re-enter into the marketing of properties with confidence. Thanks for your publication . . . today the buyer will be as well-informed as the seller . . . I'm closed!

Susan Ross, *Arcadia, CA*

Your book. . . has proven its value to me as a real estate salesman. Our clients cover the full range from the novice to the sophisticated investor. Let me add that I even place residential home buyers in the investor category because of their need to fully understand today's real estate dynamics. I previously have found myself in a position of explaining an important principle only to resort to a note pad for a rough illustration. Your book has since made this largely unnecessary. The points are covered clearly and understandably. . .
a thorough and well-organized text. It is producing results for me, and it occupies a spot reserved for only my most useful references.

Raymond G. Cole
Deutscher Associates, Inc.
Pleasant Hill, CA

362

Congratulations on your outstanding publication... members of our organization... had the opportunity to read. I noticed that real estate brokers were the first to pick up the book. Among the comments I heard were:

"This is a valuable, handy resource."
"Boy, now it will be easy to train my staff."
"I can use this to explain to my customers new investment opportunities."

...Your book is most valuable for basic consumer education for everybody. I wonder how many opportunities I have missed in the past because I did not have any idea of the basic concepts of real estate investments. We are going to alert our 200 small business organization members that your book is available because we believe that this would be a valuable service to them. Thank you for sharing.

Hank Rosendin, *Executive Director*
Mexican American Chamber of Commerce
San Jose, CA

Having served in the real estate field for over two decades... *REQE* is sound advice in a fun format of simplicity. Clear English is used with a visual explanation as well, appealing to the right side of the brain, and also the left. If this book is the first place you look for your first piace, you will truly be in the advantage point position.

George Rowan, Jr., *Founder/Director*
Continental Brokerage Co., Oakland, CA

It takes one to know one, professionalism is worth money... I am a professional and have been advising people on various assets and endeavors since 1960. Over the years I've been exposed to and reveiwed all kinds of "how to" books written by purported experts in securities, real estate, commodities and a variety of other investment vehicles which at the time were fashionable. Everyone claimed to be a professional... Generally, the resulting product was about one ounce of substance for ten ounces of paper... Your book is for the knowlege-seeking investor; it avoided cliches, wasn't loaded with meaningless filler words, and mostly useless information. The primary criterion seems to be to boil down to a reasonably sized book the most important wealth accumulating information and methods... It is profusely diagrammed and illustrated, and spiced with a generous sprinkling of topical humor... It is the definitive layperson's book on how a real estate investor can accumulate wealth by using both simple and sophisticated techniques... You obviously spent a great deal of time deciding what to *leave out*... In a book the size of the San Francisco Telephone directory are the basic (but often little known) concepts of buying, trading and selling all kinds of real estate for major profits.

Sam Elkins, *Management & Financial Consultant*
San Francisco, CA

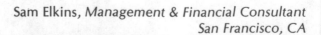

...I have a suggestion to make. Many people who are involved in numerous business transactions are concerned with the problem of disputes that can arise in connection with a particular transaction. We know that many times disputes between parties to a transaction can give rise to fairly expensive and protracted litigation. Some times parties to a transaction even use the litigation process to gain leverage. Some times a party will initiate litigation and record a *lis pendens* which notifies everyone that a lawsuit concerning a particular piece of real property is in progress. Very often it becomes difficult to sell their property as long as the *lis pendens* is in effect.

All of the above suggests that people engaging in real estate transactions may wish to take steps to minimize the impact of possible litigation. One way is to always include in a particular contract that the prevailing party will recover attorneys' fees. That way, if a person involved in a transaction is forced to incur attorneys' fees and wins the case, he can collect his fees from the losing party.

Another possibility is to include a provision in the contract that says that the parties will arbitrate all disputes pursuant to the rules of the American Arbitration Association or in accordance with Sections 1280-1294.2 of the California Code of Civil Procedure. Some times arbitration can be quicker and cheaper. It also takes out of the case the potential for a run-away verdict that can happen with a jury trial.

John N. Gulick, Jr.
Attorney at Law, San Francisco, CA

...From my background as a Northern California Investment Broker, a five-time California Association of Realtors State Director, and as a two-time Chairman of the San Francisco Board of Realtors Investment Committee... as the saying goes, I'm not an easy audience.

With the above in mind, I must say I thoroughly enjoyed your book. You took complex issues (including the politics and economics necessary to do personal estate building in the field of property ownership) and made it easy to understand and fun to read. That isn't easy. Your book contains worldly wisdom and is not only 'bricks and mortar'. You indicate that many of the thoughts and concepts have been the work of others, and you were merely the compiler. I say that if you rent a space, hire an architect, install a top chef, and have a successful restaurant called Roy's Place, then the credit for the final effort chiefly belongs to you. Good job!

Now... suggestions for the updated version... I say place less importance on inflation as a reason to purchase real estate. You can create value and equity appreciation through diligence and 'value add' concepts. I think inflation will be less important as a reason to buy real estate in the 1980s. I also think that an accurate gross income multiplier is simpler for the average investor, and also less susceptible to maniuplation than dogmatic fixed expense percentages (that are commonly used in a cap rate). The 1980s investor will hear new words like 'cash flow, depreciation, and investment.'

The 1970s investor heard 'feeding the alligator, out-of-pocket, and speculation.'

John Robert Associates
San Francisco, CA

...There are two types of deeds of trust used in real estate. The one most people are familiar with is the purchase money deed of trust. This is usually carried back by the seller of a property, at a rate 1% below the market rate on conventional first loans. The loans are usually for three to five years. If a seller decides to sell their note, then a discount will have to be given to the investor so that the yield is attractive.

The other type of deed of trust is called a "hard money" or "equity loan." These loans are generally 3% higher than conventional loans, and for only two years, and with a prepayment penalty if paid off sooner than two years. There is no discount given to the investor.

Other differences between the loans... A purchase money deed of trust (mortgage) (1) can be by any lender, (2) must be made at time of purchase, and for the purchase of the property, and (3) there is usually no deficiency judgment. A hard money or equity loan (deed of trust or mortgage) (1) is made after the ownership of property transfers to borrower, and (2) there usually is a deficiency judgment....

Mike Lakich, *Mortgage Broker/Appraiser*
Lakich Realty
Auburn, CA

You have one hell of a fantastic book. There are only two things I don't like. One is that none of the royalty checks will be in my name (I bet there will be plenty of them), and second is the title. *Real Estate Quick and Easy* does not do the book justice. It makes it all sound too simple, as if it's just for beginners. There are people who have been in the business for thirty years who would not understand half the ideas you have... so I know it *was* not quick and easy for you to put it together.... It *was* worth the effort. This is a book the real estate world needs.

Joseph N. Marino
Author of *Magic Contracts*
Publisher of *Creative Concepts in Real Estate Investing*

I use the amortization table in your appendix (the book's, that is) in working with first time buyers.

For example, if they tell me they can afford $1,000 per month loan payment, and have a down-payment of $20,000, I can tell them immediately they are in the $120,000 price range. This way I don't waste my time or theirs by showing them houses in the $150,000 range. I simply look at the monthly payment rate, based on current interest rates (12%), with a 30-year amortization, and determine the total loan amount, *i.e.*, $100,000, and then add the down payment to it.

Byron Rife, *Branch Manager*
RE/MAX Spring Realty
Manhattan Beach, CA

Having been involved in multiple real estate transactions... individual ownership, syndications and partnerships...there is no doubt in my mind that the single most important element is property management.

The right people must be obtained from the on-site manager to the property management company. It is the key element to survival in this temperamental people business. It is not so much the correct financing, finding the properties, etc., but the actual property inspections, collecting rents, getting rid of improper tenants, having good leases with teeth in them, and having tenants adhere to the regulations.

If good tenants are maintained by management... there is no problem with rents, payment of loans, or debt... provided the initial financing was structured correctly.

Edward J. Yarolin, M.D.
Santa Clara, CA

I could have been more profitable in my real estate buying and developing if I had read **REQE** and followed your ideas before I started. I have a few ideas for you... How to figure profit "percentagewise." Profit is always figured from the selling price.

Selling price $150, cost $100, profit is 1/3, or 33 1/3%.
Selling price $200, cost $100, profit is 1/2, or 50%.
Selling price $300, cost $100, profit is 2/3, or 66 2/3%.

For net cost... figure the cost of the product plus overhead: rent, utilities, sales costs plus the costs of "flooring"... interest either paid out, or lost by not earning interest on cash invested waiting for a sale.

Another thought... How a banker relates to time.
Yesterday is like a cashed check. All you can do is use the knowledge gained.
Tomorrow is like a note. You may never get paid.
Today is cash. To be used wisely for the benefits to be derived.

John W. Weiss, *President*
JW Enterprises
Creator of Self Awareness Programs
Castro Valley, CA

...I think that the proper attitude in a real estate transaction is, "I care, but I don't care *that* much." Many people get emotionally tied up during negotiations and sabotage the deal. Fear creates blocks. Play it loose. Desperation shows and it can cost you a lot of money.

...Also, a goal of "win win" for all parties will aid in having smooth and meaningful results. The best transactions are right and fair for all parties....

Sam Butler
Real Estate Broker, Merrill Lynch Realty

... This is certainly a comprehensive graphic overview of fundamental realty concepts.

Prentice-Hall, Inc., book publishers
Englewood Cliffs, NJ

I enjoyed the article you wrote and think you should include it in your next edition. It went as follows:

IF YOU THINK PRICES ARE HIGH NOW... WAIT UNTIL NEXT YEAR.

Probably every investor that ever lived has thought, or stated, "If I only bought last year, or ten years ago...."

I wish that I had bought fifteen billion years ago. The lastest scientific theories tell us that all of the matter in the universe, at that time, could fit in a grain of sand. I believe the Seller would have been fair, and as a buyer I would have offered favorable terms. The offer would include a life estate for the Seller, who would no doubt occupy the premises in perpetuity. The terms would include: nothing down with a fully amortized sixteen billion year loan. First payment to start as soon as buyer was able to occupy a minimum of one acre of habitable land. No balloon payments, but right to sub-divide the property, and transfer a portion of the loan to credit worthy nations of the buyer's choice. The total number of transfers not to exceed one hundred... for any one subject planet. The loan to be variable, with adjustments to the interest rate every ten thousand years, and the interest rate to be based on the Universal Price Index (UPI). The UPI to be calculated from the average CPI (Consumer Price Index) of all occupied planets in the universe.

On the day of the last payment on the loan, there would be a "burning of the mortgage" celebration. The celebration to take place on a star of the Seller's choice, with both the star and the mortgage to be vaporized with an appropriate blinding flash.

Michael McKenna
Program Director, Court Services
Sacramento CA

You may want to inform your readers that the "documentary transfer tax" (a tax on the sale of property) is in force in many cities in California. The tax is usually 5% of the sales price, and can be quite a shock to people who do not know about it.

Diane Sadusky
Pacific Union Residential Brokerage Co., Inc.
San Francisco

. . . *REQE* has been helpful to me in my profession. Forming real estate syndications has been my main business for the last seven years. I have bought and sold over 300 million dollars of real estate as a syndicator.

I have found your book helpful in explaining real estate intricacies to my investors. For many people, their first investment in real estate, other than the purchase of their own home, is through syndication. Your book helps to clearly explain mortgage investments, subordination and multiple ownership. I can show an investor the answers to questions in a manner that is understandable and not confusing by using terms and language that only an agent or veteran of the business understands.

Prices of real property have gone up so fast and so high that for many people the only way they can participate in the benefits of purchasing real estate is by purchasing through syndications. More agents are getting into the syndication field every day and I am sure that they too will find your book a useful tool. I would recommend making your book a part of every salesperson's kit.

I am presently syndicating the purchase of two hotels in Atlantic City, New Jersey. The purchase price is $18,500,000 with a 30% downpayment; the investors will receive a completely tax-sheltered return of $825,000 per annum. The return in projected to exceed 20% cash-on-cash in less than four years. *REQE* will be useful in illustrating the benefits of this transaction to potential investors.

Michael McDonald, Vice President
Realty Acquisition Management & Marketing Corp. (RAMMCRP)

Real Estate Quick and Easy has always been my top recommendation as a great "starter book." As everybody knows, more money has been made by individual real estate investors than in all other forms of business combined. Even when real estate goes into a slump after too much speculation, those who can hold on for the longer term will invariably come out ahead. Those who buy with the idea of holding "forever" will never get stuck in a bad deal. Only those who count on a rising market or a quick flip of property sometimes get disappointed. And, of course, the tax advantages of real estate make it all worthwhile even if property prices were constant. I made millions in real estate so I could afford to write. In my book, *Think Like A Tycoon* I told how anyone could make a million dollars within two years. I even talked about keeping a low profile, so that the IRS and building inspectors wouldn't come down on you too hard. But being a famous author is NOT keeping a low profile, and the IRS which didn't appreciate my books, or funny cartoons about tax avoidance soon fixed my wagon. After spending $3,000,000 on an investigation and trial, they had me sentenced to a Federal Prison Camp in California, where it costs the government another $30,000 a year to keep me housed, guarded and fed. While here, I'm working on several new books. They may get me tossed in the pokey again! But where else can I get three square meals, a warm shower anytime, and a safe and quiet place to write? While here I would be glad to hear from my old friends and fans in the real estate business.

Bill "Tycoon" Greene
Lecturer, prisoner, and national best-selling author
PO Box 850, Mill Valley, CA 94942

Liked your book a lot . . .
Wrote a column on real estate . . . hope you like it.

REAL ESTATE TIPS

AS I AM NOW the proud owner of actual real estate, I feel that I can, with confidence, pass on the information I have gleaned during this process.

The first rule of home buying is: Anywhere you want to live you can't afford. This leaves places you don't want to live. Select the one you don't want to live in least.

This is your dream house.

Next it is time to make an offer. The current owner of the home (or seller, in real estate jargon) will have produced a fictional number which represents the selling price. The buyer (that's you) then provides an equally fictional number which represents the price the buyer is willing to pay.

This process is not without irony. The seller, who is trying to unload the house, praises it to the skies and values it highly. The buyer, who desires the house, does his best to indicate what a disgusting little hovel it is.

Then the buyer and the seller (frequently accompanied by anywhere from two to 16 real estate agents) drink many cups of coffee and say offensive things to one another in a calm and even tone of voice.

This is called negotiation.

AT THE END, a document with many, many clauses is signed, and the real fun begins. You have entered escrow.

Escrow is a concept straight out of Tolkien. It is a land of sea serpents and monsters, dark caves, endless plains, hags with snake hair, sudden explosions. All the hobbits and other friendly folk have long since been exterminated; you're on your own in escrow land.

At the edge of this uncharted territory, in a dank and foul-smelling cave, surrounded by simpering toads, lives the Title Company. In order to cross escrow land, you must pay an enormous sum of money to the Title Company. The Title Company does nothing in exchange for this money, except agree not to kill you.

Soon after, you wil undoubtedly have your first encounter with the Termite People. The Termite People, you have been warned, are all thieves. They will demand a large sum of money to come and "inspect" your new home.

This inspection typically consists of a Termite Person standing on your front lawn, gazing at your home and saying, "You've got a problem there." He then announces that for $10,000 he will seek to eliminate the problem.

The Termite People are the chosen minions of the Title Company, who use them to wage all-out war on its sworn enemy, the loathsome Powder Post Beetle. There has not been a Powder Post Beetle sighted in North America since the French and Indian Wars, but the Termite People nevertheless pretend to kill great quantities of them each year.

If they don't, the Title Company will force them to enter escrow.

AT THE CENTER of escrow land, on the top of the highest mountain, where the dark clouds lower eternally, is the Bank. The Bank has other names — sometimes it is called S&L, which stands for Slothful and Lethargic; sometimes it is called a Mortgage Company, which stands for no craven excuses from the likes of you.

Whatever it's called, it will agree to lend you enough money to make up the difference between the "down payment" (so called because you feel so down after paying it) and the actual purchase price of your home, in exchange for your immortal soul, the still-beating heart of your first-born, and all the money you could ever hope to earn in your lifetime.

And then it will want "points." Very simply, "points" are the insult which is traditionally added to injury.

After you've made your deal with the Bank, you are allowed to straighten your shoulders and march proudly into the soft sunlight of Propertyowner Land.

Now all you have to worry about is fire, flood, earthquake, pestilence, famine and Unforeseen Acts of God.

— JON CARROLL, Columnist
San Francisco Chronicle

EDITOR'S NOTE:

Starting with the tenth edition we will publish letters to the author that we believe are of value in keeping you informed for the 1990's.

Many of the letters are from distinguished teachers, lecturers and authors.

It has been our dream to explain the concepts of real estate with illustrations . . . We receive inquiries about American real estate practices from our subscribers. We will recommend your book.

JUNKO NIKKAWA
JUTAKU-SHIMPO-SHA INC.,
REAL ESTATE BOOK PUBLISHERS
TORANOMON BUILDING
TOKYO, 105 JAPAN

THE EVOLUTION OF NETWORKING

Old and proven methods of locating commercial and investment properties for clients as well as advertising such properties on behalf of sellers are becoming extinct, almost as certainly as a change in world conditions wiped out the existence of the dinosaurs. The volume of real estate property information and clients' wants that saturates the marketplace, locally and nationally, is so massive it far exceeds the ability of the human brain to properly utilize this data.

NATIONAL TRENDS

The challenge becomes even more intense when you realize that close to eighty percent of commercial/investment property sales are made on properties that are OPEN LISTINGS, bringing about a drastic need for methods that differ from the historic and typical methods utilized in marketing residential property where agents work almost entirely with Exclusive Listings. Commercial agents move cautiously in a world of secrecy, jealously guarding the identity of their open listings, yet frustrated in their efforts to maximize the exposure of the property to potential buyers. These prospects are no longer just in their local community but may be found at the other end of the nation or even in foreign countries. One owner of a Lake Tahoe shopping center recently wrote to his agent stating that a sales effort should proceed but not to place the property in MLS (Multiple Listing Service), not to discuss the matter with any tenants, not to talk to the property manager, and in effect maintain the identity confidential.

This agent states, **"Great listing. Go out and sell it, but don't discuss it with anyone!"**

This example is not uncommon. Owners of better properties generally are careful in protecting the peace and tranquility of their tenants. Also, there is a strong feeling by some sophisticated sellers that a property has a better chance of selling quickly and for a better price and terms if it is not over-exposed to the marketplace.

NATIONAL DEMANDS

One vital factor in this changing industry is the need of today's national corporations who buy and sell properties without regard to geographical boundaries. The inevitable question for the local, independent broker is, "Will I lose this company's business right in my own backyard because I can't help them sell a property in Chicago or buy one in San Francisco?" How can the independent broker compete with the giant national real estate companies? In short, Realtors are combining their power by joining forces in what has popularly come to be known as NETWORKING.

THE SOLUTION

I believe the best method to accomplish this is with a well designed *computer matching program*.

Victor Hugo said, "There is nothing so powerful as an idea whose time has come." Networking IS an idea whose time has come for the commercial real estate industry. Clients demand it, independent brokers need it, and technology is making it happen.

The 'perfect' networking tool should offer: SIMPLICITY OF USE, VAST NUMBERS OF ACTIVE MEMBER USERS, AND A HUGE DATA BANK (every type of property).

The key questions or CATEGORIES are: Cap Rate desired; Cash on Cash desired, Type, Quality and Term of Lease, Age of Property, Future Growth Potential, Size of Property, i.e., square footage/acreage/number of units, Exchange Information, and Zoning, to mention a few.

If the Property and the Buyer's wants MATCH high in these categories, wouldn't you say this is a lead worth checking? If an agent is going to play telephone tag, the LEAD should look like a good fit.

JOHN KOCKOS
COMMERCIAL REAL ESTATE BROKER & DEVELOPER
PRESIDENT OF INVESTMENT PROPERTIES
COMP-U-MATCH
P.O. BOX 692-R
BURLINGAME, CA 94010
(415) 348-8118

Concise, educational—and humorous! That's the latest edition of your fine work, "REAL ESTATE QUICK & EASY."

It's great to read an author who clearly sees his job is to HELP HIS READERS TO UNDERSTAND—not dazzle them with how hard it is to know what the author knows.

The secret? Simple words and facile graphics, which make clear the underlying concepts of real estate. Without this base, dealing in real estate is like flying backwards—awfully dangerous.

Of course, Anthony Schools is proud that you are one of our San Francisco graduates. Keep up the fine work!

W.A. "BILL" McALWEE, *DIRECTOR*
ANTHONY SCHOOLS
2220 MOUNTAIN BLVD.
OAKLAND, CA 94611

INVESTING IN COMMERCIAL - INDUSTRIAL REAL ESTATE

Your book is an excellent working tool to use in dealing with COMMERCIAL AND INDUSTRIAL REAL ESTATE. When I speak of commercial and industrial real estate, I am not referring to agricultural properties, farm and ranch properties, or business opportunities, which are personal property. Commercial property has many meanings, but it always has a "C" attached to the zoning classification.

Commercial property normally includes improved property, such as retail buildings, office buildings, restaurants, service stations, buildings housing service-type businesses, and unimproved land under a C zoning designation. Of course neighborhood, community and regional shopping centers are commercial property. One must be careful with service stations, for they are sometimes re-zoned as residential property sites once the station is closed down.

Industrial property is any property used for manufacturing/assembly purposes, distribution (such as truck terminals), wholesaling and warehousing.

Most commercial properties are evaluated using the *'Income Approach'* with the capitalization of net income its most prominent feature. The scheduling of income versus current operating income, if any, and the projection or analysis of operating expenses require considerable sophistication on the part of an investor.

On the other hand, in the evaluation of industrial property the investor should also consider the *'Replacement Cost Approach'* and the *'Market Value By Comparison Approach'* with respect to improved property.

Today, more so than ever before, the prospective buyer should seek expert advice to determine the feasibility of purchase. This should be done prior to making an offer to purchase or signing a Purchase Agreement And Deposit Receipt. My *Screening Check List* would include the following:

1. Hire an appraiser to make an appraisal, preferably an MAI designee.
2. Retain the services of a tax expert to explain the tax consequences, preferably a CPA accountant.
3. Obtain the services of a specialist in planning and zoning matters to check the zoning regulations and Master Plan for the appropriate city and county with jurisdiction over the parcel; preferably an attorney specializing in land use with close ties to the political establishment.
4. Retain the services of an attorney specializing in real estate law to review all documents requiring your signature, and any existing leases.
5. Consult with an expert in property management to assist you with understanding management requirements for the subject property; to explain the expenses you will incur as owner; and to point out present and future maintenance requirements.
6. Consult with an expert in commercial or industrial leasing, if you do not plan to occupy the entire building or premises yourself for the anticipated life of your investment. If you want to sell the property and lease it back for your own use, you will want to be familiar with the leasing market. A real estate broker specializing in commercial or industrial leasing would be the preferable party. You should try to avoid hiring the services of any real estate agents concerned with the pending transaction.

7. Engage the services of engineers, contractors, space planners, and/or architects, depending on the type of building and the type of construction, to inspect the premises from top to bottom; and to check with the appropriate government agencies regarding any existing building and fire code violations or improvements required with a change in ownership and/or occupancy.

8. Consult with a real estate financial expert. If it is a very small property, your friendly banker or bankers may very well provide you with the desired assistance. It is wise to shop around when dealing with mortgage bankers. One should seek the advice of a non-interested third party financial consultant, banker or one who has no potential financial investment in the prospective purchase.

9. Select a real estate agent that you have trust and confidence in to represent you as the buyer. It doesn't have to be the same agent as the seller's agent.

LOCATION, LOCATION, LOCATION adequately describes the philosophy of the most successful investors. Many investors do not have the opportunity to select the best location due to the law of supply and demand. An investor like Donald Trump can pay the price for the best location. Union Square in San Francisco has a limited number of properties available. Rodeo Drive in Beverly Hills is "hot" for retail properties . . .but for how long? Silicon Valley is short of land for development . . . so developers are building elsewhere. There are still thousands of excellent locations for buyers of real property around the country, in particular for purchases under one million dollars.

If you can't handle a small investment, the next best thing is to participate in a partnership investment program. Form your own partnership, and act as the general partner; or invest in someone else's limited partnership, if you want to buy into multi-million dollar properties as your real estate investment vehicle.

There is a shortage of prime properties in the most select locations, as mentioned above, but the investor should not be discouraged. If one does a thorough job of screening a property, some very good investments should turn up right around the corner from the best location, location, location sites.

Commercial and industrial real estate investments can be most rewarding. But the demand far outstrips the supply. One has to be very careful in buying a commercial or industrial building. You must do your homework. You must have staying power.

The vacancy factor is high, especially in office buildings . . . over 20% nationally in class A & B buildings in 1987. Factories can stay vacant for years and eventually require conversion to offices or retail, such as with the outlet stores in Reading, Pa. Hence, an investor seeking a steady income stream must beware of the vacancy factor; the need for reserve funds to make the mortgage payments; taxes and other expenses . . . depending upon the lease agreement. One must be very careful of purchasing a property with lease agreements providing a negative cash flow.

After doing an analysis of the property, residential or commercial, do not hesitate to make an offer to buy. The asking price may appear to be beyond reason, but you may be pleasantly surprised to have the seller counter-offer with favorable price and terms. Properties are frequently listed at prices beyond what a prudent buyer would pay. Of course, there is always a risk when purchasing real estate.

CLAY SANDERS
COMMERCIAL REAL ESTATE BROKER, LEASING CONSULTANT
INSTRUCTOR AT EUROPEAN UNIVERSITY OF AMERICA
P.O. BOX 64071-R
SAN FRANCISCO, CA 94164
(415) 771-9200

THE AUTHOR (ON RIGHT) BEING INTERVIEWED ON SONNY BLOCH'S
NATIONAL TELEVISION PROGRAM.

Roy, two years ago I purchased a condo from you in a building you condo-converted.
It was a definite win/win deal. I love the place.

You massaged the price and terms (ROT-POT) to my exact requirements. Both my
broker and attorney had never even heard of the terms you wrote. The concept of
structuring the second loan payments as a function of the first loan payments, i.e., zero
the first year, $50 per month the second year and $200 per month the third year, was
the clue that turned a perpetual renter into a potential land baron.

I also like the way you always use odd dollar amounts, e.g. if $170,000 is too much,
and $145,000 is too little . . . you come up with $163,450 to close the deal.

Finally I find it interesting that you sell to other real estate authors. The Robert Allen
Group purchased and sold your condo adjacent to mine.

TOM JOHNSON
DISTRICT SALES MANAGER
AVIS LEASING CORP.
SAN MATEO, CA

I really appreciate the way your book presents complex issues in an easily under-standable way and with humor.

Part of my duties at Bank of America involve training real estate loan administration personnel. We provide internal workshops for our employees. With your permission we will use parts of your book for our internal reference manual and give credit to the source.

LINDA J. DEWBERRY
VICE PRESIDENT, BANK OF AMERICA
REGIONAL LOAN ADMINISTRATION MANAGER
SAN FRANCISCO, CA

I think it is important to know the difference in interest savings and time, when comparing a 15 year loan vis a vis a standard amortized 30 year loan. It would look like this:

PRINCIPLE BALANCE
OR DEBT
REMAINING

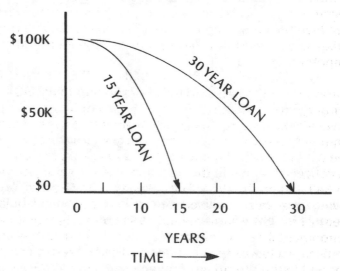

Note the faster "drop-off" or equity position gain with the 15 year loan. With the 30 year loan 5% (approximate percentages) goes to principle the first decade of the loan, 20% in the second decade, and the remaining 75% goes to principle in the last decade.

RICHARD D. STORY, PHARM MPH
NORTHRIDGE, CALIF.

AUTHOR COMMENT:

Mr. Story's point is well received and so published. I would offer the thought that it is still better to have a 30 year loan with option to "pay down." It is easier to pay down a 30 year loan in 15 years than it is to ask permission to extend a 15 year loan to 30 years. Always leave yourself negotiating room.

THE CHANGING WORLD OF THE INDEPENDENT REAL ESTATE MARKET ANALYST/APPRAISER

The latter part of the 1980's has brought with it dramatic changes in the real estate market analytical and appraisal professions. These changes are primarily the result of three major socio-economic forces. The first I call "Forward Spin," the second I refer to as the "Environmental Circle," and the third I've named the "Outer-limit Money Line." Let me illustrate what's going on by explaining these forces one at a time.

Forward Spin denotes ideas or things whose time has not quite come, but is around the corner. The general public, the competent real estate broker, the property manager, developer and syndicator is now demanding that appraisers be full economic analysts capable of looking around corners with the same kinds of skills that have been required of planning economists for decades. The underlying cause of this pressure being exerted on the appraiser is that people in the USA and around the world have now become so mobile that they are moving to different locales, at least four times during their working careers. This ever-increasing constant shift of the population and all of the social impacts that go with it are forcing the appraiser and/or the market analyst to rely more and more on high tech data inputs to carry out an assignment. The message here is that the more high tech we become as a nation, the more high tech the appraiser must become to survive professionally. The appraiser/ market analyst must now be continually upgrading and changing their skills to remain competent.

Environmental Circle is my way of expressing what I refer to as the ever increasing environmental restrictions being imposed on real estate parcels with good intentions. However, like all good things, when all of these restrictions exist together, in a given community, state or county, they can significantly affect the overall price of land and drive out industry and home buyers as a trade for preserving environment. For instance, it is conceivable that in the next fifty years a major portion of the USA will live in the Sun Belt and on the West Coast. Prices in these areas, especially California, are moving up at an accelerated rate, due to the scarcity of land, caused primarily by recently enacted environmental ordinances. The point I am making here is not that environmental restrictions are bad but rather that they are with us and that they have significantly changed the way the appraiser needs to analyze real estate. They must now, and in the future, be continously aware of how each of these restrictions affect a specific parcel of real estate as well as the real estate market generally.

Outer Limit Money Line is what I have titled that attitude which is harbored by many lending institution officers that appreciation will take care of their decision to lend more money on a given property than that which is prudent to make it a secure asset. This carefree attitude has caused the failure of more of the banks and saving and loans in the past 3 years than any other factor. The tendency has been for the public to blame the appraisers for these failures. In some instances this has been true, but the proven cases are few. As a result of these failures the various levels of government have stepped forward to impose new regulations to govern the work of the appraisers. For example, there is legislation pending in the Congress of the United States to create a national appraisal policy; there are recently passed laws in several states which now have licensing requirements or have required that the appraisal be certified, rather than the appraiser, such as the recently enacted law in California. The Federal Home Loan Bank Board entered the regulation picture three years ago and issued its own set of guidelines. The FHLBB is now requiring, by law, that savings & loan institutions set up their own guidelines, with some basic restrictions set forth by the FHLBB, and that they create their own panels of approved appraisers.

In summary, the impact of these three socio-economic forces on the independent market analyst/appraiser is that they, now and in the future, need to subscribe to the best printed and on line data services applicable to the real estate marketplaces served and must provide clients with sophisticated reports. Providing these clients with fully supported conclusions backed by solid economic data is the best way for the small independent market analyst/appraiser of the future to compete with growing national and multinational firms.

Dr. H. William Brown is Vice Chairman/Director of Real Estate Services for IPEC — Investment Property Economic Consultants — which is an international real estate market analysis/appraisal firm. Dr. Brown has analyzed and appraised real estate in 50 states of the USA, and in 13 nations of Europe, South and Central America, the Middle East and Asia. Dr. Brown is also available to represent foreign investors seeking particular types of commercial real estate on the West Coast of the United States.

DR. H.W. BROWN
IPEC
2351 POWELL STREET, SUITE 515
SAN FRANCISCO, CALIFORNIA 94133
U.S.A.
(415) 362-1313

I teach Real Estate at the College of Alameda, and appreciate your ability to demythologize what is normally an incredibly boring subject. I have had great success using your explanations and drawings to explain the esoteric subjects of Triple Net Leases, Options, Wrap Around Loans, and 1031 exchanges.

I think generally, the subject is so humorless that most people only study it as a means to an end, viz., a R.E. license. It is through books such as yours that the lightheartedness may actually make a concept clear, so that students can actually use the idea in the real world. So thank you for your humor, for your demystification, and for your ability to make a complicated concept accessible to the student.

The suggestions I have are:

ON CALCULATORS

A financial calculator should be the best tool anyone with even a modicum of interest in real estate can own. The books that come with them make most functions easy to understand. Mortgage tables have become obsolete.

It is through the hands-on use of a financial calculator that one can learn:
• the time value of money,
• the cost to finance a house,
• the effect of early payments on home loans,
• the yield of a mortgage,
• the differences between various mortgages,
• and all of the other variables in these deliciously complicated money instruments.

Not many people can answer the question: Which is better;
• to receive $1100 in one year or
• receive $1610 in 5 years or
• receive $500 in 5 years and $181 per month?

Yet that is the kind of thinking that a successful investor must understand. There is no quicker way to that understanding than through an inexpensive financial calculator.

The exciting thing about these machines is that you can begin to make very good judgements about how to handle your own home mortgage. Should you double-up on payments? Should you pay semi-weekly? Should you pay your mortgage off completely? These questions were very difficult to handle when there were only tables and books to use to look up the interest, the principle and balance of loans. With calculators you can now ask "what if": I change the time to amortize, or change the interest rate, or change the payment? What would be the most profitable to me?

An investor or real estate professional who understands the time value of money is far ahead of most people. It is the subject with the greatest potential for profit and the least understood by the average investor. This was understandable before the days of these calculators, but now you must, at least, be conversant with the concepts programmed into a financial calculator.

A simple calculator that figures the five basic variables in a loan is sufficient. (These variables are: Number of Payments, Interest, Present Value, Payment, and Future Value.) Calculators that figure Internal Rate of Return, various depreciation schedules, and that are programmable are generally more than most people need since you would seldom make these calculations in the field. They should be done on a small computer with a printout.

So one major road to success in real estate is in understanding the time value of money and the mathematics of mortgages. That understanding can come very easily by knowing how to work your financial calculator. I would note pg. 175 of your book.

ON NEGOTIATING

To be a successful player in the real estate investing game you must know human nature and be a good negotiator. By learning a few facts about how people communicate, about their wants, needs and values, you can structure a situation where you will get just what you want out of a real estate deal. If you do not consider what your opponent wants, you probably will fail in developing a successful transaction.

Some facts to consider in being a successful negotiator:

• The single most important thing in successful negotiating is to know your adversary. What does he/she want out of the deal? How can you give it to them in such a way that they are satisfied? Just knowing that a seller wants monthly payments and not all cash gives you a great deal of leverage in bargaining process.

• A cliche in the business is that "the first one to mention price loses." So be cautious, and get the other person to state the bargaining price.

• "Your price, my terms; your terms, my price." This maxim is central to knowing how to structure a transaction that is satisfactory to all parties.

• "Never give in; trade off" means if you must give in on an item, demand something else in return. "All right, I'll offer you $50,000 more, but you have to give me your 1984 Jaguar."

• "You make your profit when you buy, you realize that profit when you sell" is an old negotiating saying that should keep you honest when confronting a seller. You seldom make up for paying too much for a property.

• "He who cares most, loses." You are allowed only one emotional purchase in real estate, and that is your own house. Emotion will only cloud your thinking and cause you to over-bid. Never fall in love with a piece of investment property.

• Negotiating does not always have to be an adversarial process. If you know what your opponent wants, you can structure a transaction where you both feel you have the best deal. Some writers call this a "win-win" situation.

• Know your limits before you meet for the negotiating process. Bargaining can be so stressful that you may fall back on emotion and forget your logic. So know ahead of time how far you will go, and what is the highest or lowest price you will consider.

There are many other tips for the successful investor and negotiator. If you read only one book on the subject you will be so far ahead of 90% of the population. You will, by comparison, be a professional negotiator. I would note pg. 69 of your book.

Thanks again for a fine book.

JON RICHARDS,
REAL ESTATE INSTRUCTOR, COLLEGE OF ALAMEDA
LICENSED REAL ESTATE BROKER
ACTIVE MANAGEMENT COMPANY
P.O. BOX 31451
SAN FRANCISCO, CA 94131
(415) 824-1864

Entering a lease or contract is an important transaction. Before you commit yourself to your next real estate venture, here are some tips for a successful negotiation.

1. Look at the lease negotiation from the point of view of the other side. What do they need? What are they likely to ask for? What might their priorities be? Getting an insight into their thinking process won't increase the likelihood of your making concessions. Rather it will give you an understanding of how to deal with their positions more successfully and with greater strength.

2. If you find it difficult to reach agreement because the rent is too high, explore other considerations such as painting, repairs, appliances, longer terms, less increases, or options to renew for an additional period. All of these are worth money. The landlord might be more willing to spend money in this way rather than accepting less rent. The rent income of a building determines the amount of mortgage the landlord can get.

3. If the landlord is not looking for new mortgage financing, the reverse is true. If the tenant spends money on the premises, the landlord might take less rent.

4. Do research on what the property is leasing for. A real estate agent can help you. Understanding the market value is an essential ingredient of preparation.

5. Try to deal with the party who can actually close and sign the lease. Beware when you deal with an agent with limited authority.

6. Your negotiation will be different in a rising market than it will be if the market is falling. In the former, paying the asking price may make good sense. Negotiation does not mean trying to get it cheaper.

7. Are you getting what you negotiated for? Have the premises been inspected by knowledgeable people to be sure your expectations will be met.

8. If you plan to make improvements on the premises, is the term of the lease long enough to make the expenditure worth while?

9. It is all right to show great interest in the property. The other side owns it. But remember that there's usually another piece of property that will serve you as well.

10. Every landlord and tenancy is a relationship. To create a lasting one, both parties must want to sustain it. One of the best ways of doing so is to bring about a negotiated outcome in which everyone is a winner. Such a conclusion is the best insurance that everyone will implement the outcome.

GERARD I. NIERENBERG
AUTHOR OF THE COMPLETE NEGOTIATOR AND THE ART OF NEGOTIATING
PRESIDENT OF THE NEGOTIATION INSTITUTE OF NEW YORK
230 PARK AVENUE
NEW YORK CITY, NEW YORK 10169

P.S. THE ART OF NEGOTIATING is available in software on a diskette from:

EXPERIENCE IN SOFTWARE, INC.
2039 SHATTUCK AVENUE
BERKELEY, CA 94704

★ ★ ★

LITIGATION PREVENTION

I have attempted to keep the format organized, clear, and simple.

QUESTION: How can buyers, sellers, and agents avoid becoming victims of the current "litigation explosion"?

ANSWER: 1. Sellers—Disclose!
2. Buyers—Do your homework!
3. Brokers/Agents—Disclose and do your homework!

1. SELLER DISCLOSURES

A. Duty: Sellers have a duty to truthfully disclose all facts known to them which materially affect the value or desirability of the property and are not known by or obvious to the buyer after a casual inspection of the property.

B. Disclosure Form: California and many other states now require sellers to provide buyers with a detailed Transfer Disclosure Statement—although there appears to be no penalty for noncompliance. Also, various other specific disclosures are required by statute (e.g., IRS Certificate of Nonforeign Status; condominium documents; Flood, Earthquake or Toxic Waste Zones, etc.)

C. Timing: Seller disclosures should be made ASAP for the following reasons:
- With his eyes thus opened, buyer won't be able to hammer the seller's price down after they're in contract.
- Buyer and seller are less likely to waste their time on an unworkable deal when the facts are known up front.

- In California, buyers can rescind their offers if the Disclosure Statement is made after acceptance of the offer.

D. Content: Examples of material facts sellers must disclose are:
- Illegal units, zoning or code violations
- Notices, citations, or lawsuits affecting the property
- Encroachments
- Structural defects
- Flooding, soil, or drainage problems
- Serious neighborhood noise problems or nuisances

2. SUGGESTIONS FOR BUYERS

A. Yes . . . The old strict rule of "caveat emptor" (buyer beware) is seldom now applied. And the buyer's failure to inspect or investigate is not a defense to intentiona fraud by the seller.

B. But . . . A buyer's negligence in protecting his own interests will make recovery against a seller more difficult when the seller's misrepresentation has been only negligent, or innocent. Furthermore, when the sale is "as is" or involves income property, a greater burden is placed upon the buyer to protect his own interests.

C. Therefore, All Buyers Should:

- Thoroughly inspect the property using a checklist— obtainable from books or property inspection services. (Pages 48 to 50 in your book).
- Get a written competitive market analysis from your agent and/or acquaint yourself with the market.
- Ask for a written disclosure statement from seller and start a list of questions to ask seller or seller's agent.
- Make up a list of the conditions that you will want to put in the purchase contract. The more conditions you have, the more "outs" you have and the better the deal you'll get (since you can hammer the seller on price if the conditions within seller's control aren't met).
- If neither you nor your broker is confident in drafting the purchase contract, a visit to an attorney can be a good investment. The more specific and detailed the contract, the less chance of later misunderstandings.
- Before signing, read and understand all parts of the purchase contract.
- If you are buying income property, verify income, expenses and vacancies. Smart buyers do rent and vacancy surveys, as well.

3. BROKERS AND AGENTS

A. Duty to Inspect: Listing agents in California and many other states now have a duty to conduct a reasonably diligent inspection and disclose to buyers all material facts affecting value and desirability of the property that are not known by the buyer.

B. Dual Agency Disclosure: California agents must also disclose to both buyer and seller which party they are representing and whether they are acting as exclusive or dual agents.

C. Duties to Buyer and Seller: Agents have a fiduciary duty of utmost care, honesty and loyalty to their clients. In addition, agents owe both parties a duty of reasonable skill, honesty, fair dealing and good faith.

Furthermore, many states have now imposed upon the agent a duty to disclose to both buyer and seller (even if only one is a client) all facts known to the agent which materially affect the value or desirability of the property unless those facts are known to, or within the diligent observation of the parties.

4. CONCLUSION

The standard of care imposed upon all parties in real estate transactions, and the willingness of those parties to take each other to court if they perceive a wrong, is greater than ever before. Protect yourself by disclosing and doing your homework!

*** The "Trade-Off Department" ***

II. IMPORTANT QUESTION EVERY SELLER OF INVESTMENT REAL ESTATE MUST FIRST ASK:

Am I really better off selling and putting my equity into a larger property (as my agent recommends)?

A. BENEFITS OF SALE VS. REFI:

1. Permits you to take out all of equity, instead of leaving in the property the 20-30% equity most refi lenders require.
2. Somewhat higher tax write-offs (unless you do a S1031 exchange) because the basis in the new property will be higher, permitting greater depreciation.
3. Particular facts about the property may make it unsuitable for your present needs (e.g., too distant, too management intensive, intolerable negative cash flow, etc.).
4. If you have coowner problems (e.g., partner, divorcing spouse) you may have to sell because neither can afford to buy out the other.
5. You may anticipate that your property won't appreciate or be a good investment in the future.
6. You may want to consolidate your properties, especially if you're now driving all over town managing them.

B. BENEFITS OF REFI VS. SALE:

1. Lower fees—loan points of 1-3% instead of broker commissions of 6%. This huge "bite" really cuts your rate of return unless you hold for a long time.
2. Less risk—because you are familiar with your own property, whereas any new property is an unknown, and because you have 2 properties, rather than having all your money tied up in one.
3. Lower taxes and insurance costs.
4. It's less time-consuming and less aggravating to refi than to sell and buy.
5. Although your total write-offs will decrease, your interest write-off will be greater than it was and you don't have any taxable gain (or exchange deadlines) to worry about.
6. You keep your same neighbors, schools and local friends.

*** The "Trade-Off Department" ***

I. IMPORTANT QUESTION EVERY BUYER OF REAL ESTATE MUST FIRST ASK:

Am I really better off occupying the residence I'm buying? Or does it make more economic sense to buy a non-owner occupied residence and continue renting?

A. BENEFITS OF OWNER-OCCUPANCY:

1. Pride of Ownership.
2. No tenant hassles and no landlord hassles!
3. Less property management burden, since property is so close and accessible.
4. More secure (no possibility of eviction).
5. Better loan terms: (a) About 1% lower interest rate
   (b) Better leverage (only 10% downpayment vs. 20% down)
6. You can always move in for 6-12 months, and then move out again and possibly get the best of both alternatives!
7. You can remodel and design the property to your personal taste.
8. You set the rules. You don't have to follow lease restrictions. So keep the dog.

B. BENEFITS OF NON-OWNER-OCCUPANCY (PUT TENANT IN YOUR BUILDING):

1. You can stay in the beautiful apartment in the nice neighborhood that you can't afford to buy.
2. Even if you lose your job, you don't have to worry as much about monthly loan payments, since the property will break even sooner or later.
3. More tax benefits, since you can depreciate the purchase costs, plus write off all expenditures for maintenance or further improvements—none of which you can do with "A."
4. You can always move into the house after giving proper notice to the tenant.
5. You can have amenities, not possible in your price range, e.g., Olympic pool, tennis courts, etc.
6. If you need more friends it is less lonely in a garden apartment complex with club house and social activities, and collect rent from your tenant in your building.

JOHN H. O'REILLY,
ATTORNEY AT LAW
SAN FRANCISCO CITY COLLEGE, REAL ESTATE LAW INSTRUCTOR
456 MONTGOMERY STREET, SUITE 900
SAN FRANCISCO, CA 94104
(415) 392-2860

Roy, I like your personal letters to illustrate ideas.

An easy way to determine the amount you can borrow from a lending institution is as follows:

HOME EQUITY BORROWING GUIDE

Current market value
of your home $ _____

x 80% $ _____

Less the balance due on
any loans $ _____

Equity loan potential $ _____

To illustrate, if your home is worth $200,000, then 80% of value is $160,000.

If you have $100,000 in loans, then the potential amount you can borrow is $60,000.

LARRY LUCHOK
ULTRASTONE DISTRIBUTOR
SAUSALITO, CALIFORNIA

The question is frequently asked, "Why go to the extra expense of an architect for a remodeling job costing only a few thousand?"

It is a matter of cultural evolution, or how far one has moved out of the cave.

Most real estate agents and prospective buyers concerns are with the number of bedrooms, the amount of plumbing, and the total square feet. Any good carpenter can satisfy these numerical requirements for creature comforts in response to a sincere request and proper payment.

Seeking shelter is a fundamental need second only to eating and sleeping. However, satisfying the biological needs of the flesh within a larger, smoother, less craggy cave, is hardly cultural evolution.

To create a center for your being, to express your larger self, to dramatize the act of inhabitation through a magnificent gesture requires the kinship and empathy of a sensitive architect. Your alignment with the combined talents of an artist and engineer (architect) presents an opportunity for you both to re-create, to re-model the center of your universe.

In remodeling your architect must maintain an "archaeologists' morality" about the re-shaping of what already exists. Nothing should be covered or changed except through the exercise of prudence. Re-modeling is a process of "selective elimination" incurred through aesthetic and engineering decisions. The next step is the "critical act" of addition, i.e., solving the problems of universal disarray. The architect adapts and relates the structure to natural law and the environment by insinuating miracles of organization into the plan. An atmosphere is created of space and things from which the inhabitant, whether fully conscious or not, derives countenance and sustenance.

The architects fees generate such an atmosphere of support and nurture to the human spirit, that they are transformed into an investment instead of a cost.

LEE AARON WARD
ARCHITECT AIA
FRANK LLOYD WRIGHT APPRENTICE
NAPA, CALIFORNIA
(707) 253-7737

I'd like to pass on a few thoughts about real estate investment after recent tax reform.

I think President Reagan best put things into perspective when he said, "If our current tax structure were a TV show, it would either be 'Foul-ups, Bleeps and Blunders,' or 'Gimme a Break.'"

Tax changes of 84, 86, 87 & 88 undoubtedly wounded real estate investors, but most other tax sheltered opportunities were killed outright! For the average guy wanting a tax advantaged investment, real estate is the only game in town.

In particular, the tax benefits of home ownership appear safe from even the tax-hungriest pol, in Washington. Mortgage interest (with some limitations) and real estate tax deductions can still be written off on both primary and second residences. We can still trade our homes without tax on gains and can sell at age 55 and escape taxes on $125,000 of gain altogether.

Home offices still provide deduction opportunities. NOTE that when depreciation has been claimed on a home office, it is recaptured (taxed) in the year of the sale—even if the home is "rolled over" into another residence. TIP: Avoid this rule by discontinuing the use of the home office at least 6 months prior to or in the year of the sale.

Home equity loans of up to $100,000 provide *fully* deductible interest regardless of how the money is used. This is important to remember because most other type of consumer interest is losing its deductibility. TIP: Get a home equity loan or line of credit on your first or second home and use it for major purchases, such as your next car! Some banks are offering equity loans which can be accessed by credit cards.

Also surviving "tax deform" are savings in shifting income from higher to lower tax bracket family members. EXAMPLE: Transfer your office building to a trust for your children and lease it back. Result: Deductions from your maximum bracket for rents and income to children's minimum bracket!

It may help your readers to understand the complexities of the Tax Code if they know it is used for purposes other than to raise money: (1) Social, e.g., low income tax incentives; (2) Political, e.g., oil and gas tax breaks and (3) Economic, e.g., accelerated depreciation deductions to stimulate capital spending by businesses.

Roy, I hope you like my work on the Tax Code Quick & Easy your pages 303 to 305.

FREDERICK W. DAILY, J.D., LL.M.
TAX ATTORNEY
TAX SEMINAR LECTURER ON RADIO AND TELEVISION
479 BUENA VISTA EAST, SUITE 300
SAN FRANCISCO, CA 94117
(415) 626-4046

Author's comment: I can't make these concepts simple . . . they already are simple.